HOW TO HOLD IT ALL TOGETHER WHEN YOU'VE LOST YOUR JOB

Townsend Albright

Printed on recyclable paper

 **VGM Career Horizons**
a division of *NTC Publishing Group*
Lincolnwood, Illinois USA

Library of Congress Cataloging-in-Publication Data

Albright, Townsend.
    How to hold it all together when you've lost your job/Townsend Albright.
        p. cm.
    Includes bibliographical references.
    ISBN 0-8442-4395-7 (pbk.)
    1. Unemployed—Services for—United States.   2. Unemployed—United
States—Life skills guides.   3. Job hunting—United States.
    I. Title.
    HD5724.A4793   1996
    650.14—dc20   95-30142
                                                                                          CIP

Published by VGM Career Horizons, a division of NTC Publishing Group
4255 West Touhy Avenue
Lincolnwood (Chicago), Illinois 60646–1975, U.S.A.
©1996 by NTC Publishing Group. All rights reserved.
No part of this book may be reproduced, stored in a retrieval
system, or transmitted in any form or by any means,
electronic, mechanical, photocopying, recording or otherwise,
without the prior permission of NTC Publishing Group.
Manufactured in the United States of America.

5 6 7 8 9 0 VP 9 8 7 6 5 4 3 2 1

Contents

Negotiating Your Best Separation Package 165

Preface

On September 27, 1994, the American Management Association released their annual survey on downsizing, based on a survey of 713 major domestic companies. Their conclusion: *downsizing works best when it becomes a permanent practice.* The massive corporate restructuring of U.S. industry that began in the late 1980s is by no means over. Of companies surveyed by the association, 26 percent made it clear they plan to slash their workforces by June 30, 1995. If history repeats itself, this number will continue to grow. In 1993, 21.6 percent of companies interviewed said they planned to eliminate jobs by the end of June, 1994. In reality, 47.3 percent cut employment by roughly 9.2 percent of their workforces.

Corporate layoffs have touched each one of us in some way. If you are among the unemployed you have experienced this trauma first-hand. My wife and I have two daughters who attend college, a home with a mortgage, and plenty of installment debts. And we have financially survived unemployment! To keep our family afloat, I researched, unearthed, and tapped into every available public financial resource for the unemployed and low-income worker. This financial knowledge and assistance became the cornerstone of our new lifestyle and helped us to avoid financial disaster when I was unemployed. *You can too! How to Hold It All Together When You've Lost Your Job* gives specific examples and the tools to help you manage key issues affecting your unemployed lifestyle to your best advantage so you can financially survive and achieve your job search goal. You will learn:

- How to prepare an unemployment survival budget you can live on

- How to re-negotiate your fixed expenses (mortgage, auto and other installment debts)

- How to slash your discretionary "impulse" purchases

- How to craft your least expensive insurance safety net

- How to take advantage of all the financial assistance available to you through federal, state and local agencies, assistance that can mean the difference between financial survival or financial ruin during a lengthy period without a paycheck.

In addition, you'll benefit from proven insights on constructing your own successful job-search campaign and on the array of government programs available to those of you who want to improve your current career skills, train for a new career, or start your own business. The last two chapters discuss how to become a savvy worker who knows everything that is happening in his or her work environment and how to negotiate your best separation package from your exit interview.

The information, advice, case histories, and worksheets provide the tools for overcoming the paralyzing stress and financial ruin so many experience when unemployed. Knowing how to avoid these crises will make it much easier for you to achieve success in your job search.

Acknowledgments

I want to express my gratitude to the following people and organizations who provided information and shared their expertise with me about the material and topics I have addressed in *How to Hold It All Together When You've Lost Your Job*: Bill Holland, Assistant to the Director, Illinois Department of Employment Security
Tom Lorenz, Ombudsperson, Illinois Department of Public Aid
Rochelle Heard, Advocacy Director, The Public Welfare Coalition
Doug Dobmeyer, Executive Director, The Public Welfare Coalition
Linda and Michael Murphy, The Signet Group Outplacement Consultants
Trish Svehla, Svehla Consultants, Inc.
and the many informed and cooperative government agency personnel who shared their perspectives and expertise with me.

Introduction

How to Hold It All Together When You've Lost Your Job is a practical, nuts and bolts manual written to prepare you for the worst scenarios you could face during your transition and to give you the tools you'll need to survive financially as you navigate the turbulent waters of your job search.

Throughout the late 1980s and during the early 1990s, corporate America laid off workers at a rate of 2,200 per day. Causes of this working-person's disaster include the "merger mania" of the 1980s when companies piled up debts they now find difficult to repay; the introduction of increasingly sophisticated technology that replaces manufacturing, managerial, administrative, and financial personnel; and the corporate relocation of manufacturing facilities to other countries. We all have been affected in one way or another by this global corporate reconfiguration.

Corporate restructuring is not about to end. The American Management Association's downsizing survey revealed that businesses that cut their workforces *at least twice* between 1989 and 1994 reported gains in productivity and in operating profits. Nearly 58 percent of companies that had gone through multiple downsizings indicated that their incomes had increased. Of the companies surveyed, 43 percent experienced an improvement in worker productivity.

What do these facts mean to us? Simply that as long as businesses believe they can profitably produce more goods and services while employing fewer workers, they will continue to downsize.

Nor are state and local government workers immune from being slashed from payrolls as these public bodies bring their budgets into balance. Every year since 1991 an average of 100,000 state and local government employees have lost their jobs. And due to reductions in the armed services, even more men and women are seeking careers in a shrinking private job market.

Although our national unemployment rate has dropped from seven percent during most of 1993 to close to six percent for most of 1994, this is not the complete story. Federal statistics on unemployment do not include those workers who can find only lower paying part-time and temporary work, or have to settle for jobs below their skill level. They do not include the discouraged workers who have given up looking for work altogether.

Undoubtedly, this is a traumatic, high-anxiety time for all workers whether they are employed in the private or public sector. This book will help you deal with these challenges by taking you step-by-step through a process that will assure your survival.

Although every chapter contains valuable information, certain chapters are particularly recommended for readers in specific employment situations. You may wish to read these chapters first, depending on your own circumstances.

- Have you just become unemployed? Read Chapters 1, 2, 3, 4, and 7. Think about the case studies presented in these chapters. Then roll up your sleeves and *complete the worksheets*. These worksheets are the core of this book.

- Have you been unemployed and conducting your job search for several months? Chapters 2, 3, and 5 are essential reading for you. Crunch your numbers. Be honest with yourself. Study Chapter 6 and contact your local Private Industry Council. Then read Chapter 1. The information covered there will help you keep your job search on course.

- Are you concerned that you could lose your job? You have the opportunity to do some "crisis planning." Begin by reading and following the recommendations outlined in Chapter 7. Then study Chapter 8. The analysis of the exit interview and strategies that you can use to obtain your best separation package are essential reading for you. Next, read and complete the worksheets in Chapters 2 and 3. Then read Chapter 4. This chapter explains just about everything you need to know about collecting unemployment compensation.

Then read the rest of the chapters. Outplacement professionals tell us that the average wage earner will experience as many as five job/career changes during his or her working years. This book will help you master these challenges.

(*Note: Sample tax forms are provided throughout the book to demonstrate how they are to be filled out. Be sure you use the form that applies to the year you are filing.*)

Keeping Yourself Going When You Are Unemployed

The thrust of this book is three-fold:

- To provide you with the tools that will ensure your financial survival, teach you how to use them, and introduce you to government assistance programs that you can weave into your financial safety net during your unemployment

- To teach you how to assess your life skills, craft a successful job search campaign, and introduce you to government programs that offer training that will help you upgrade your professional talents, retool for a new career, or start your own business

- To advise you how to position yourself to your best financial advantage should you face unemployment again

This first chapter is critical. In it, you will find practical advice that will help you grapple and cope with the emotionally charged issues that accompany the shock of job loss, as well as an Action Plan that provides the environment, structure, and resources you will need to develop and implement a successful job search campaign.

Why Me? Coming to Grips with Your Emotions

Job loss is a shock. It is abrupt. Your daily routine is shattered. Your relationships with your co-workers are severed. And your means of economic support—*your livelihood*—is taken away from you.

It is normal and natural for a trauma of this magnitude to produce the most basic human fears and emotions: denial, anger, and guilt. Job loss especially affects individuals who have spent their entire careers working for one company. It doesn't matter how long rumors of merger, downsizing, or rightsizing have circulated around your office or plant. Realizing and accepting that important relationships in your life have been severed will help you cope with your stress. Your goal must be to redirect your energies into accepting your situation and to moving forward—in other words, into *acceptance* and *hope*.

Virtually every day, we read or hear about another major corporate layoff. Yesterday IBM eliminated 5,000 positions. Today Proctor and Gamble announced it will downsize 13,000 workers. *You are not alone!* By concentrating your efforts on the present and by re-framing your future you will bolster your self-esteem and be able to proceed with confidence.

It helps us if we understand why employers reduce staff and eliminate positions. Some of the most common reasons are:

- To complete mergers and acquisitions that caused duplication of staff and work functions

- To restructure and concentrate only on the most profitable products and services

- To cut costs (labor costs are usually the first to be cut) to remain profitable in a competitive business environment

- To discharge employees who no longer fit the employer's needs

The following scenario is a classic example of what can happen if you allow yourself to lose your self-confidence over job loss. These emotions can be so paralyzing that it becomes almost impossible for you to begin the tasks necessary for a successful job search.

> John, who is in his forties, lost his job as a district manager of a major auto parts distributor. The parent company reorganized geographically and laid off 2,000 employees, from hourly workers up to district-level managers. John had spent his entire career with "his company." He was a company man who played by the rules. Although he received an adequate severance package, he blamed his company and himself for his job loss.

> Julie, John's wife, is an accountant and their children are about to enter high school. While their lifestyle is now crimped, their current money problems are not yet serious. And because John resented the thought of anyone stooping to "go on welfare," he procrastinated for three weeks before applying for unemployment benefits.

> Instead, John withdrew. He refused to talk about his employment situation with his friends or associates and procrastinated on his job search. He dropped his regular workday schedule. Many mornings he slept in. Eventually John became involved in household projects, convincing himself that he was doing something useful by improving the value of his home.

> John was practicing avoidance. He denied the reality of his job loss. Family tensions concerning his lack of a job search plan began to grow.

> Then John fell into a classic trap known as "the second bathroom syndrome." He decided to construct an office in the unfinished attic. He had already used up half of his 26-week unemployment compensation benefit period and had only made half-hearted attempts to find a job by answering newspaper ads and by making a few phone calls for interviews with search firm recruiters. John's case, sad to say, is far from unique.

Your Job Search Action Plan

One industry has mushroomed during the late 1980s and early 1990s—outplacement counseling services. Outplacement counselors can be either company-sponsored or private. Outplacement services are provided by three sources—your employer, private counselors and through civic and religious organizations.

Counseling is an invaluable benefit. It helps you:

- Work through the trauma of job loss

- Prepare an effective and professional résumé

- Learn to write your cover letters and follow-up thank you notes

- Develop your networking skills

Private outplacement packages are expensive. They can easily cost several thousand dollars. However their tailored approach can be very helpful to high-income executives who have lost their jobs. If your employer did not offer you outplacement counseling, and you need to conserve cash during unemployment, turn to self-help programs. Civic organizations (such as Rotary, Kiwanis, or local chambers of commerce), libraries, community colleges, religious groups, and organizations such as 40 PLUS and the American Association of Retired People (AARP) offer excellent job search programs for the unemployed. Speakers cover every topic related to your job search. Most are free. Whatever avenue you choose, you have to muster the discipline and marshal the resources you need to conduct an effective job search. The rest of Chapter 1 takes you through this process step by step.

Know yourself

Assess your skills, interests, and abilities, as well as your strengths and weaknesses. Knowing your strengths and weaknesses—what you can do well and what you cannot do well—is the first step in planning a successful job search plan. Begin by developing a list of skills and abilities that reflect your background and work experience. Next, rate yourself as objectively as possible. Then list your accomplishments; they are proof of your capabilities.

Don't rush your work! It could take you hours or days to complete this work, and the self-analysis is critical to your future success. After you complete these lists, ask yourself whether your co-workers, subordinates, and superiors would agree with them. These lists call for intuitive thinking and are not precise. You could have similar replies in different categories. The lists will, however, help you form a clear picture of yourself, one which you will continue to evaluate as you develop your job search plan.

Rate Your Skills

Instructions. Think carefully about each skill listed and determine if it applies to you and your career. If it does, rate yourself and list key accomplishments that resulted from using that skill.

Rate yourself in the following manner:

An exceptionally well-developed skill	4
A strong skill	3
An average skill	2
An underdeveloped skill	1

SKILLS	RATING

Administrative
How I...

Plan and organize my activities   _____

Meet my deadlines   _____

Handle detail   _____

Accomplishments:

_____

_____

_____

Managerial
How I...

Lead and motivate others   _____

Establish my own and others' goals and objectives _____

Build rapport and motivate others   _____

Accomplishments:

_____

_____

_____

SKILLS	RATING

Social-interactive
How I work effectively with…

My peers	_____
My bosses	_____
My subordinates	_____
My customers and clients	_____
Am I a team player?	_____

Accomplishments:

_____

_____

_____

Personal
My judgment in…

Logical thinking	_____
Decision making	_____
Setting priorities and achieving them	_____
Managing conflict	_____

Accomplishments:

_____

_____

_____

Technical
These skills are clearly defined and broadly understood. Examples include computer proficiency (WordPerfect, Lotus 1–2–3, etc.) and professional certifications (CPA, CLU, etc.).

Accomplishments:

_____

_____

_____

***Create your own
home office***

Create a quiet space in your home where you can:

- Make uninterrupted phone calls

- Write letters

- Keep files about:

  1) who you contacted

  2) what position

  3) when to follow up

  4) target company lists

  5) future contacts

  6) replies to job advertisements

- Keep your appointment calendar

- Keep your expense log

- Keep your matching stationary for résumés and letters

Remember: you are marketing your most important product—*Yourself*!

Upgrade your computer skills. Become proficient in using WordPerfect, Microsoft Word, or any of the software programs that enable you to create letters and résumés that look professional. If you aren't yet computer literate, enroll in an evening course at your local high school, community center, or community college. This leaves you free to contact prospective employers during the day. Some computer literacy is essential for just about every position in today's job market.

If you do not own a computer and cannot afford to buy one, use one of the computers that are available at your local public library. If you haven't learned computer skills, purchase a used typewriter that corrects errors. They are inexpensive because computers have made them virtually obsolete. Don't rely upon secretarial services. They are expensive. Your résumés and cover letters have to fit into their workload, and this can delay your schedule by several days. What's more, if the service makes errors, it could take one or two days to correct them. In today's competitive job market, time is critical. Become self-reliant.

Finally, install a second phone line if your household gets a lot of calls. Potential employers need to be able to reach you. And by all means, make sure you have an answering machine that works.

Prepare your networking and target company lists

Eighty percent of all jobs are filled through networking. Networking simply means talking to people who can help you in your job search. Perhaps they can make contacts or give you the names of people who are decision-makers who might need or know someone who needs a person having your background and skills. Your network for your job search includes your supporters and your professional contacts. Your supporters include your friends, former employers, supervisors, co-workers and subordinates, and your minister, priest or rabbi. They are:

- People who like you and will help you

- People who know your qualifications

- People who have contacts they can use to introduce you to decision-makers

You can make professional contacts through:

- Trade associations

- Community organizations (Jaycees, Rotary, chambers of commerce, etc.)

- Religious affiliations (Knights of Columbus, B'nai Brith, etc.)

- Family activities (Boy Scouts or Girl Scouts, PTA, children's sports teams and leagues)

- Labor organizations

- Alumni associations

Target those companies located in your geographic area and/or nationwide that are well-managed and growing, and employ people who have your career skills.

Help-wanted ads and search firms

While you are networking, make sure you read the help-wanted sections of your local newspapers. If you live in a rural area, obtain a copy of the Sunday edition of your state's and neighboring cities' largest daily newspapers. Sunday editions usually offer the largest help-wanted sections.

Each Tuesday *The Wall Street Journal* publishes a listing of available positions in its Marketplace section. This is a good source for white-collar employment opportunities. *The National Business Employment Weekly*, published by Dow Jones, Inc., is available on Mondays and is a compilation of the previous week's available positions advertised in all geographically based editions of *The Wall Street Journal*. You will want to read the many well-written articles that address every issue related to job search. In today's economy, the competition for jobs is fierce. The typical help-wanted advertisement generates several hundred résumés. Look for all of these papers in the reference section of your local public library.

Read trade journals. They are an excellent source for employment leads. The articles they publish will keep you abreast of current trends, newly developed products and services, and corporate happenings in your career field. You might learn about a company that is moving into your area that will need to hire someone with your skills!

Search firm recruiters are another contact, especially for higher-level positions. Recruiters work for their client firms, *not for you*. They charge their clients a fee, typically 30 percent to 33 percent of the successful job candidate's first year's salary. Search firm recruiters are extremely exacting when it comes to matching a candidate's qualifications with their client's wants and needs for a particular position.

There are two types of search firm recruiters:

Retainer. Recruiters on retainer are employed by a company to find the perfect person to fill a specific position. They receive their professional fee for professional services whether or not they fill the position. Companies use retainer search firms to fill high-level positions.

Contingency. Recruiters who work on a contingency basis have no contract with a client company. They do not receive a fee unless the candidate they present is hired for the job. Contingency recruiters most often work to fill low- to mid-level management positions.

Many recruiters specialize in filling positions in specific professions. An excellent source for recruiters is *The Directory of Executive Recruiters*, published by Kennedy Publications.

Don't rely on recruiters to do your job search for you. These sobering statistics will show you how difficult it is to land a job through a recruiter. In 1993, recruiters filled approximately 7,000 managerial positions nationwide. Industry sources tell us that search firms received over 700,000 résumés that same year. Thus, your odds are about 100 to 1 that you will find employment by delegating your job search to a recruiter.

Action plan advice

The key components of a successful job search Action Plan are:

1. Concentrating on your networking—for job search contacts and to gather information about different, yet related careers that fit your set of skills

2. Answering advertisements that call for your specific experience and career skills

3. Broadcasting your credentials to as many search recruiters as possible and making sure you get placed in their search firms' data banks

Addenda to
Chapter 1

Job Search and Career Resources

There are many books and directories that can help you plan your job search, prepare professional résumés, and write cover letters. Others list names of potential employers, their addresses, whom to contact, and a brief description about what they do. This is a small list. The reference librarian at your public or community college library, or the staff at your local bookstore can help you select further reading tailored to your specific needs and objectives.

Books

Studner, Peter K. *Super Job Search*. Los Angeles: Jamenair, Ltd., 1987.

Block, Deborah Perlmutter. *How to Make the Right Career Moves*. Lincolnwood, Ill.: VGM Career Horizons, 1990.

Bolles, Richard N. *What Color Is Your Parachute?* Berkeley: Ten Speed Press, 1994.

Figler, Howard. *The Complete Job Search Book*. New York: Henry Holt and Co., 19—.

U.S. Department of Labor, Employment and Training Administration and the U.S. Employment Service. *Dictionary of Occupational Titles*. Washington: 1993.

This informative dictionary, available in most public libraries or from VGM Career Horizons, lists:

- Over 12,700 jobs, and is divided into job categories such as banking, machine trades and sales

- Job categories by occupational groups such as bank tellers, nursing, etc.

- Job descriptions

- Required skills

Directories

The Job Book Series. Bob Adams, Inc., Holbrook, Mass.

- Supplies up-to-date information on most major corporations and gives specific contact names

- Written for most large U.S. metropolitan areas

How to Get A Job Series. Surrey Books, Chicago, Ill.

- Contains similar material to *The Job Book Series*

- Covers large metropolitan areas in the United States and Europe

Leadership Directories. Montar Publishing Company, New York.

- Provides a "who's who" for corporate, financial, legal, international, and governmental organizations

The Directory of Executive Recruiters. Kennedy Publications, Fitzwilliam, NH.

- Lists retainer and contingency recruiters

- Describes various industries and their functions

- Explains the search business, offers advice on résumé preparation and working with search professionals

IRS Form 2106 and instructions

Most job search expenses are tax-deductible and can be itemized on IRS Form 2106. The sample form completed here will give you an idea of how to fill out Form 2106. *Be sure to use an updated form, available from the IRS or your local post office or library, as certain items may change slightly from year to year.*

Form **2106**

Department of the Treasury
Internal Revenue Service   (O)

Employee Business Expenses

▶ **See separate instructions.**

▶ **Attach to Form 1040.**

OMB No. 1545-0139

19

Attachment
Sequence No. **54**

Your name DONALD JONES	Social security number 326 19 4567	Occupation in which expenses were incurred JOB SEARCH

Part I   **Employee Business Expenses and Reimbursements**

STEP 1   Enter Your Expenses

		Column A Other Than Meals and Entertainment		Column B Meals and Entertainment	
1	Vehicle expense from line 22 or line 29	**1**	709 05		
2	Parking fees, tolls, and transportation, including train, bus, etc., that **did not** involve overnight travel	**2**	313 70		
3	Travel expense while away from home overnight, including lodging, airplane, car rental, etc. **Do not** include meals and entertainment	**3**			
4	Business expenses not included on lines 1 through 3. **Do not** include meals and entertainment	**4**	1584 61		
5	Meals and entertainment expenses (see instructions)	**5**			1002 01
6	**Total expenses.** In Column A, add lines 1 through 4 and enter the result. In Column B, enter the amount from line 5	**6**	2607 36		1002 01

Note: *If you were not reimbursed for any expenses in Step 1, skip line 7 and enter the amount from line 6 on line 8.*

STEP 2   Enter Amounts Your Employer Gave You for Expenses Listed in STEP 1

7	Enter amounts your employer gave you that were **not** reported to you in box 1 of Form W-2. Include any amount reported under code "L" in box 13 of your Form W-2 (see instructions) . . .	**7**	–0–		–0–

STEP 3   Figure Expenses To Deduct on Schedule A (Form 1040)

8	Subtract line 7 from line 6	**8**	2607 36		1002 01
	Note: *If both columns of line 8 are zero, stop here. If Column A is less than zero, report the amount as income on Form 1040, line 7.*				
9	In Column A, enter the amount from line 8 (if zero or less, enter -0-). In Column B, multiply the amount on line 8 by 50% (.50) .	**9**	2607 36		501 00
10	Add the amounts on line 9 of both columns and enter the total here. **Also, enter the total on Schedule A (Form 1040), line 20.** (Qualified performing artists and individuals with disabilities, see the instructions for special rules on where to enter the total.) . . . . ▶	**10**		3108 37	

For Paperwork Reduction Act Notice, see instructions.   Cat. No. 11700N   Form **2106** (1994)

Form 2106 (1994)   Page **2**

Part II	**Vehicle Expenses** (See instructions to find out which sections to complete.)			

Section A.—General Information

			(a) Vehicle 1	**(b)** Vehicle 2
11	Enter the date vehicle was placed in service	11	11 / 31 /94	/ /
12	Total miles vehicle was driven during 1994	12	111,000 miles	miles
13	Business miles included on line 12	13	2,445 miles	miles
14	Percent of business use. Divide line 13 by line 12	14	22.3 %	%
15	Average daily round trip commuting distance	15	25 miles	miles
16	Commuting miles included on line 12	16	4,500 miles	miles
17	Other personal miles. Add lines 13 and 16 and subtract the total from line 12	17	4,055 miles	miles

18	Do you (or your spouse) have another vehicle available for personal purposes?	[X] Yes [ ] No
19	If your employer provided you with a vehicle, is personal use during off duty hours permitted? [ ] Yes [ ] No [X] Not applicable	
20	Do you have evidence to support your deduction?	[X] Yes [ ] No
21	If "Yes," is the evidence written? Kept a daily log	[X] Yes [ ] No

Section B.—Standard Mileage Rate (Use this section only if you own the vehicle.)

22	Multiply line 13 by 29¢ (.29). Enter the result here and on line 1. (Rural mail carriers, see instructions.)	22	709	05

Section C.—Actual Expenses

			(a) Vehicle 1		**(b)** Vehicle 2	
23	Gasoline, oil, repairs, vehicle insurance, etc.	23				
24a	Vehicle rentals	24a				
b	Inclusion amount (see instructions)	24b				
c	Subtract line 24b from line 24a	24c				
25	Value of employer-provided vehicle (applies only if 100% of annual lease value was included on Form W-2—see instructions)	25				
26	Add lines 23, 24c, and 25 . .	26				
27	Multiply line 26 by the percentage on line 14 . . .	27				
28	Depreciation. Enter amount from line 38 below	28				
29	Add lines 27 and 28. Enter total here and on line 1.	29				

Section D.—Depreciation of Vehicles (Use this section only if you own the vehicle.)

			(a) Vehicle 1		**(b)** Vehicle 2	
30	Enter cost or other basis (see instructions)	30				
31	Enter amount of section 179 deduction (see instructions) .	31				
32	Multiply line 30 by line 14 (see instructions if you elected the section 179 deduction) . . .	32				
33	Enter depreciation method and percentage (see instructions) .	33				
34	Multiply line 32 by the percentage on line 33 (see instructions) . .	34				
35	Add lines 31 and 34	35				
36	Enter the limitation amount from the table in the line 36 instructions	36				
37	Multiply line 36 by the percentage on line 14 . . .	37				
38	Enter the **smaller** of line 35 or line 37. Also, enter this amount on line 28 above	38				

♲ *Printed on recycled paper*   ☆ U.S. GPO:1994-375-326

19__

**Department of the Treasury
Internal Revenue Service**

Instructions for Form 2106
Employee Business Expenses
Section references are to the Internal Revenue Code.

Paperwork Reduction Act Notice

We ask for the information on this form to carry out the Internal Revenue laws of the United States. You are required to give us the information. We need it to ensure that you are complying with these laws and to allow us to figure and collect the right amount of tax.

The time needed to complete and file this form will vary depending on individual circumstances. The estimated average time is:

Recordkeeping . . . . 1 hr., 38 min.

**Learning about the law
or the form** . . . . 19 min.

Preparing the form . . . 1 hr., 13 min.

**Copying, assembling, and
sending the form to the IRS** . . 42 min.

If you have comments concerning the accuracy of these time estimates or suggestions for making this form more simple, we would be happy to hear from you. You can write to both the IRS and the Office of Management and Budget at the addresses listed in the Instructions for Form 1040.

General Instructions
Purpose of Form

Use Form 2106 if you are an employee deducting expenses attributable to your job.

See the chart at the bottom of this page to find out if you must file this form.

Changes To Note

● Beginning in 1994, the deductible portion of business meal costs and entertainment expenses has been reduced from 80% to 50%.

● The standard mileage rate has been increased to 29 cents for each mile of business use in 1994.

● Employees who use the standard mileage rate (if claiming vehicle expense) and are not reimbursed by their employers for any expense may be able to file new **Form 2106-EZ,** Unreimbursed Employee Business Expenses. See Form 2106-EZ to find out if you qualify to file it.

Additional Information

If you need more information about employee business expenses, you will find the following publications helpful:

Pub. 463, Travel, Entertainment, and Gift Expenses

Pub. 502, Medical and Dental Expenses

Pub. 529, Miscellaneous Deductions

Pub. 534, Depreciation

Pub. 587, Business Use of Your Home

Pub. 917, Business Use of a Car

Pub. 946, How To Begin Depreciating Your Property

Specific Instructions
Part I—Employee Business Expenses and Reimbursements

Fill in ALL of Part I if you were reimbursed for employee business expenses. If you were not reimbursed for your expenses, fill in only Steps 1 and 3 of Part I.

Step 1—Enter Your Expenses

Line 1—Enter your vehicle expenses from Part II, line 22 or line 29.

Line 2—Enter parking fees, etc., that did not involve overnight travel. Do not include transportation expenses for commuting to and from work. See the line 15 instructions for the definition of **commuting.**

Line 3—Enter expenses for lodging and transportation connected with overnight travel away from your **tax home.** You cannot deduct any expenses for travel away from your tax home if the period of temporary employment is more than 1 year. Do not include expenses for meals and entertainment. For details, including limitations, see Pub. 463.

Generally, your **tax home** is your main place of business or post of duty regardless of where you maintain your family home. If you do not have a regular or main place of business because of the nature of your work, then your tax home is the place where you regularly live. If you do not fit either of these categories, you are considered an itinerant and your tax home is wherever you work. As an itinerant, you are not away from home and cannot claim a travel expense deduction. For more details on tax home, see Pub. 463.

Line 4—Enter other job-related expenses not listed on any other line on this form. Include expenses for business gifts, education (tuition and books), home office, trade publications, etc. For details, including limitations, see Pub. 463 and Pub. 529. If you are deducting home office expenses, see Pub. 587 for special

---

Who Must File Form 2106

A Were you an employee during the year? — **No** → Do not file Form 2106. See the instructions for Schedule C, C-EZ, E, or F.

Yes ↓

B Did you have job-related business expenses? — **No** → Do not file Form 2106.

Yes ↓

C Were you reimbursed for any of your business expenses (count only reimbursements your employer **did not** include in box 1 of your Form W-2)? — **No** → **D** Are you claiming job-related vehicle, travel, transportation, meals, or entertainment expenses? — **Yes** → File Form 2106 (but see **Notes** below).

D ... — **No** ↓

C **Yes** ↓

F Did you use a vehicle in your job in 1994 that you also used for business in a prior year? — **No** → **E** Are you a qualified performing artist or an individual with a disability claiming impairment-related work expenses? See the line 10 instructions for definitions. — **Yes** → File Form 2106 (but see Notes below).

F **Yes** ↓

H Are your deductible expenses more than your reimbursements (count only reimbursements your employer **did not** include in box 1 of your Form W-2)? For rules covering employer reporting of reimbursed expenses, see the instructions for line 7. — **No** → Do not file Form 2106.

E — **No** → Do not file Form 2106. Enter expenses on Schedule A, line 20. These expenses include business gifts, education (tuition and books), home office, trade publications, etc.

H **Yes** ↓

G Is either **1** or **2** true?
  1 You used the actual expense method in the first year you used your vehicle for business.
  2 You used a depreciation method other than straight line for this vehicle in a prior year. — **No** → File Form 2106 (but see **Notes** to the right).

G **Yes** ↓

File Form 2106.

Notes

● Generally, employee expenses are deductible only if you itemize your deductions on Schedule A (Form 1040). But **qualified performing artists** and **individuals with disabilities** should see the instructions for line 10 to find out where to deduct employee expenses.

● Do not file Form 2106 if none of your expenses are deductible because of the 2% limit on Schedule A (Form 1040); that is, Schedule A, line 26, is zero.

Cat. No. 64188V

instructions on how to report your expenses. If you are deducting depreciation or claiming a section 179 deduction on a cellular telephone or other similar telecommunications equipment, a home computer, etc., get **Form 4562,** Depreciation and Amortization, to figure the depreciation and section 179 deduction. Enter the depreciation and section 179 deduction on line 4.

Do not include expenses for meals and entertainment, taxes, or interest. Deductible taxes are entered on lines 5 through 9 of Schedule A. Employees cannot deduct car loan interest.

Note: *If line 4 is your only entry, do not complete Form 2106. Instead, enter your expenses directly on Schedule A, line 20.*

Line 5—Enter your allowable meals and entertainment expense. Include meals while away from your tax home overnight and other business meals and entertainment. Instead of actual cost, you may be able to claim the "standard meal allowance" for your daily meals and incidental expenses while away from your tax home overnight. Under this method, you deduct a specified amount, depending on where you travel, instead of keeping records of your actual meal expenses. However, you must still keep records to prove the time, place, and business purpose of your travel. See Pub. 463 to figure your deduction using the standard meal allowance.

Step 2—Enter Amounts Your Employer Gave You for Expenses Listed in Step 1

Line 7—Enter the amounts your employer (or third party) gave you for expenses shown in Step 1 that were NOT reported to you in box 1 of your Form W-2. This includes any amount reported under code "L" in box 13 of Form W-2. Amounts reported under code "L" are certain reimbursements you received for business expenses that were not included as wages on Form W-2 because the expenses were treated as meeting specific IRS substantiation requirements.

Generally, when your employer pays for your expenses, the payments should not be included in box 1 of your Form W-2 if, within a reasonable period of time, you (a) accounted to your employer for the expenses, AND (b) were required to return, and did return, any payments not spent (or considered not spent) for business expenses. If these payments were included in box 1, ask your employer for a corrected Form W-2.

Accounting to your employer means that you gave your employer documentary evidence and an account book, diary, or similar statement to verify the amount, time, place, and business purpose of each expense. You are also treated as having accounted for your expenses if either of the following applies:

• Your employer gave you a fixed travel allowance that is similar in form to the per diem allowance specified by the Federal Government and you verified the time, place, and business purpose of each expense. See Pub. 463 for more details.

• Your employer reimbursed you for vehicle expenses at the standard mileage rate or according to a flat rate or stated schedule, and you verified the date of each trip,

mileage, and business purpose of the vehicle use. See Pub. 917 for more details.

Allocating Your Reimbursement. If your employer paid you a single amount that covers both meals and entertainment, as well as other business expenses, you must allocate the reimbursement so that you know how much to enter in Column A and Column B of line 7. Use the following worksheet to figure this allocation.

Worksheet

1. Enter the total amount of reimbursements your employer gave you that **were not** reported to you in box 1 of Form W-2 . . . . . _____

2. Enter the total amount of your expenses for the periods covered by this reimbursement . . . . . _____

3. Of the amount on line 2, enter your total expense for meals and entertainment . . . . . . _____

4. Divide line 3 by line 2. Enter the result as a decimal (to at least two places) _____

5. Multiply line 1 by line 4. Enter the result here and in Column B, line 7 . . _____

6. Subtract line 5 from line 1. Enter this result here and in Column A, line 7 . _____

Step 3—Figure Expenses To Deduct on Schedule A (Form 1040)

Line 10—Special Rules. If you are a qualified performing artist (defined below), include your performing-arts-related expenses in the total on Form 1040, line 30. Write "QPA" and the amount in the space to the left of line 30. Your performing-arts-related business expenses are deductible whether or not you itemize deductions on Schedule A. The expenses are not subject to the 2% limit that applies to most other employee business expenses.

A **qualified performing artist** is an individual who (1) performed services in the performing arts as an employee for at least two employers during the tax year, (2) received from at least two of those employers wages of $200 or more per employer, (3) had allowable business expenses attributable to the performing arts of more than 10% of gross income from the performing arts, and (4) had adjusted gross income of $16,000 or less before deducting expenses as a performing artist. To be treated as a qualified performing artist, a married individual must also file a joint return, unless the individual and his or her spouse lived apart for all of 1994. On a joint return, requirements (1), (2), and (3) must be figured separately for each spouse. However, requirement (4) applies to the combined adjusted gross income of both spouses.

If you are an **individual with a disability** and are claiming impairment-related work expenses (defined below), enter the part of the line 10 amount attributable to those expenses on Schedule A, line 28, instead of on Schedule A, line 20. Your impairment-related work expenses are not subject to the 2% limit that applies to most other employee business expenses.

Impairment-related work expenses are the allowable expenses of an individual with physical or mental disabilities for attendant care at his or her place of employment. They also include other expenses in connection with the place of employment that enable the employee to work.

See Pub. 502 for more details.

Part II—Vehicle Expenses

There are two methods for computing vehicle expenses—the Standard Mileage Rate and the Actual Expense Method. In some cases, you must use the Actual Expense Method instead of the Standard Mileage Rate. Use the following two flowcharts to see which method you should use. Rural mail carriers should see the line 22 instructions instead of using the flowcharts for special rules that apply to them.

If you have the option of using either the Standard Mileage Rate or Actual Expense Method, you should calculate your expenses using each method, and use the method most advantageous to you. However, when completing Form 2106, fill in only the sections that apply to the method you choose.

For Vehicles Placed in Service After 1980

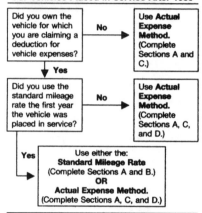

For Vehicles Placed in Service Before 1981

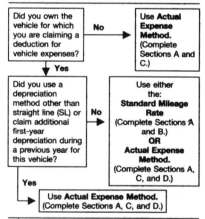

Section A.—General Information

All individuals claiming vehicle expenses must complete Section A.

If you used two vehicles for business during the year, use a separate column for each vehicle in Sections A, C, and D. If you used more than two, attach a computation using the format in Sections A, C, and D.

Line 11—Date placed in service is generally the date you first start using your vehicle. However, if you first start using your vehicle for personal use and later convert it to business use, the vehicle is treated as placed in service on the date you started using it for business.

Line 12—Enter the total miles you drove each vehicle during the year for all purposes. However, if you converted your vehicle during the year from personal to business use (or from business to personal use), enter the total miles only for the months during which you drove the vehicle for business purposes.

Line 13—Do not include commuting miles on this line; commuting miles are not considered business miles. See the line 15 instructions for the definition of **commuting**.

Line 14—Divide line 13 by line 12 to figure your business use percentage. However, if you converted your vehicle during the year from personal to business use (or from business to personal use), multiply this percentage by the number of months during which you drove the vehicle for business purposes and divide the result by 12.

Line 15—Enter your average daily round trip commuting distance. If you went to more than one work location, figure the average.

Generally, **commuting** is travel between your home and a work location. However, travel between your home and a work location is not commuting if you meet ANY of the following conditions:

1. You travel to a temporary work location outside the metropolitan area where you live and normally work. A temporary work location is one at which you perform services on an irregular or short-term basis (generally a matter of days or weeks).

2. You have at least one regular work location away from your home and you travel to a temporary work location in the same trade or business, regardless of the distance.

3. Your home is your principal place of business under section 280A(c)(1)(A) (for purposes of deducting expenses for business use of your home) and you travel to another work location in the same trade or business, regardless of whether that location is regular or temporary and regardless of distance.

Line 16—If you do not know the total actual miles you used your vehicle for commuting during the year, figure the amount to enter on line 16 by multiplying the number of days during the year that you used each vehicle for commuting by the average daily round trip commuting distance in miles. However, if you converted your vehicle during the year from personal to business use (or from business to personal use), enter the miles you used your vehicle for commuting only for the same period of time you drove your vehicle for business purposes.

Section B.—Standard Mileage Rate

If you do not own the vehicle, skip Section B and go to Section C.

You may use the standard mileage rate instead of actual expenses to figure the deductible costs of operating a passenger car, including a van, pickup, or panel truck. If you want to use the standard mileage rate for a car placed in service after 1980, you must do so in the first year you place your car in service. In later years, you may deduct actual expenses but you may not use a depreciation method other than straight line. If you do not use the standard mileage rate in the first year, you may not use it for that car for any subsequent year.

You may also deduct state and local personal property taxes. Enter state and local personal property taxes on Schedule A, line 7.

Line 22—If you are a rural mail carrier (defined below) and you use the standard mileage rate to figure your vehicle expense, multiply the number of miles on line 13 by 43.5 cents (.435) instead of 29 cents.

You may use the higher mileage rate if you (1) were an employee of the U.S. Postal Service in 1994, (2) used your own vehicle to collect and deliver mail on a rural route, and (3) did not claim depreciation for the vehicle for any tax year beginning after 1987.

If you are also claiming the standard mileage rate for mileage driven in another business activity, you must figure the deduction for that mileage on a separate Form 2106.

See Pub. 917 for more details.

Section C.—Actual Expenses

Line 23—Enter your total annual expenses for gasoline, oil, repairs, insurance, tires, license plates, or similar items. Do not include state and local personal property taxes or interest expense you paid. Deduct state and local personal property taxes on Schedule A, line 7. Employees cannot deduct car loan interest.

Line 24a—If you rented or leased a vehicle during the year instead of using one you own, enter the cost of renting. Also, include on this line any temporary vehicle rentals not included on line 3, such as when your car was being repaired.

Line 24b—If you leased a vehicle for a term of 30 days or more after June 18, 1984, you may have to reduce your deduction for vehicle lease payments by an amount called the **inclusion amount**. You may have to enter the inclusion amount on line 24b if—

The lease term began:	And the vehicle's fair market value on the first day of the lease exceeded:
During 1994	$14,900
During 1993	$14,300
During 1992	$13,700
During 1991	$13,400
After 1986 but before 1991 . .	$12,800

If the lease term began after June 18, 1984, but before January 1, 1987, see Pub. 917 to find out if you have an inclusion amount.

See Pub. 917 to figure the inclusion amount. Enter the inclusion amount on line 24b. If you have no inclusion amount, leave line 24b blank.

Line 25—If during 1994 your employer provided a vehicle for your business use and included 100% of its annual lease value in box 1 of your Form W-2, enter this amount on line 25. If less than 100% of the annual lease value was included in box 1 of your Form W-2, skip line 25.

Section D.—Depreciation of Vehicles

Depreciation is an amount you can deduct to recover the cost or other basis of your vehicle over a certain number of years. In some cases, you may elect to expense, under section 179, part of the cost of your vehicle in the year of purchase. For more details, see Pub. 917.

Line 30—Enter the vehicle's actual cost or other basis (unadjusted for prior years' depreciation). If you traded in your vehicle, your basis is the adjusted basis of the old vehicle (figured as if 100% of the vehicle's use had been for business purposes) plus any additional amount you pay for your new vehicle. Reduce your basis by any diesel fuel tax credit, qualified electric vehicle credit, or deduction for clean-fuel vehicles you claimed. For any vehicle purchased after 1986, add to your basis any sales tax paid on the vehicle.

If you converted the vehicle from personal use to business use, your basis for depreciation is the smaller of the vehicle's adjusted basis or its fair market value on the date of conversion.

Line 31—If 1994 is the first year your vehicle was placed in service and the percentage on line 14 is more than 50%, you may elect to deduct as an expense a portion of the cost (subject to a yearly limit). To calculate this section 179 deduction, multiply the part of the cost of the vehicle that you choose to expense by the percentage on line 14. The total of your depreciation and section 179 deduction cannot be more than $2,960 multiplied by the percentage on line 14. Your section 179 deduction for the year cannot be more than the income from your job and any other active trade or business on your Form 1040.

Caution: *If you are claiming a section 179 deduction on other property, or you placed more than $200,000 of section 179 property in service during the year, use Form 4562 to figure your section 179 deduction. Enter the amount of the section 179 deduction allocable to your vehicle (from Form 4562, line 12) on Form 2106, line 31.*

Note: *For section 179 purposes, the cost of the new vehicle does not include the adjusted basis of the vehicle you traded in.*

Example:

Cost including taxes	$15,000
Adjusted basis of trade-in . .	– $ 2,000
Section 179 basis	= $13,000
Limit on depreciation and section 179 deduction	$ 2,960

Smaller of:

Section 179 basis, or	
Limit on depreciation and section 179 deduction	$ 2,960
Percentage on line 14	x 75%
Section 179 deduction	= $ 2,220

Line 32—To figure the basis for depreciation, multiply line 30 by the percentage on line 14. From that result, subtract the full amount of any section 179 deduction (and half of any investment credit taken before 1986 unless you took the reduced credit).

Page 3

Line 33—If you used the standard mileage rate in the first year the vehicle was placed in service and now elect to use the actual expense method, you **MUST** use the straight line method of depreciation for the vehicle's estimated useful life. Otherwise, use the chart below to find the depreciation method and percentage to enter on line 33. (For example, if you placed a car in service on December 1, 1994, and you use the method and percentage in column (a), enter "200 DB 5%" on line 33.) To use the chart, first find the date you placed the vehicle in service (line 11). Then, select the depreciation method and percentage from column (a), (b), (c), or (d). For vehicles placed in service before 1994, use the same method you used on last year's return unless a decline in your business use requires a change to the straight line method. For vehicles placed in service during 1994, select the depreciation method and percentage after reading the explanation for each column below.

Column (a)—You may use column (a) only if the business use percentage on line 14 is more than 50%. The method in this column, the 200% declining balance method, will give you the largest deduction in the year your vehicle is placed in service. This column is also used for vehicles placed in service before 1987 and depreciated under ACRS (accelerated cost recovery system).

Column (b)—You may use column (b) only if the business use percentage on line 14 is more than 50%. The method in this column, the 150% declining balance method, will give you a smaller depreciation deduction than in column (a) for the first 3 years. However, you will not have a "depreciation adjustment" on this item for alternative minimum tax purposes. This may result in a smaller tax liability if you must file **Form 6251**, Alternative Minimum Tax—Individuals.

Column (c)—You must use column (c), or column (d) if applicable, if the business use percentage on line 14 is 50% or less. The method in this column is the straight line method over 5 years. It is optional if the business use percentage on line 14 is more than 50%.

Note: *If your vehicle was used more than 50% for business in the year it was placed in service and used 50% or less in a later year, part of the depreciation and section 179 deduction previously claimed may have to be added back to your income in the later year. Figure the amount to be included in income on **Form 4797**, Sales of Business Property.*

Column (d)—You must use column (d) if you placed your vehicle in service before 1987 and you elected the straight line method over a recovery period of 12 years.

Caution: *If you placed other business property in service during the year you placed your vehicle in service (for any year after 1986), or you used your vehicle predominantly within an Indian reservation, you may not be able to use the chart shown below. See Pub. 534 for the proper depreciation rate to use.*

Depreciation Method and Percentage Chart

Date Placed in Service	(a)	(b)	(c)	(d)
Oct. 1—Dec. 31, 1994	200 DB 5%	150 DB 3.75%	SL 2.5%	
Jan. 1—Sept. 30, 1994	200 DB 20%	150 DB 15%	SL 10%	
Oct. 1—Dec. 31, 1993	200 DB 38%	150 DB 28.88%	SL 20%	
Jan. 1—Sept. 30, 1993	200 DB 32%	150 DB 25.5%	SL 20%	
Oct. 1—Dec. 31, 1992	200 DB 22.8%	150 DB 20.21%	SL 20%	
Jan. 1—Sept. 30, 1992	200 DB 19.2%	150 DB 17.85%	SL 20%	
Oct. 1—Dec. 31, 1991	200 DB 13.68%	150 DB 16.4%	SL 20%	
Jan. 1—Sept. 30, 1991	200 DB 11.52%	150 DB 16.66%	SL 20%	
Oct. 1—Dec. 31, 1990	200 DB 10.94%	150 DB 16.41%	SL 20%	
Jan. 1—Sept. 30, 1990	200 DB 11.52%	150 DB 16.66%	SL 20%	
Oct. 1—Dec. 31, 1989	200 DB 9.58%	150 DB 14.35%	SL 17.5%	
Jan. 1—Sept. 30, 1989	200 DB 5.76%	150 DB 8.33%	SL 10%	
Jan. 1, 1987—Dec. 31, 1988	MACRS*	MACRS*	SL*	
June 19, 1984—Dec. 31, 1986	ACRS*		SL*	SL 8.333%
Jan. 1, 1983—June 18, 1984				SL 8.333%
Jan. 1—Dec. 31, 1982				SL 4.167%

*Enter your unrecovered basis, if any, on line 34. See Pub. 917 for more information.

Line 34—If during the year you did not sell or exchange your vehicle (or you sold or exchanged your vehicle that was placed in service in 1987 or 1988), multiply line 32 by the percentage on line 33. If during the year you sold or exchanged your vehicle that was placed in service: **(a)** Before 1987, enter -0- on line 34 for that vehicle; **(b)** After 1988, multiply the result for line 34 by 50% and enter on line 34. However, do not multiply by 50% if you originally placed the vehicle in service during the last 3 months of a year after 1988. Instead, multiply the result for line 34 by the percentage shown below for the month you disposed of the vehicle:

Month	Percentage
Jan., Feb., March	12.5%
April, May, June	37.5%
July, Aug., Sept.	62.5%
Oct., Nov., Dec.	87.5%

Line 36—Using the chart below, find the date you placed your vehicle in service. Then, enter on line 36 the corresponding amount from the **Limitation** column. If your vehicle was placed in service before June 19, 1984, skip lines 36 and 37 and enter on line 38 the amount from line 35.

Date Vehicle Was Placed in Service	Limitation
Jan. 1—Dec. 31, 1994	$2,960
Jan. 1—Dec. 31, 1993	$4,600
Jan. 1—Dec. 31, 1992	$2,650
Jan. 1—Dec. 31, 1991	$1,575
Jan. 1, 1987—Dec. 31, 1990	$1,475
Apr. 3, 1985—Dec. 31, 1986	$4,800
Jan. 1—Apr. 2, 1985	$6,200
June 19—Dec. 31, 1984	$6,000

Learning to Live on Less

Now is the time to confront reality. Are you currently unemployed? Do you have a hunch—or does the company grapevine suggest—that the ax might soon fall? Are you simply taking precautions because of the uncertain job environment facing all workers today? You should prepare a budget that provides you and your family with your basic needs, insures against catastrophe, and enables you to maintain a quite basic but viable lifestyle.

Take pencil in hand and begin making some cold, hard financial decisions about how you will survive. There is no way of knowing how long you could be looking for work—a few weeks, several months, or more than a year. This chapter is the core of the book. Our family had to crunch numbers and cut expenses, and we survived. Hundreds of people who have attended my seminars on financial survival have worked through these same exercises and negotiated with their creditors. They, too, have survived.

Your first step is to determine where you are today. Begin by preparing a budget that reflects your current living expenses. Before you can plan a budget for the future, you need to know what you are spending now. Use the budget worksheets on the next two pages to begin assessing what comes in and what needs to go out.

Your Current Personal Monthly Budget

		Amount
Regular monthly income:		
Previous (current) salary	$	_____
Interest		_____
Dividends		_____
Rental income		_____
Other		_____
TOTAL Monthly Income	$	_____
Regular Monthly Obligations:		
Rent or mortgage payments	$	_____
Car payments		_____
TV/appliance payments		_____
Repayment of loans		_____
Medical/dental plan or insurance		_____
Life insurance premiums		_____
Other insurance premiums (auto, home)		_____
Miscellaneous regular payments (credit cards)		_____
TOTAL	$	_____
Personal Living Expenses (for entire family):		
Clothing (purchasing, cleaning, repair)	$	_____
Doctor/dentist bills (not covered by plan or insurance)		_____
Education		_____
Membership dues		_____
Gifts and contributions		_____
Auto maintenance, gas, parking fees		_____
Travel (apart from auto payments, insurance, gas, parking, and maintenance)		_____
Food (home and away)		_____
Books, newspapers, magazines		_____
Spending money, allowances		_____
Entertainment		_____
TOTAL	$	_____

Household Operating Expenses:

Telephone	$ _____
Gas and electricity	_____
Water	_____
Sewer charges	_____
New home fixtures, furniture	_____
Repairs, maintenance	_____
Other household expenses	_____
TOTAL	$ _____

Taxes:

Federal, state, and local income taxes	$ _____
Property taxes	_____
Other taxes	_____
TOTAL	$ _____

Expense Summary:

Regular monthly obligations total	$ _____
Personal living expenses total	_____
Household operating expenses total	_____
Taxes	_____
TOTAL MONTHLY EXPENSES	$ _____

BUDGET SUMMARY

TOTAL monthly income	$ _____
(less) TOTAL monthly expenses	$ _____

Next, add up all your sources of ready cash. These sources include:

• Savings	$ _____
• Severance pay (total amount you will receive over your severance period)	$ _____
• Income from unemployment compensation (26 weeks plus any extended benefits)	$ _____
• Market value of company vested pension and profit-sharing plans	$ _____
• Cash values and accumulated dividends from your life insurance policies	$ _____
• Market value of IRAs, stocks, and bonds	$ _____
• Spousal or other family income	$ _____
TOTAL readily available financial resources:	$ _____

Now total all your sources of ready cash. Divide your total sources of ready cash by twelve, as it could be twelve months before you find employment. This is crisis planning. You must allow for a worst-case scenario. Since this is survival time, you and your family have to pull together both financially and emotionally. Look for part-time work as you job search. Other family members can do the same. For now, assume that no one in your family will be working who doesn't already have a job.

Many self-help manuals written about crisis finance emphasize slashing your discretionary impulse spending and reducing your everyday living expenses by modifying your buying habits. I agree that most people, with some guidance, are able to accomplish this goal, and offer practical advice about how you can do this.

It is absolutely crucial for you to learn how you can reduce your *fixed costs* (mortgage, car payments, credit card and installment payments, insurance premiums, etc.) since these obligations take precedence over all of your other expenses. Defaulting on fixed obligations is the major cause of personal bankruptcy.

I have been successful in accomplishing these tasks and will teach you how you can succeed. This labor takes time, perseverance, and persuasion on your part. You will need to be patient, as your creditors can be slow to modify your payment contracts. It is worth the effort, however, because what follows are the most important steps you can take to avoid financial disaster.

Becoming an Intelligent Penny Pincher

There are many ways to evaluate one's financial priorities. Certainly it is the height of folly to take an expensive trip or have one last fling at shopping to refresh yourself before you begin your job search. This irresponsible behavior only compounds your financial difficulties. Enough said.

Unemployment requires being mature and disciplined in your approach and taking stock of little ways to cut back on your spending. One method that might seem impractical but is a good way to begin is to decide between the things you like and those you don't like.

For example, if you enjoy a well-manicured lawn and a well-maintained home, dispense with the lawn service and workpeople and learn how to be a "do it yourselfer," if this is not already part of your lifestyle. Here are words of caution: if you don't know how to fix something, learn before you try. Plumbers and electricians can be expensive.

If you and your family enjoy gourmet food, forget the expensive restaurants and pricey cuts of meat and purchase one of the many cookbooks that offer recipes for delicious, nutritious, and adventuresome meals on a tight budget.

To conserve energy, turn off lights when you leave a room, and your TV and radio when you are not there to enjoy them. Caulk around windows and doors, and install storm windows. By eliminating drafts you save a bundle in heating costs.

Alcohol and tobacco are expensive. This is an ideal time to quit smoking and to cut back on costly liquor and wine consumption.

If you have more than one vehicle, drive the one that is more economical to operate. Take public transportation to save on gas and parking fees.

Stop all purchases on credit unless they are *absolutely* essential. You will need to pay off those balances, not add to them. *Cash is king!*

Make sure you keep up your personal appearance. You don't need to purchase a new wardrobe. You do need to wear clean and pressed clothes and shined shoes, and keep your hair well-groomed. Good grooming makes you feel better, plus it sends a message to your family and friends that you "have it together." Good grooming and appearance are essential if you are to be successful networking and interviewing as you seek a new job.

Slashing Your Fixed Expenses

As important as personal lifestyle modifications are, there is additional scaling back you can do to conserve your resources. Where else should you turn for help in order to cut your current expenses? Talk to your creditors.

Before you learn how to work with your lending institutions and other creditors to significantly reduce your mortgage and other fixed obligations, it's helpful to know what your lenders do with your loans. This will help you understand one important reason why your creditors should be willing to help you.

Most banks and credit corporations group or package mortgage loans and sell them to large banks or investment bankers, who in turn convert them into a vast array of mortgage-backed securities or pools. These pools are then marketed to insurance company, pension fund, mutual fund, and bank portfolio managers. Bankers and mortgage companies sell loans in order to free up cash to make more loans, collect more fees, and keep their loan portfolios in line with current interest rates. Automobile finance corporations and major credit card issuers package and market consumer loans for the same reasons. The prime concern of the ultimate purchaser of your mortgage and auto loan is to keep cash flowing, maintaining steady interest and principal payments. Lenders and bankers always want to anticipate problems so they have the time to solve them as quickly and painlessly as possible.

One thing many borrowers don't realize is how early they can begin arranging debt restructuring or moratoriums on payments. It is imperative that you discuss immediately your drop in income with your banker and with your other creditors, in order to secure as much assistance from them as you can. Tell them you lost your job. Remind them that you have always been prompt with your payments and that you have an excellent credit rating. Additionally, tell them that you are asking all of your creditors for help during your job search. You will be pleasantly surprised to learn that many creditors will lighten your payments from the first day you are out of work.

The process you use to reduce your mortgage and other fixed payments should follow these steps:

1. Meet with your banker. Request that the bank allow you to modify (reduce) principal or interest payments on your mortgage until you find employment or for one year—whichever is shorter. Your request gives the bank a reasonable time frame in which to operate. It may also give you an opportunity to extend the agreement if you are still looking for work after a year.

2. Ask your banker or collections manager to help you draft a letter that explains why you are making your request. Or ask him or her to check to see that it is worded appropriately and meets the requirements of the institution that purchased your loan.

3. If your request is approved, the lending institution will have you sign a Loan Modification Agreement which stipulates your new repayment terms. In my situation I was able to negotiate payment of "interest only" for one year. (A sample agreement is provided in the Addenda to this chapter).

4. Work with your banker or credit company in the same manner to restructure your auto loans.

5. Write to all of your creditors and inform them of your unemployment situation and your desire to work out the most equitable repayment plan for both parties.

Remember: Lenders are vigilant. If you fall behind on a payment they will write or phone you to learn if there is a problem. Once you fall behind you have lost much of your bargaining leverage. They will look upon you as someone in financial crisis. Your best defense is a good offense.

Understand that loan defaults reflect as negatively on the lender as they do on you. Lenders want problem-free loans and should be willing to work out acceptable terms for you if they understand your situation. It is crucial that you present it to them in a courteous and well thought out manner *before* it becomes a problem!

It takes time to restructure your loan payments. Indeed, it can take anywhere from a week or two for your banker to present your request to his or her loan committee, and two or three months to hear from the ultimate owner of your mortgage. Persevere! Most of us have little experience solving complex financial problems. Success will bolster your confidence and boost your morale. You will know that you are doing everything you can to work through a difficult, stressful situation.

There are two critically important facts. Lenders cannot call your loans if they learn you are unemployed as long as you are current on your payments and are not otherwise violating the terms of your contracts. Because your lender reduced your payment schedule doesn't mean your lender reduced the amount of your loan. Usually your lender will stipulate in the agreement contract that you will make a "balloon" payment of all outstanding principal in addition to your last loan payment. Your lender will charge you interest on this additional unpaid principal balance.

What to Do if You Are Strapped for Cash

If you find yourself strapped for cash, either because of your lack of savings and severance dollars or because of credit card and other installment debts, contact your city or county agency that works with people who have overextended themselves with debt, have lost their source of income, or both. These agencies are usually called the Department of Consumer Affairs or the Department of Consumer Assistance, and are staffed with counselors who will help you craft a reasonable repayment plan with your creditors. Your counselor might even be able to persuade your creditors to waive their finance charges, which could net an annual savings to you of up to 22 percent on your unpaid installment balances.

Not-for-profit social service organizations such as United Charities have credit counselors who can help you work out a repayment plan on your consumer non-secured debt. The only charge is a small donation. Another source of help nationwide is the creditor-funded Consumer Credit Counseling Service. Their toll-free number is 1-800-388-2227. Bankers and creditors often prefer to work directly with these agencies. This takes a burden off of your shoulders.

A meeting with a credit counselor is confidential and is for your benefit. Make an appointment to work with one of these agencies *before* you become delinquent. You will save yourself from losing your credit rating, from becoming embroiled in lawsuits and repossessions, and from facing bankruptcy.

Consider the situation that one couple found themselves in when they *both* lost their jobs. They met with a reputable consumer counseling service. Their story illustrates what a counselor can do for you.

> Hugh and Mary lived on the edge. Both were "power shoppers" who had spent to the limit on their store charges and credit cards. They were committed to large monthly home mortgage payments. Their combined annual income was $110,000, but they were both laid off within a month of each other. They realized that they had to quickly readjust their priorities and their lifestyle. They both considered personal bankruptcy, but decided to first seek another solution to their financial dilemma.

> Hugh began collecting unemployment compensation. Fortunately, Mary found employment as an office manager. Her new take-home pay was half that of her previous salary. The couple met with their banker and were able to negotiate a mortgage modification agreement which allowed them to pay only the interest on their home mortgage, and deferred their principal payments for one year. Their banker recommended that they work with a reputable consumer credit counseling agency that could help them with their unsecured charge debts. The agency was able to:

1. Work out a monthly repayment schedule of three percent of their outstanding retail and credit card debts

2. Reduce most and completely eliminate some of their monthly retail interest costs

3. Reduce their credit card interest on unpaid balances from 19.8 percent to an average of 8 percent

4. Request and obtain from their public utilities and phone company a delinquent debt repayment plan

5. Offer them budget and financial reassessment counseling

6. Arrange for Hugh and Mary to pay the agency each month, with the agency directly paying their creditors

Of course, Hugh and Mary had to give up all their charge privileges. They also sold their two-year-old Jeep Cherokee, using the proceeds to pay off their auto loan. They kept their older car for basic transportation. The two of them had no choice but to stop all impulse buying. The following table shows their "before" and "after" budgets.

	Monthly Budget Before	Monthly Budget After
Net take-home pay	$5900	$2910*
Expenses		
Mortgage	$2100	$1100
Insurance	400	200
Auto loan	500	—
Private club (dropped membership)	150	—
Retail & credit card charges	1200	275
Living expenses	1700	1250
Total	$6050	$2825
Cash cushion	<150>	<85>

Crafting a Survival Budget

At this point you should have a clear sense of your own financial obligations and how and where you can obtain

*Mary's monthly salary was $2000. Hugh received $910 in unemployment compensation.

assistance with them. Now it's time to prepare your own Survival Budget. First, total all your financial resources.

My Monthly Survival Resources

My Resources:

Total savings—divide by 12	$ _____
Total severance—divide by 12	_____
Remaining unemployment compensation—divide by 12	_____
Cash values and accumulated dividends from life insurance policies—divide by 12	_____
Spouse's and/or other family income	_____
Stocks and bonds	_____
Market value of your vested pension and profit-sharing plans (less 10 percent tax penalty) —divide by 12*	_____
Market value of your IRAs (less 10 percent penalty tax)—divide by 12*	_____
Total readily available financial resources	$ _____

Now prepare your own Survival Budget using the following worksheets.

*Tap into the cheapest money available first. Your IRA, 401K and pension dollars are the most expensive money you can use. You are also borrowing from your future. Assess the tax implications before you tap into your investments. You want to avoid finding yourself moved into a higher tax bracket just when you have no current income.

Current Personal Monthly Survival Budget

Your Monthly Obligations	Possible percentage savings from current monthly payment	Amount
Regular Monthly Obligations		
Rent or mortgage payments	40%	$ _____
Car payments	50%	$ _____
TV/appliance payments	40–80%	$ _____
Repayment of loans	40–60%	$ _____
Medical/dental plan or insurance will double, assuming you convert		$ _____
Life insurance premiums can double or triple unless you purchase term insurance		$ _____
Other insurance premiums (auto, home)	10–30%	$ _____
Miscellaneous regular payments (credit cards)	50–70%	$ _____
TOTAL	_____%	$ _____
Personal Living Expenses (for entire family)		
Clothing (purchasing, cleaning, repair)	60%	$ _____
Doctor/dentist bills (not covered by plan or insurance usually the same; don't sacrifice your health!)		$ _____
Education: apply for financial aid for your kids	60%	$ _____
Membership dues: ask to become an associate or pay dues only to those groups who can help you with job search	80%	$ _____
Gifts and contributions: not until you have a job!	100%	$ _____
Auto maintenance, gas, parking fees	30%	$ _____
Travel (apart from auto payments, insurance, gas, parking, and maintenance): travel only if necessary and inexpensive	90%	$ _____
Food (home and away)	30%	$ _____
Books, newspapers, magazines: buy newspapers for job search; borrow books and magazines from public library	50%	$ _____
Spending money, allowances	80%	$ _____
Entertainment: rent videos, have friends over, etc.	80%	$ _____
TOTAL	_____%	$ _____

Your Monthly Obligations	Possible percentage savings from current monthly payment	Amount
Household Operating Expenses		
Telephone: install cheapest service	30%	$ _____
Gas and electricity: energy assistance can reduce costs	20%	$ _____
Water	same	$ _____
Sewer charges	same	$ _____
New home fixtures, furniture: enjoy what you own!	100%	$ _____
Repairs, maintenance: become a do-it-yourselfer	60%	$ _____
Other household expenses	100%	$ _____
TOTAL	_____%	$ _____
Taxes		
Federal, state, and local income taxes: unemployment compensation benefits are taxable— take advantage of low-income tax credits		$ _____
Property taxes	same	$ _____
Other taxes	same	$ _____
TOTAL		$ _____
Expense Summary		
Regular monthly obligations total	40–50%	$ _____
Personal living expenses total	40–60%	$ _____
Household operating expenses total	40–60%	$ _____
Taxes: property, same; income, lower		$ _____
TOTAL MONTHLY EXPENSES		$ _____
SURVIVAL BUDGET SUMMARY		
Financial resources, prorated monthly		$ _____
(less) TOTAL monthly survival expenses		$ _____

You now know how long you can financially survive your job search. Become a conserver rather than a consumer! Remember that your days of seeking employment won't last forever. Your Survival Budget will enable you and your family to get through the lean days ahead. Having your new budget before you should significantly reduce your stress. It may boost your morale to know that you are doing everything possible to get through this financially difficult period.

Consider talking to your banker about taking out a home equity loan. This will allow you to use the equity you have built up in your home or condo for basic living expenses. This is not a gift to you from your banker. You are, in fact, using up your greatest asset. If you are fortunate enough to be able to get by without tapping into your resources, seal your credit cards in an envelope. Use your remaining credit limits to pay for any emergency expenses that arise during your unemployment. There is no excuse for not preparing yourself to live within your Survival Budget.

Become familiar with the Loan Modification Agreement in the Addenda to this chapter. This agreement legally provides for your mortgage modifications.

Finally, it is possible that you qualify for the Earned Income Credit. The EIC is a special credit for workers and reduces the taxes you owe. In 1994, if your total taxable and nontaxable earned income was less than $23,755 (if you have one qualifying child) or $25,296 (if you have more than one qualifying child) you would have been eligible for this credit. The credit in 1994 was as high as $2,038 (for those with one qualifying child) and up to $2,528 (for those with more than one qualifying child). Earned income credit can give you a refund even if you don't owe any tax. If you did not have a child living with you, earned less than $9,000, and you or your spouse were at least age 25, the credit in 1994 would have been as high as $306. You will find a sample Schedule EIC in the Addenda to Chapter 2. This is a simple form to complete. The IRS will figure your credit for you if you wish. You will also find a sample Form W (Advance Payment Certificate). The earned income limits change from year to year. If you are eligible for advance payments in any given year, you may receive up to or above $100 a month. You may qualify for earned income credit if your income falls within the limits due to your job search, part-time work, or the salary of your new job.

Addenda to
Chapter 2

Loan Modification Agreement

This is provided as an example. Request the appropriate loan modification agreement form from your bank.

LOAN MODIFICATION AGREEMENT
(Providing for Adjustable Rate and Balloon)

This Loan Modification Agreement ("Agreement") made this **10th** day of _____**May**_____, 19 ____, between ____**DONALD P. and SHIELA JONES**_____ ("Borrower") and ____**FIRST NATIONAL BANK**_____ ("Lender"), amends and supplements (1) the Mortgage, Deed of Trust or Deed to Secure Debt (the "Security Instrument"), dated _____ and recorded in Book or Liber _____, at page(s) _____, of the ___**Note**____

(Name of Records)

Records of _____, and (2) the Note bearing the same date as, and secured by,

(County and State, or other Jurisdiction)

the Security Instrument, which covers the real and personal property described in the Security Instrument and defined therein as the "Property", located at _____,

the real property described being set forth as follows:

(Property Address)

(YOUR PROPERTY DESCRIPTION)

In consideration of the mutual promises and agreements exchanged, the parties hereto agree as follows (notwithstanding anything to the contrary contained in the Note or Security Instrument):

1. As of _____, the amount payable under the Note and the Security Instrument (the "Unpaid Principal Balance") is U.S. $_____, consisting of the amount(s) loaned to the Borrower by the Lender and any interest capitalized to date.

2. The Borrower promises to pay the Unpaid Principal Balance, plus interest, to the order of the Lender. XXXXXXX XXXXXXXXXXXXXXXXXXXXXXXXXXXXXXXXXXXXXXXXXXXXXXXXXXXXXXXXXXXXXXXXXX XXXXXXXXXXXXXXXXXXXXXXXXXXXXXXXXXXXXXXXXXXXXXXXXXXXXXXXXXXXXXXXXXXXX XXXXXXXXXXXXXXXXXXXXXXXXXXXXXXXXXXXXXXXXXXXXXXXXXXXXXXXXXXXXXXXXXXXX XXXXXXXXXXXXXXXXXXXXXXXXXXXXXXXXXXXXXXXXXXXXXXXXXXXXXXXXXXXXX If on _____ (the "Maturity Date"), the Borrower still owes amounts under the Note and the Security Instrument, as amended by this Agreement, the Borrower will pay these amounts in full on the Maturity Date.

    The Borrower will make such payments at _____ or at such other place as the Lender may require.

3. If all or any part of the Property or any interest in it is sold or transferred (or if a beneficial interest in the Borrower is sold or transferred and the Borrower is not a natural person) without the Lender's prior written consent, the Lender may, at its option, require immediate payment in full of all sums secured by this Security Instrument.

    If the Lender exercises this option, the Lender shall give the Borrower notice of acceleration. The notice shall provide a period of not less than 30 days from the date the notice is delivered or mailed within which the Borrower must pay all sums secured by this Security Instrument. If the Borrower fails to pay these sums prior to the expiration of this period, the Lender may invoke any remedies permitted by this Security Instrument without further notice or demand on the Borrower.

LOAN MODIFICATION AGREEMENT—Single Family—Fannie Mae Uniform Instrument   Form 3179 2/88

4. The Borrower also will comply with all other covenants, agreements, and requirements of the Security Instrument, including without limitation, the Borrower's covenants and agreements to make all payments of taxes, insurance premiums, assessments, escrow items, impounds, and all other payments that the Borrower is obligated to make under the Security Instrument; however, the following terms and provisions are forever canceled, null and void, as of the date specified in paragraph No. 1 above:

   (a) all terms and provisions of the Note and Security Instrument (if any) providing for, implementing, or relating to, any change or adjustment in the rate of interest payable under the Note; and

   (b) all terms and provisions of any adjustable rate rider or other instrument or document that is affixed to, wholly or partially incorporated into, or is part of, the Note or Security Instrument and that contains any such terms and provisions as those referred to in (a) above.

5. Nothing in this Agreement shall be understood or construed to be a satisfaction or release in whole or in part of the Note and Security Instrument. Except as otherwise specifically provided in this Agreement, the Note and Security Instrument will remain unchanged, and the Borrower and Lender will be bound by, and comply with, all of the terms and provisions thereof, as amended by this Agreement.

_____ (Seal)   _Donald P. Jones_ _____ (Seal)
                              Lender   Borrower

By: _____   _Shiela Jones_ _____ (Seal)
                                                               Borrower

Schedule EIC (Earned Income Credit)

Be sure to use an updated form, available from the IRS or your local post office or library, as certain items may have changed.

SCHEDULE EIC (Form 1040A or 1040) Department of the Treasury Internal Revenue Service (10)	**Earned Income Credit** **(Qualifying Child Information)** ▶ Attach to Form 1040A or 1040. ▶ See instructions on back.	OMB No. 1545-0074 **19__** Attachment Sequence No. **43**
Name(s) shown on return JAMES T. AND LAURA SMITH		Your social security number 31549 9738

Before You Begin . . .

- Answer the questions on page 44 (1040A) or page 27 (1040) to see if you can take this credit.
- If you can take the credit, fill in the worksheet on page 45 (1040A) or page 28 (1040) to figure your credit. **But if you want the IRS to figure it for you, see page 40 (1040A) or page 24 (1040).**

Then, complete and attach Schedule EIC only if you have a qualifying child (see boxes on back).

Information About Your Qualifying Child or Children

If you have more than two qualifying children, you only have to list two to get the maximum credit.

Caution: *If you don't fill in all the lines that apply, it will take us longer to process your return and issue your refund.*	**(a) Child 1**	**(b) Child 2**
1 Child's name (first, initial, and last name)	THOMAS P. SMITH	LAURA L. SMITH
2 Child's year of birth	19_75_	19_79_
3 If child was born **before 1976** AND—		
a was a student **under age 24** at the end of 1994, check the "Yes" box, **OR**	[X] Yes	[ ] Yes
b was permanently and totally disabled (see back), check the "Yes" box	[ ] Yes	[ ] Yes
4 If child was born **before 1994,** enter the child's social security number	387 49 2501	387 52 7204
5 Child's relationship to you (for example, son, grandchild, etc.)	SON	DAUGHTER
6 Number of months child lived with you in the U.S. in 1994	12 months	12 months

TIP: Do you want the earned income credit added to your take-home pay in 1995? To see if you qualify, get **Form W-5** from your employer or by calling the IRS at 1-800-TAX-FORM (1-800-829-3676).

For Paperwork Reduction Act Notice, see Form 1040A or 1040 instructions.   Cat. No. 13339M   **Schedule EIC (Form 1040A or 1040) 1994**

Instructions

Purpose of Schedule

If you can take the earned income credit and have a qualifying child, use Schedule EIC to give information about that child. To figure the amount of your credit, use the worksheet on page 45 of the Form 1040A instructions or page 28 of the Form 1040 instructions.

Line 1

Enter each qualifying child's name.

Line 3a

If your child was born **before 1976** but was under age 24 at the end of 1994 and a student, put a checkmark in the "Yes" box.

Your child was a **student** if he or she—

● Was enrolled as a full-time student at a school during any 5 months of 1994, or

● Took a full-time, on-farm training course during any 5 months of 1994. The course had to be given by a school or a state, county, or local government agency.

A **school** includes technical, trade, and mechanical schools. It does not include on-the-job training courses or correspondence schools.

Line 3b

If your child was born **before 1976** and was permanently and totally disabled during any part of 1994, put a checkmark in the "Yes" box.

A person is **permanently and totally disabled** if **both** of the following apply.

1. He or she cannot engage in any substantial gainful activity because of a physical or mental condition.

2. A doctor determines the condition has lasted or can be expected to last continuously for at least a year or can lead to death.

Line 4

If your child was born **before 1994,** you must enter his or her social security number (SSN) on line 4. If you don't enter an SSN or if the SSN you enter is incorrect, it will take us longer to issue any refund shown on your return. If your child doesn't have a number, apply for one by filing **Form SS-5** with your local Social Security Administration (SSA) office. It usually takes about 2 weeks to get a number. If your child won't have an SSN by April 17, 1995, you can get an automatic 4-month extension by filing Form 4868 with the IRS by that date.

Line 6

Enter the number of months your child lived with you in your home in the United States during 1994. Do not enter more than 12. Count temporary absences, such as for school, vacation, or medical care, as time lived in your home. If the child lived with you for more than half of 1994 but less than 7 months, enter "7" on this line.

Exception. If your child, including a foster child, was born or died in 1994 and your home was the child's home for the entire time he or she was alive during 1994, enter "12" on line 6.

Qualifying Child

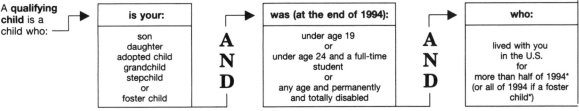

If the child was married or is also a qualifying child of another person (other than your spouse if filing a joint return), special rules apply. For details, see page 47 of the Form 1040A instructions or page 28 of the Form 1040 instructions.

IRS Form W–5 Earned Income Credit Advance Payment Certificate

Be sure to use an updated form, available from the IRS or your local post office or library, as certain items may change slightly from year to year.

Form **W-5**

Department of the Treasury
Internal Revenue Service

**Earned Income Credit
Advance Payment Certificate**

19__ __

Instructions

Purpose

Use Form W-5 if you are eligible to get part of the earned income credit (EIC) in advance with your pay and choose to do so. If you choose not to get advance payments, you can still claim the EIC on your 1995 tax return.

Caution: *At the time this form went to print, Congress was considering legislation that would (1) allow certain members of the Armed Forces stationed outside the United States to claim the EIC and get advance payment of the EIC for 1995, (2) require the reporting of social security numbers for qualifying children born before November 1, 1995, and (3) make most nonresident aliens ineligible to claim the EIC for 1995. For later information about this legislation, get Pub. 553, Highlights of 1994 Tax Law Changes.*

What Is the EIC?

The EIC is a special credit for certain workers. It reduces tax you owe. It may give you a refund even if you don't owe any tax. For 1995, the EIC can be as much as $2,094 if you have one qualifying child; $3,110 if you have more than one qualifying child; $314 if you do not have a qualifying child. See **Who Is a Qualifying Child?** later. But you **cannot** get advance EIC payments unless you have a qualifying child.

Who Is Eligible To Get Advance EIC Payments?

You are eligible to get advance EIC payments if **all three** of the following apply:

1. You have at least one qualifying child.

2. You expect that your 1995 earned income and adjusted gross income will each be less than $24,396 (including your spouse's income if you expect to file a joint return).

3. You expect to be able to claim the EIC for 1995. To find out if you may be able to claim the EIC, answer the questions on page 2. If you expect to file **Form 2555**, Foreign Earned Income, or **Form 2555-EZ**, Foreign Earned Income Exclusion, for 1995, you **cannot** claim the EIC.

How Do I Get Advance EIC Payments?

If you are eligible to get advance EIC payments for 1995, you may be able to get up to $105 a month added to your take-home pay. To get advance EIC payments, fill in the Form W-5 at the bottom of this page. Then, detach it and give it to your employer. If you get advance payments, you **must** file a 1995 Form 1040A or Form 1040.

You may have only **one** Form W-5 in effect with a current employer at one time. If you and your spouse are both employed, you should file separate Forms W-5.

This Form W-5 expires on December 31, 1995. If you are eligible to get advance EIC payments for 1996, you must file a new Form W-5 next year.

Note: *You may be able to get a larger credit when you file your 1995 return. For details, see Additional Credit on page 2.*

Who Is a Qualifying Child?

Any child who meets **all three** of the following conditions is a **qualifying child:**

1. The child is your son, daughter, adopted child, stepchild, foster child, or a

descendant (for example, your grandchild) of your son, daughter, or adopted child.

Note: *An adopted child includes a child placed with you by an authorized placement agency for legal adoption even if the adoption isn't final. A foster child is any child you cared for as your own child.*

2. The child is under age 19 or a full-time student under age 24 at the end of 1995, or is permanently and totally disabled.

3. The child lives with you in the United States for more than half of 1995 (for all of 1995 if a foster child). If the child does not live with you for the required time because the child was born or died in 1995, the child is considered to have lived with you for all of 1995 if your home in the United States was the child's home for the entire time he or she was alive in 1995.

Note: *Temporary absences such as for school, medical care, or vacation count as time lived with you.*

Married child.—If the child is married at the end of 1995, the child is a qualifying child only if you may claim the child as your dependent or the following **Exception** applies to you.

Exception. You are the custodial parent and would be able to claim the child as your dependent, but the noncustodial parent claims the child as a dependent because—

• You signed **Form 8332**, Release of Claim to Exemption for Child of Divorced or Separated Parents, or a similar statement, agreeing not to claim the child for 1995, or

(Continued on page 2)

Give the lower part to your employer; keep the top part for your records.
...... Detach along this line ......

Form **W-5**

Department of the Treasury
Internal Revenue Service

**Earned Income Credit
Advance Payment Certificate**
▶ Give this certificate to your employer.
▶ This certificate expires on December 31, 1995.

OMB No. 1545-1342

19__ __

Type or print your full name

JAMES T. SMITH

Your social security number
315 : 49 : 9738

Note: *If you get advance payments of the earned income credit for 1995, you **must** file a 1995 Form 1040A or Form 1040. To get advance payments, you **must** have a qualifying child and your filing status must be any status **except** married filing a separate return.*

		Yes	No
1	I expect to be able to claim the earned income credit for 1995, I do not have another Form W-5 in effect with any other current employer, and I choose to get advance EIC payments . . .	✓	
2	Do you have a qualifying child? . . .	✓	
3	Are you married? . . .	✓	
4	If you are married, does your spouse have a Form W-5 in effect for 1995 with any employer? . . .		✓

Under penalties of perjury, I declare that the information I have furnished above is, to the best of my knowledge, true, correct, and complete.

Signature ▶ *James T Smith*　　　　Date ▶

Cat. No. 10227P

Questions To See If You May Be Able To Claim the EIC for 1995

1   Do you have a qualifying child? Read **Who Is a Qualifying Child?** on page 1 before you answer this question. If the child is married, be sure you also read **Married child** on page 1.

☐ **No. Stop here.** You may be able to claim the EIC but you **cannot** get advance EIC payments.

☑ **Yes.** Continue.

Caution: *If the child is a qualifying child for both you and another person, the child is your qualifying child only if you expect your 1995 adjusted gross income to be* **higher** *than the other person's adjusted gross income. If the other person is your spouse and you expect to file a joint return for 1995, this rule doesn't apply.*

2   Do you expect your 1995 filing status to be Married filing a separate return?

☐ **Yes. Stop here.** You **cannot** claim the EIC.

☑ **No.** Continue.

3   Do you expect that your 1995 earned income and adjusted gross income will each be less than $24,396 (less than $26,673 if you have more than one qualifying child)? If you expect to file a joint return for 1995, include your spouse's income when answering this question.

TIP: To find out what is included in adjusted gross income, you can look at page 1 of your 1994 Form 1040EZ, Form 1040A, or Form 1040.

☐ **No. Stop here.** You **cannot** claim the EIC.

☑ **Yes.** Continue. But remember, you **cannot** get advance EIC payments if you expect your 1995 earned income or adjusted gross income will be $24,396 or more.

4   Do **you** expect to be a qualifying child of another person for 1995?

☑ **No.** You may be able to claim the EIC.

☐ **Yes.** You **cannot** claim the EIC.

● You have a pre-1985 divorce decree or separation agreement that allows the noncustodial parent to claim the child and he or she gives at least $600 for the child's support in 1995.

Qualifying child of more than one person.—If the child is a qualifying child of more than one person, only the person with the **highest** adjusted gross income for 1995 may treat that child as a qualifying child. If the other person is your spouse and you expect to file a joint return for 1995, this rule doesn't apply.

Reminder.—You must get a social security number for a qualifying child born before 1995.

What If My Situation Changes?

If your situation changes after you give Form W-5 to your employer, you usually will need to file a new Form W-5. For example, you should file a new Form W-5 if any of the following applies for 1995:

● You no longer have a qualifying child. Check "No" on line 2 of your new Form W-5.

● You expect your filing status to be Married filing separately, you expect to be a qualifying child of another person, or you expect your earned income or adjusted gross income to be $24,396 or more. Check "No" on line 1 of your new Form W-5.

● You no longer want advance payments. Check "No" on line 1 of your new Form W-5.

● Your spouse files Form W-5 with his or her employer. Check "Yes" on line 4 of your new Form W-5.

Note: *If you get the EIC with your pay and find you are not eligible, you must pay it back when you file your 1995 Federal income tax return.*

Additional Information

How To Claim the EIC

If you have at least one qualifying child, fill in and attach **Schedule EIC** to your 1995 Form 1040 or Form 1040A. In addition to other information, the social security number of your qualifying child born before 1995 must be shown on Schedule EIC. To figure your EIC, use the worksheet in your 1995 Form 1040 or Form 1040A instruction booklet.

Additional Credit

You may be able to claim a larger credit when you file your 1995 tax return because your employer is not permitted to give you more than $1,257 of the EIC in advance with your pay. You may also be able to claim a larger credit if you have more than one qualifying child. But you must file your 1995 tax return to claim any additional credit.

Privacy Act and Paperwork Reduction Act Notice

We ask for the information on this form to carry out the Internal Revenue laws of the United States. Internal Revenue Code sections 3507 and 6109 and their regulations require you to provide the information requested on Form W-5 and give the form to your employer if you want advance payment of the EIC. As provided by law, we may give the information to the Department of Justice and other Federal agencies. In addition, we may give it to cities, states, and the District of Columbia so they may carry out their tax laws.

The time needed to complete this form will vary depending on individual circumstances. The estimated average time is: **Recordkeeping,** 7 min.; **Learning about the law or the form,** 9 min.; and **Preparing the form,** 26 min.

If you have comments concerning the accuracy of these time estimates or suggestions for making this form simpler, we would be happy to hear from you. You can write to both the **Internal Revenue Service,** Attention: Tax Forms Committee, PC:FP, Washington, DC 20224; and the **Office of Management and Budget,** Paperwork Reduction Project (1545-1342), Washington, DC 20503. **DO NOT** send this form to either of these offices. Instead, give it to your employer.

Your Financial Safety Net: Insurance

I am not an insurance professional. However, I was responsible for designing and managing an employee benefits program for one company during my career. I have the personal knowledge and the professional experience to tell you that it is crucial for you to maintain a basic personal risk management program throughout your unemployment.

In this chapter, you will learn how to craft the least expensive insurance program that will meet your needs and how to figure the dollar amount of coverage you need for life insurance, medical insurance, disability insurance, and homeowner's and vehicle coverage.

Additionally, you'll discover how to save premium dollars, pick a financially sound insurance company, and select your insurance agent.

Your Insurance Needs

Webster's Third International Dictionary defines insurance as a "device for the elimination or reduction of an economic risk to all members of a large group by employing a system of equitable contributions out of which losses are paid." You need insurance in order to avoid financial catastrophe. Insurance coverage provides:

- Assistance in your economic survival

- Indemnification in case of economic loss

- A basis for credit (no bank will lend you money for a mortgage or home equity loan unless your home is insured against loss)

- Peace of mind

When you were working your employer paid an amount equal to what you paid into your social security account (FICA). Your employer also paid between 25 and 40 percent over and above your gross earnings for premiums to insure you for unemployment compensation benefits, group life, health and disability, and for liability during business travel. These are all part of the employee benefits package which is designed to protect your economic security. Your benefits were part of your compensation.

As we know, life is uncertain, and job loss is a traumatic event. Psychologists tell us it is second only to the death of a spouse in terms of the stress and upheaval it creates in our lives. Now, more than ever, you want to minimize your and your family's exposure to the risk of injury and illness, destruction of property, liability, and loss of life.

Let's begin assessing your insurance needs by preparing an inventory of your coverage by category. After you study this chapter and consult with your agent, you will want to compare your current coverage to the amount of coverage you need to carry during your unemployment. Use the space provided on the following page to do this.

Your Medical Coverage

	Insured	Company	Policy maximum	Deductible	Co-insurance	Stop-loss	Premium
1.	_____	_____	_____	_____	_____	_____	_____
2.	_____	_____	_____	_____	_____	_____	_____

Continuing Your Coverage with COBRA

It is important for you to carry health (medical expense) insurance in order to avoid medical bankruptcy. COBRA, the Consolidated Omnibus Budget Reconciliation Act, gives you the option of continuing your health insurance coverage after you lose your job. The act applies to employers who provide health benefits to a group of 20 or more employees. If you elect to continue your benefits under COBRA, you will pay your former employer's share of the premium in addition to your own. For most people, this means your health premiums will double and there will be an additional administrative fee of up to two percent.

COBRA is a lifesaver for you and your dependents as the act allows you to continue your coverage regardless of your medical condition. You become eligible for COBRA coverage because your group coverage terminated due to one of these qualifying events:

Qualifying Events	Duration of Continuation Coverage
1. Termination of employment (except for "gross misconduct")	Up to 18 months
2. Reduction of the employee's hours which results in a loss of coverage	Up to 18 months
3. The death of an employee	Up to 36 months
4. Divorce	Up to 36 months
5. A dependent child no longer meets the definition of an eligible dependent	Up to 36 months

In the event of an employee's death, dependent coverage under his or her group plan automatically continues for the time period, if any, specified in the plan. The COBRA continuance option takes effect after the end of that period if the surviving spouse or heirs request it.

Termination of continued coverage

Coverage ends when any of the following events occur:

- Your employer ceases to provide a group health plan to employees

- You fail to pay your premium when due

- You become a covered employee under any other group health plan, after the date of election

- In the case of a spouse: when the spouse remarries and gains coverage under another group health plan

- Your specified duration period ends

Election

The human resources person at your company will give you an election (acceptance) form to sign and return which states that you want to continue your coverage. You need to complete the form and return it to your employer within 60 days of your termination date.

How you pay for continued coverage

Remember that under COBRA you pay the entire cost of your coverage, including what your employer was contributing. The amount and the method of payment are explained in your election form. You must make your first payment to your previous employer no later than 45 days from the date of election. You must make additional payments in a timely manner, usually on the 25th day of the month, for coverage for the following month.

How to Save on Insurance Premiums

First, sign up for your continuation coverage. Then, if you have no pre-existing medical problems and are in good health, shop for carriers offering policies that only cover hospitalization, emergency care, and surgical expenses. You will pay for routine visits to the doctor and for prescription drugs. These catastrophic illness policies usually do not provide coverage for maternity, mental illness, or for substance abuse. Most carriers offer a range of deductibles and out-of-pocket minimums. Your typical premium savings can be as much as 40 percent of the cost of traditional insurance plans with comparable deductibles and out-of-pocket minimums. Blue Cross–Blue Shield of Illinois is one of a number of companies offering such a plan. Some insurance companies offer guaranteed renewable short-term (three and six month) medical policies. It's best to explore every opportunity and buy the least expensive health insurance coverage that meets your specific needs.

If you are between the ages of 50 and 64, consider joining the American Association of Retired Persons (AARP). Membership in the AARP is only eight dollars a year and is available to anyone over 50. AARP offers two excellent Group Hospital Indemnity Benefits plans. AARP's address is 601 E. Street, N.W., Washington, D.C. 20049.

Getting health coverage when you have a serious medical problem

If you or a family member has a serious medical condition, new health insurance will be prohibitively expensive. On top of the cost, most insurance companies have a one or two-year waiting period before they will pay medical costs for the condition. You should definitely continue your COBRA coverage. While still covered, you can also explore an alternative. Call your state's Department of Insurance Commissioners. Most states offer enrollment in a pooled risk program for those who cannot otherwise buy insurance. Requirements vary with each state, but most programs require a six month waiting period on pre-existing conditions. Many programs will allow you to waive this waiting period if you have an incurable illness and are willing to pay a higher premium.

Choosing the Coverage That's Right for You

Let's examine how two families with entirely different medical situations chose health insurance packages that worked the best for them. Try to place yourself in their shoes. It will help you determine what you should look for when seeking insurance.

Don lost his job because of a plant closing. He and his wife Martha are in their late thirties and have one daughter. All three are in excellent health. When Don learned that his COBRA insurance premiums would rise from $250 to $500 per month (plus a two percent administrative fee) he opted for a new major medical policy with a high deductible ($1000 per family member). The monthly premiums for this new policy were less than $200. He also dropped his group life coverage (which he had to convert to whole life 30 days after his severance period ended) and purchased an individual convertible term life policy having a face amount that covered the unpaid balance on his home mortgage and auto loans as well as one year's income should he die. (More about this later.) By taking these steps, Don provided himself and his family with the necessary coverage in case of disaster. More immediately, he conserved cash he would need during his job search.

Sheila and Ken faced a different situation. After losing her job, Sheila elected to continue her COBRA medical coverage and converted her group life to an individual policy even though this meant hefty premium increases. She and her husband Ken both have serious health problems and have large prescription drug expenses. Sheila knew that most health and life policies normally exclude benefits for pre-existing conditions for either one or two years. It made sense for Sheila to continue her coverage with COBRA because her risk of incurring costs from a serious illness was much greater than the reward of saving premium dollars.

Both of these families met with their insurance agents to review their homeowners' and auto insurance plans. They asked their agents if they could save on insurance costs by increasing deductibles or by dropping unnecessary coverage.

If you or your spouse is pregnant, elect to continue your group healthcare coverage. Your new carrier will classify the pregnancy as a pre-existing condition and will either pay you no benefits at all, or only up to the policy's pre-existing benefit limit, if your new contract has one. These amounts average $1000. A difficult pregnancy could cost many thousands of dollars more.

Disability income insurance

Many employers offer disability income insurance coverage to their employees. Often this coverage is the least discussed and is the least understood part of your financial safety net.

Your Disability Income Coverage

Insurance company	Policy number	Monthly income	Benefits start	Benefits end	Monthly premium
_____	_____	_____	_____	_____	_____
_____	_____	_____	_____	_____	_____

60 percent of your gross monthly income: $_____

The policy features of disability income insurance include:

1. Group policy

2. Personal policy

3. Association policy

4. Non-cancelable & guaranteed renewable

5. Guaranteed insurability

6. Your own occupation

7. Any occupation

8. Partial disability

9. Residual disability

10. Inflation rider

Do you need disability coverage?

There are some statistics you should know. Before you reach 40, the likelihood of your becoming disabled for at least 90 days is more than three times greater than your chance of dying. If you are between the ages of 50 and 60, your risk of disability is two to one. Insurers tell us that if a person experiences a disability that lasts for more than 90 days, he or she can expect that they will be disabled for at least five years. A disability caused by a serious accident will not only stop your job search efforts, but will also substantially increase your medical and associated care expenses.

If you have already been laid off and did not elect to purchase an individual continuation disability policy, but that privilege remains in your severance contract, contact your former company's disability insurer to convert to an individual policy. It is easier to convert during your severance period (when pre-existing conditions do not apply) than apply independently later.

If your previous employer did not provide this coverage, purchase a non-cancelable, guaranteed renewable policy from a financially sound insurer. Make sure that the policy insures 60 percent of your monthly gross income and has a reasonable definition of disability. The policy should specify that you qualify for disability if, as a result of injury or sickness, you are unable to engage in the substantial and material duties of your regular occupation. Insurers call this your "Own Occupation."

Author's tip: As long as you pay your disability premiums with after-tax dollars, any benefit dollars you receive are tax-free and do not affect any other benefits for which you are eligible through Social Security or other government agencies.

Life insurance

Job loss is traumatic. The stress associated with job loss causes us to become more accident prone and can activate or worsen any existing physical condition. It is critical for you to maintain adequate life insurance coverage.

Your Life Insurance Inventory

Insurance company	Type of policy	Death benefit	Cash value	Policy loan	Annual premium
_____	_____	_____	_____	_____	_____
_____	_____	_____	_____	_____	_____
Totals:		_____	_____	_____	_____

Policy Beneficiaries:

Primary Beneficiary _____

Secondary Beneficiary_____

If you don't know what type of policy you own, look at the bottom of the front page of your contract. You will find a brief statement defining your policy: whole life, variable life, term, or universal life. Each year your insurer will send you a statement on your policy's anniversary date. This statement lists your policy's accumulated cash value and dividends, less any outstanding premium loans. If you can't find your policy, contact your insurance agent to find out the current amount of cash values and any outstanding policy loans. If you own older whole life policies, you can borrow against their accumulated cash values to help pay for your basic living expenses. You can use your annual policy dividends to help pay your premiums.

How much life insurance do you need?

As you cut your expenses, ask yourself this important question: "If I should die, will those I care about suffer economic loss?" If you believe they will, you need life insurance. Life insurance guarantees that the person or persons who could suffer economic loss in the event of your death will be indemnified for that loss. In other words, it provides a safety net for the people you care about.

There is a minimum amount of coverage you must carry at the lowest cost to you while you are unemployed. The amount you need to carry depends upon your personal circumstances. Make a list of the financial obligations your heirs would be responsible to pay. Below is a list of some typical obligations. Modify this list to reflect your own circumstances.

Your Insurance Needs

Item	Amount
Federal income tax and funeral expenses	$ _____
Estate and inheritance taxes (if any)	$ _____
Debts:	
Mortgage principal balance due	$ _____
Installment debts:	
Auto	$ _____
Credit cards	$ _____
Retail	$ _____
Current bills	$ _____
Special obligations:	
Contracts	$ _____
Divorce (alimony and child support payments)	$ _____
Pledges	$ _____
Business	$ _____
Family Emergency Fund (One year's gross income)	$ _____
Total financial obligations you must fund by insurance	$ _____

You now have an accurate picture of the minimum amount of coverage that will be needed to meet your financial obligations should something happen to you.

Next, let's talk about your employer group life insurance. Your group life coverage will end 31 days after your termination. During this time you can elect to convert all or part of your group insurance to an individual whole life policy without a medical exam. Whole life premiums are more expensive than group life, which is term insurance. You cannot convert your group life to an individual term life policy.

If you have medical problems you will want to convert at least part of your group coverage regardless of the cost. If you are healthy and under age 60, however, you might consider buying annual renewable convertible term insurance. Your immediate goal in buying term insurance is to spend the least amount of your out-of-pocket cash for protection.

Asset insurance

Almost everyone is familiar with insurance that covers personal assets. Lenders require homeowners to purchase insurance before they will grant you a mortgage. States mandate that drivers insure their vehicles. Review your policies so that you know exactly what you are insuring. Then we'll cover ideas that could help save on your premiums.

Your Residence/Real Estate Insurance Coverage

Company	Deductible	Contents	Liability maximum	Medical maximum	Flood	Special riders	Annual premium
_____	_____	_____	_____	_____	_____	_____	_____
_____	_____	_____	_____	_____	_____	_____	_____

Your Vehicle Insurance Coverage

Company	Deductible	Comprehensive	Liability maximum	Medical maximum	Car rental expense	Un- or under-insured vehicle	Emergency road service	Annual premium
_____	_____	_____	_____	_____	_____	_____	_____	_____
_____	_____	_____	_____	_____	_____	_____	_____	_____

Your total residence/real estate insurance premium(s) $_____

Your total vehicle insurance premium(s) $_____

Your total asset insurance premiums $_____

Reviewing Your Insurance Policies

Review your coverage with your agent to uncover other areas where you can save valuable premium dollars. Be sure to ask your agent about all of the ways you might be able to save money, such as increasing your deductibles or installing safety devices in your home.

Check your policies to make sure you are not insuring something on a rider on your homeowner's or renter's policy that you no longer own.

There are also a number of questions to ask your agent when you review your vehicle coverage. Money-saving options could include good-driver and low-mileage discounts, higher deductibles, and dropping collision coverage on older cars. Ask about these and other cost-effective options.

Work with your professional agent, who can help you develop the best insurance package at the lowest cost without sacrificing your liability coverage.

Choosing the Right Insurance Agent and Carrier

A professional agent will empathize with your situation, understand your needs, and develop the best coverage package at the least cost. Talk to as many agents as you need to, until you find one with whom you feel comfortable.

Ask about the agent's background. Most career insurance professionals have taken courses to become designated as Chartered Life Underwriters (CLUs) or as Certified Financial Planners (CFPs).

Ask your agent about the A.M. Best and Company rating of any carrier recommended to you. Best's analyzes the financial strength of insurance companies and assigns a risk rating to them. Any recommended carrier should carry a minimum of an "A" rating for the past five years.

You may also want to meet with the agent or broker who sells insurance to your former employer, to learn about converting your group benefits.

Mastering the Unemployment Office

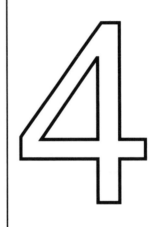

What should you bring?

What should you expect?

What should you know?

How much will you get?

Chapter 4 will explain everything you need to know to tackle the unemployment office: how you qualify, what can disqualify you, what information you need to bring, and what determines the amount of money you will receive. Chapter 4 will be especially helpful to those of you who are facing imminent unemployment, and government and military personnel who believe they will be affected by budget reductions and base closings. If you are currently collecting unemployment benefits and were laid off—or your work schedule was reduced—because of increased imports, read the section discussing Trade Assistance Benefits. You might qualify for additional monetary allowances and job training and job search benefits. Otherwise, proceed to Chapter 5.

Registering with the Department of Employment Security

The purpose of state unemployment offices (in some states called bureaus or departments of Employment Security) is to process claims for unemployment insurance benefits. The unemployment office might seem to you like a cold and austere world populated by sullen clients and grim bureaucrats. As you learn to surmount its quirks and learn your "survival ropes," dealing with the unemployment office will become easier.

First, accept the fact that in the eyes of civil servants, everyone is created equal. In the world of the unemployment office, it makes no difference if you were a senior vice president of XYZ Corporation or one of its assistant shipping clerks. You are applying for and you are entitled to benefits if your job was *insured work* for an employer who is subject to the law—one who is required to make payments (as taxes) to your state under your state's Unemployment Insurance Act. *Leave your ego at home.*

Most of the civil servants you will encounter are genuinely conscientious and caring people who are working within the rules and regulations of the system. Because of funding cutbacks, you can expect to find little "new blood." Most employees are entrenched and they know the rules and regulations. If you bring the proper information and treat them in a courteous and cooperative manner, they will do their best for you. However, if you attempt to cover your loss of dignity by treating your counselor in a rude or hostile way, your actions could jeopardize your main source of income during your transition. Agencies' statistics indicate that claimants who create difficulties for their interviewers are disqualified for benefits more than twice as often as are cooperative claimants.

Although procedures vary from state to state, the routine is essentially the same. Locate the address of the office closest to your home in the yellow or white pages. Take a deep breath and step inside the office. You will be asked to stand in line. Next, an expediter will take your name, assign you a number, and hand you a benefit application form for you to complete. Then you will sit at one of the tables and complete the form. At that point, you could wait and wait for a counselor to call your name for your initial interview. Unemployment offices are busy places.

Important tips

1. On your first visit, especially if you must travel a long distance to reach your nearest unemployment office, make sure you arrive early in the day. It will only add to your frustration to have driven 50 or 60 miles to apply for benefits only to be told in the late afternoon, after a long wait, that there is not enough time left to process the rest of the claimants that day, and that you will have to come back the next day.

2. Don't phone the office. You might be given incorrect information. Due to the increased number of claimants and government cutbacks on hiring, counselors are often too overwhelmed to help claimants over the phone. They are too busy assisting claimants in person to answer questions over the phone and, after they process their claimants, they have paperwork to complete.

You need to bring the following information with you to your initial interview:

1. Your Social Security card.

2. Any unemployment insurance forms your employer has given you.

3. Employer names, addresses, and dates of employment for the last 18 months. In states that keep wage records, a claimant only need give the name of his or her last employer to the counselor.

4. Your evidence of earnings, such as payroll check stubs and withholding statements (W–2 Forms).

5. If you are a former federal employee, bring your Standard Form 8 and Personnel Action Form 50, or any other documents that prove that you worked for the federal government.

6. If you were in the military, bring a copy of your DD Form 214 and your Social Security card. Also bring

your record of employment, if any, both before and/or after your military service during the last two years.

Be prepared to provide complete information about:

1. Why you are unemployed

2. Wages earned including dismissal pay, vacation pay, retirement pay, and any other earnings

3. Names and birth dates of your children under 18 who are supported by you, and the name or names of any child over 18 years supported by you who cannot work because of illness or disability

4. Your spouse's Social Security number, if supported by you, and information about your spouse's employment in your state during the last two years

5. Your efforts to find another job

You should file your claim during the first week of unemployment. There is no best time to visit the unemployment office. However, some offices suggest that you arrive about 45 minutes before the doors open since the lines become long around 10:00–10:30 A.M. Agency personnel will tell you that Mondays, Tuesdays, and Wednesdays are the worst days to come. Thursdays and Fridays are better. Most people are terminated on Friday, at the end of the workweek, or on a Monday before the workweek begins. Most people rush to their unemployment office the same or the following day to file for benefits, where they wait in long lines. The first in are usually the first out, and Fridays tend to be the least crowded days.

Some advice from a survivor

Be prepared to spend several hours waiting when you go for your initial determination interview. Take along a good book or a tablet of paper and a pocket calculator so you can work on your Survival Budget or draft letters to your creditors. Use this time productively. It will:

1. Help reduce your feelings of frustration

2. Eliminate the chance of you engaging in negative and depressing conversations with others who are waiting—many of whom are hostile and will direct their resentment at everything and everyone remotely associated with their misfortune

3. Provide time for you to complete some very important tasks

Your initial interview

At your initial interview your counselor will review your application form. Whether or not you will receive benefits depends upon a factual examination of your case. Tell your interviewer all the details honestly and show him or her any documentation that substantiates your story. Never lie or omit important details. Your interviewer has worked with thousands of claimants and has heard every story there is to tell. Lying now could disqualify you and take you off the benefit eligibility rolls for one year or more. You could even be charged with a misdemeanor for committing fraud.

In Illinois, for example, if you give false or misleading information or hold back any information in order to draw benefits to which you are not entitled, you may be subject to a $500 fine or six months in jail *or both*. In addition to these possible criminal penalties, you may not draw benefits again until you have served a number of "penalty weeks" (or two years have elapsed from the time your ineligibility began) and you have either repaid the amount of fraudulent benefits you have received or that amount has been recovered from benefits otherwise payable to you.

Your interviewer will ask you why you left your job. Explain why you left. If you were laid off as part of a mass layoff due to restructuring, or because your employer had no work for you, you should experience little problem in qualifying for benefits. This is why many companies define their terminations as "permanent layoffs" or "layoffs with packages." Their human resources people feel that this method is more humane. They believe it spawns less anger and bad feelings toward the company. Moreover, they want to avoid the hassle and additional paperwork involved with denial of benefit appeals.

Your interviewer wants to know why you were terminated and who was at fault. Your interviewer most likely will request that you write a brief explanation about why you were discharged. For example, your best efforts did not meet the work standards of your employer. State your reason honestly and don't leave out any pertinent information. Omit unnecessary facts that could slant your argument against you. If you were discharged for gross misconduct committed on the job, you will be disqualified (sometimes only partially) from receiving any benefits.

Facts and Definitions You Need to Know

The federal government has yet to publish a handbook for the unemployed worker that explains his or her rights. Each state's Department of Employment Security issues a handbook that explains your rights, how to apply for benefits, what to do if your claim is denied, and other pertinent information and procedures. Below is some of the information that you can find in your state's handbook.

- Your *benefit year* is the full year—52 weeks from the date of your first valid claim. During this period you can draw all awarded checks—up to 26—regardless of the number of times you are laid off. For example, if your first valid claim date is February 6, 1996, your benefit year will continue through February 5, 1997. Taking part-time work might not prevent you from receiving benefits, as long as your weekly gross earnings don't exceed a certain percentage of your weekly benefit amount.

- If you live in a wage report state (for example, Illinois), your *base period* consists of the first four of the last five completed calendar quarters, unless your benefits year begins in March. There are four calendar quarters: January–March, April–June, July–September, and October–December. If you live in a wage request state (for example, New York), the base period for determining your benefit amount would cover the twelve preceding months before you filed for benefits. For example, if you filed your claim on March 6, 1996, your benefit amount would be determined by the amount of wages you earned between March, 1995 and February, 1996.

Waiting to file could mean a change in your base period that might affect your benefit amount. If you wait too long, your period of unemployment might be counted as part of your base period, thus reducing your benefits.

- Your *total weekly benefits* are the amount of benefits you will be paid for any week in your benefit year if you are out of work and meet all of the eligibility requirements (unless you have already exhausted all your benefits). You may receive *partial benefits* equal to the difference between that part of your earnings which doesn't exceed a certain percentage of your weekly benefit amount and the weekly benefit amount for total unemployment. Different states will use different percentages if they offer partial benefits. It pays for you to accept part-time work during your job search!

- Under certain circumstances you can file a *combined wage claim* if you have worked in more than one state, either to qualify for benefits or to increase your benefits. Inform your counselor about your situation.

- Any state to which you have just moved will act as an agent in helping you file an *interstate claim* to draw benefits from your *home state*. This is also true in the District of Columbia, Puerto Rico, the Virgin Islands, and Canada.

- You must be *available for work* during any week for which you claim benefits. You must be willing and able to accept suitable employment, which normally means a full-time job. You are not available for work if:

  1. You are sick and cannot work on any day

  2. You are away on vacation

  3. You must stay at home to keep house or care for your family

  4. You have retired and will not accept a suitable job

  5. After losing your last job you move to a community where your chances of getting a job are definitely not as good as those in the community you left

  6. The kind of wages, hours, or work conditions you insist upon unreasonably limit your chances of getting a job

  7. Your main occupation is that of a student in attendance at or on vacation from school

However, you may be eligible for benefits if you are attending a training course to help you get a local job under special circumstances (for example, if you are a dislocated worker). If you are enrolled in such a course, be sure to apprise your counselor at your Department of Employment Security office.

You must be *actively looking for work* on your own initiative. States require you to detail your work search on your benefits claim. States also provide a Job Service or Employment Service where employers list job openings, descriptions, and salary ranges of all categories. These Job Service departments and staff are usually located adjacent to or in the same building as your local unemployment office.

Your weekly benefit amount

Each state has its own set formula for determining unemployment benefits. Some states use the amount of wages you earned during the high quarter of your base period while others use your average weekly wage during your base period. Most states require that your total earnings during your base period exceed a certain amount. These amounts are quite low. In Illinois, for example, a claimant's total earnings for insured work need only to be $1,600 in the base period to qualify. In all states, a claimant's gross wages (before taxes) determine his or her benefit amount.

Unemployed workers living in upper midwestern and northeastern states tend to receive higher benefit amounts than those living in southern and in western states. Claimants in most states are also entitled to receive dependents' benefits. Dependents include dependent children under a certain age in all states and non-working dependents, such as a spouse or parent, in some states. Your state's *Unemployment Benefits Handbook* will inform you about dependent benefit allowances.

What is insured work?

In most states the definition of "insured work" is employment for an employer who is subject to the law— one who is required to make payments to the state under the state's Unemployment Insurance Act. It will help you to know what types of work are not covered or insured in many states, and thus cannot be used as a basis for claiming benefits. Definitions of insured and uninsured work vary from state to state, but some common limitations include:

1. Railroad work covered by the Railroad Unemployment Insurance Act is not insured.

2. Certain family employment arrangements are not covered, such as a wife working for her husband, a parent working for a son or daughter, or a son or daughter under 18 years working for a parent.

3. Some government work in special job situations (for example, elected officials), or those hired to work for a short period following a disaster may not be covered.

4. Federally funded work-relief/work training are not covered.

5. Work as an insurance agent or solicitor paid solely on a commission basis is not covered.

6. Direct sellers of consumer products on a buy-sell basis, by direct commission or any similar basis in a home or in an establishment other than a permanent retail establishment may not be covered.

7. Agricultural and domestic workers are not covered in most states, unless they work for an employing unit that paid a certain sum in cash wages to the worker during any calendar quarter or year.

What Will Disqualify You for Benefits?

These or similar examples of disqualifications will apply in all states. Even if you meet all other eligibility requirements, you will not be eligible for benefits if you are disqualified. Disqualification occurs if:

1. You quit your job without good cause attributable to your employer unless you quit because of one of these exceptions: health, acceptance of another job, failure to exercise bumping privileges, sexual harassment, or unsuitable work.

2. You were discharged for misconduct connected with your work.

3. You failed, without good cause, to apply for or accept a suitable job offered to you.

   Under the law in most states, a job is *not* suitable if:

   a. The job opening exists because of a labor dispute

   b. The wages, hours, or other working conditions of the job are not as good as those that exist for the same kind of work in the same community

   c. Your safety, health, or morals may be endangered

   d. You would have to resign from or be prevented from joining a union to get or keep the job

   e. You would replace another worker under a collective bargaining agreement and cause that person to be laid off

4. You were discharged because you committed a felony or theft in connection with your work. (In this case, you may be denied *all* benefits based on wages paid to you up to the date of your discharge.)

5. You are unemployed because a labor dispute has caused a stoppage of work at the place where you work. You may be denied benefits until the stoppage ends. If you can show that you and all the other workers in your grade or classification were not participating in, or directly interested in, the labor dispute, you will not be denied benefits even though there is a stoppage.

6. You will be paid or have already received vacation pay for the same week for which you claim benefits. Such payments include vacation pay in connection with the shutdown of your plant for vacation or inventory purposes, or as a result of your separation (provided in the instance of your separation your employer properly notifies your State Department of Employment Security), or wages in lieu of notice or a back-pay award.

7. You are receiving unemployment benefits from another state or under a federal law such as the Railroad Unemployment Insurance Act for the same week for which you claim in-state benefits.

8. You are receiving workmen's compensation for a temporary disability equal to or more than the unemployment benefits you could draw for the week. If the amount is less than the benefits, you will be paid the difference.

9. You have not earned the required amount to qualify since the beginning of your prior benefit year in which you were paid benefits.

10. You will be paid or have received a retirement pension or other similar periodic payment (including Social Security) for the week for which you claim benefits. One-half of your retirement pension payment (if paid for in part by your employer) or all of your retirement pension payment (if the employer paid all of its costs) is deducted from your unemployment insurance benefits.

11. Your claim is based on wages that were earned while you worked for an educational institution as a teacher, researcher, or administrator, and you are now between academic terms or on vacation or a holiday recess and have the reasonable assurance of returning the following term. You will also be disqualified if you worked for any educational institution as a bus driver, crossing guard, cafeteria worker, clerk, etc., and are between academic terms and there is a reasonable assurance that you will return to such work in the term that immediately follows. Academic personnel might also be disqualified during a period of paid sabbatical leave.

12. You are a professional athlete between sports seasons and there is reasonable assurance that you will return to athletic services.

13. Your benefits would be based upon wages earned while you were an alien who was not a permanent resident or did not have a work permit.

Each January the U.S. Department of Labor Statistics publishes and releases the *Monthly Labor Review*. This publication gives a summary of changes in unemployment insurance legislation enacted by all state legislatures during the previous year. It is available in the reference section of your library.

How to appeal if disqualified for benefits

In today's environment of mass downsizings, some companies will try to deny benefits to as many terminated workers as they can in a misguided attempt to cut costs. Under a complex formula their unemployment taxes will rise in proportion to the number of employees they have discharged. They seem to believe that since their former employee's sense of helplessness can be large and the sums of money in unemployment benefits are relatively small, he or she will not file an appeal. Here are the appeal rights and procedures for the Illinois Department of Employment Security, which are similar to those of other states.

If your claim is contested during your initial interview, your counselor will give you a date for a determination or fact-finding interview when you can present the facts to a claims adjudicator at the Department of Employment Security office where you filed your claim. These interviews usually arise when your former employer states a different reason for termination than that given by you, for example resignation versus termination. Allegations from your former employer are normally submitted in writing or are given to the unemployment office by phone.

Present your case as reasonably as possible during your interview. If you need witnesses to help you present your case, arrange for them to attend the meeting. The fact finder must operate within the guidelines established by law. Remember that these procedures exist to aid claimants—not to suspend them—and to facilitate the process of providing your benefits.

If you are denied—stay cool. Getting angry could work against you. Instead, say "I disagree with your decision and I want to appeal. Please tell me my rights."

Filing an appeal

I have again used the Illinois Department of Employment Security's appeal procedures as an example. All states have similar procedures; check with your state's Department of Employment Security for minor local variations.

You may appeal any decision that denies you benefits. You must file your appeal within 30 days after a letter of denial has been mailed to you. If you appeal by mail, your letter must be postmarked within the time limit. Your unemployment office will help you file your appeal.

If you file an appeal, a hearing will be held before a referee who will give you an opportunity to present evidence. You will be notified in advance of the time and location of the hearing. At the hearing you will have every opportunity to present your case. You may bring witnesses to testify on your behalf.

You have additional remedies if the referee decides against you. In Illinois you may appeal to a board of review, which is an independent five-person body appointed by the governor. If you disagree with the decision of the board, you may file an appeal in the circuit court of the county in which you live.

If you file an appeal, you should continue to mail your certifications as long as you are unemployed or until you are instructed to do otherwise, even though you will not receive any benefits until your appeal is decided in your favor. Be sure to read the Statement of Claimant Rights (Illinois) included in the addenda to Chapter 4.

There are two scenarios where you should appeal if you were denied benefits during your initial interview. Appeal if:

1. You were terminated because the quality of your work did not meet your employer's standards, even though you performed to the best of your ability

2. You were terminated and your former employer declares that you resigned voluntarily

Ex-Military Personnel Benefits

To qualify for ex-military personnel benefits:

- You must have been discharged or released from the armed forces under honorable conditions

- If an officer, you must not have resigned for the good of the service

What you need to bring with you:

- A copy of your DD 214 form

- Your Social Security card

- Your record of employment, if any, before and after military service during the last two years

Here are two facts you need to know:

1. Federal law requires that military service and wages be assigned to the state where you *first* file a claim for unemployment compensation following your separation. Once assigned, *all* federal military services wages remain assigned to that state. Your benefit rights will be determined by the law of the state in which you first filed your claim.

2. You have potential re-employment rights with your pre-service employer. Your application for re-employment must be filed generally within 90 days after completion of military service, or 31 days after completion of initial active duty for training of not less than three months.

Trade Assistance Benefits

Workers who have been laid off or whose work schedule has been reduced because of increased imports may apply for Trade Adjustment Assistance under the Trade Act of 1974 as amended. These federal trade act programs are administered by your state's Department of Employment Security.

This assistance includes a variety of benefits. When you are qualified you may apply for job training, job search assistance, relocation allowances, and other employment related help. If you are eligible, a weekly Trade Re-adjustment Allowance (TRA) may be paid to you when your state unemployment insurance benefits are exhausted.

To apply for eligibility, you and your laid-off workers must first file a petition with the Office of Trade Adjustment Assistance in Washington, D.C. to establish group eligibility. Petitions may be filed by a group of three or more workers, your union representative, or an authorized representative.

Be sure to file your petition as soon as possible, as TRA weekly benefits are not payable until at least 60 days after receipt by the Office of Trade Adjustment Assistance. You can pick up forms in any state unemployment office, or you can write the U.S. Department of Labor, Employment and Training Administration, Office of Trade Adjustment Assistance, Room C-4318, 200 Constitution Avenue, N.W., Washington, D.C. 20210.

Before you proceed to Chapter 5, where you will learn about government assistance programs, how to tap into them, and what financial benefits they can offer you, you need to familiarize yourself with the benefits claim certificate and instructions, and the *Your Rights As A Claimant* declaration. The sample shown is from the state of Illinois; your state's certification form will ask for essentially the same information. If you make mistakes completing your certification it could cause a several week delay in receiving your benefits. You might also be required to appear at a fact-finding interview.

Addenda to Chapter 4

Please study the Illinois benefits claim certification form and its instructions, as well as the Illinois *Your Rights As A Claimant* declaration.

Also included is a list of current headquarters addresses for the Employment Security agencies in all states and the District of Columbia.

Claim Certification Form (Illinois)

STATE OF ILLINOIS
DEPARTMENT OF EMPLOYMENT SECURITY
CLAIM CERTIFICATION

4262

☐ **IF YOUR ADDRESS HAS CHANGED, CHECK BOX AND LIST CHANGES BELOW**

SOCIAL SECURITY NO.	LO. NO.
326194567 4	07

WEEKS COVERED BY THIS CERTIFICATION

06-12-93	06-19-93
1 WEEK ENDING	2 WEEK ENDING

FOR OFFICE USE ONLY

EXCEPTION CODES

INCOME TYPE

$	$
$	$

XYX INDUSTRIES I
FM DATE: 01-03-93
227.00 189167 A A

FOR OFFICE USE ONLY

DONALD JONES
123 HILL ROAD
BUFFALO GROVE, IL 60089

708 915 4576

DATE TO MAIL | 06-20-93

PHONE | COUNTY

COMPLETE AND <u>MAIL THIS FORM</u> TO YOUR LOCAL OFFICE ON THE DATE TO MAIL SHOWN, NOT BEFORE.

ANSWER THE QUESTIONS BELOW BY PLACING AN "X" IN THE APPROPRIATE BOX. REFER TO INSTRUCTION SHEET

DURING THE WEEKS COVERED BY THIS CERTIFICATION:

		YES	NO
A/B.	DID YOU ACTIVELY LOOK FOR WORK OR WERE YOU A MEMBER OF A UNION FROM WHICH YOU OBTAIN ALL YOUR WORK? LIST WORK SEARCH OR UNION INFORMATION BELOW.	✔	☐
C.	DID YOU REFUSE ANY OFFERS OF WORK?	☐	✔
D.	HAVE YOU RETURNED TO WORK? ENTER DATE_____	☐	✔

E.	GROSS EARNINGS IF YOU WORKED FROM 06-06-93 TO 06-12-93	LAST DAY WORKED	NUMBER OF DAYS WORKED	ENTER JOB STATUS
	$	/ /		S=STILL WORKING
	IF YOU WORKED FROM 06-13-93 TO 06-19-93			P=PART-TIME WORK
	$	/ /		L=LAID-OFF

Q=QUIT
F=FIRED
R=RETURNED TO FULL-TIME WORK

F.	IF YOU WERE UNABLE TO WORK AND/OR UNAVAILABLE FOR WORK ON A NORMAL WORK DAY, ENTER THE NUMBER OF DAYS TO THE LEFT.
G.	IF YOU EARNED HOLIDAY PAY, ENTER GROSS AMOUNT TO THE LEFT.
H.	IF YOU EARNED VACATION PAY, ENTER GROSS AMOUNT TO THE LEFT.

		YES	NO
I.	DID YOU APPLY FOR OR RECEIVE A RETIREMENT OR DISABILITY RETIREMENT PENSION INCLUDING SOCIAL SECURITY?	☐	✔
J.	DID YOU CLAIM OR RECEIVE WORKER'S COMPENSATION FOR TEMPORARY DISABILITY?	☐	✔
K.	DID YOU ATTEND SCHOOL OR RECEIVE TRAINING DURING THE WEEKS COVERED?	☐	✔
L.	HAS THERE BEEN A CHANGE IN THE NUMBER OF YOUR DEPENDENT CHILDREN? HAS A DEPENDENT CHILD REACHED THE AGE OF 18, OR HAS THE EMPLOYMENT STATUS OF YOUR SPOUSE OR YOUR MARITAL STATUS CHANGED DURING THE WEEKS COVERED?	☐	✔

LIST YOUR WORK SEARCH BELOW. KEEP A RECORD OF THIS WORK SEARCH FOR YOURSELF BECAUSE YOU MAY BE REQUIRED TO PRODUCE IT AT A LATER DATE. If you need additional space, use another sheet of paper. PLEASE PRINT.

	Contact Date	Name and Address of Contact	Person Contacted	Method of Contact	Type of Work Sought	Results
WEEK-ENDING 1	6-7-93	XYZ CORR, EVANSTON, IL	JOE SMITH	PERSON	SALES REP	NO WORK
	6-7-93	ACME TOOLS, INC. SKOKIE, IL	JIM BROWN	PERSON	V.P. MARKETING	CALL IN 2 WEEKS
	6-8-93	THE JONES GROUP, CHICAGO, IL	TOM JONES	PHONE	MARKET ANALSIS	SEND RESUME
	6-8-93	APEX CORP OAK BROOK, IL	TED ECHART	PERSON	SALES EXECUTIVE	NO WORK
	6-9-93	THE DANE MFG. CO, MADISON, WI	MARK JONES	PHONE	SALES	SEND RESUME
WEEK-ENDING 2						

IMPORTANT:
1. CONTINUE TO MAIL IN CERTIFICATIONS IF YOU FILED AN APPEAL, EVEN THOUGH YOU MAY NOT RECEIVE BENEFITS UNTIL THE APPEAL IS DECIDED.
2. IF YOU FAIL TO RECEIVE ANOTHER CERTIFICATION FORM WITHIN TWO WEEKS FROM THE DATE YOU MAILED THIS CERTIFICATION, REPORT TO YOUR LOCAL OFFICE IMMEDIATELY.
3. IF YOU ARE ELIGIBLE, YOU WILL RECEIVE BENEFITS FOR THE WEEKS CLAIMED. IF THERE IS A QUESTION ABOUT YOUR CLAIM, YOU WILL RECEIVE A CLAIMANT NOTICE OF POSSIBLE INELIGIBILTY IN THE MAIL. THIS NOTICE WILL INDICATE THE QUESTIONS INVOLVED AND WHAT ACTION IS REQUIRED BY YOU.

THIS ADDRESS MUST BE VISIBLE THROUGH THE WINDOW OF THE ENCLOSED RETURN ENVELOPE

DEPARTMENT OF EMPLOYMENT SECURITY
709 W ALGONQUIN RD
ARLINGTON HEIGH, IL 60005

Read Certification and sign below:

I hereby register for work and make claim for benefits. I certify that my answers to the questions on this form are true and correct. I know that the law provides penalties of fines and imprisonment for false statements to obtain benefits.

I understand that information submitted by me to this Department will be used by other Federal, State or local agencies and that information submitted by me to these agencies will be used by IDES in determining my eligibility for and amount of unemployment insurance benefits.

DATE 6-20-93

Donald Jones

Claimant's signature (write your name, do not print)

UI(ILL) XLF068 (REV. 08/90)

Instruction Sheet for Claim Certification Form

UNEMPLOYMENT INSURANCE CLAIM CERTIFICATION INSTRUCTIONS

THESE INSTRUCTIONS ARE VERY IMPORTANT. <u>KEEP THEM</u> AND REFER TO THEM WHEN COMPLETING YOUR CURRENT AND FUTURE CERTIFICATION FORM(S).

When you file a claim for unemployment insurance you will receive a Claim Certification form, which is used to certify for benefit credit. Your first certification form must be returned to the Local Office on the date and time assigned by your local office representative. You will mail subsequent certification forms to your Local Office on a bi-weekly basis. Certification forms must be filed in a timely manner per 56 Illinois Administrative Code Section 2720.120. If you need additional assistance, report to your Local Office (if filing an interstate claim, report to the nearest office in the area where you reside).

1. CHECK YOUR SOCIAL SECURITY NUMBER, NAME AND ADDRESS TO MAKE SURE THEY ARE CORRECT. If your social security number is wrong immediately REPORT to your Local Office. If your name or address is incorrect, make the necessary correction(s) in the space provided in the upper right hand corner of the form.

2. WEEK ENDING DATES ARE ALWAYS SATURDAY DATES. Each week starts on the Sunday prior to the week ending Saturday date. Example: If your certification has the week ending dates of 11-03-90 and 11-10-90, the beginning of the first week would be Sunday 10-28-90, the beginning of the second week would be Sunday, 11-04-90. Therefore, the certification would be covering WEEK 1 of 10-28-90 through 11-03-90, and WEEK 2 of 11-04-90 through 11-10-90. Remember, each certification is asking for the information pertaining to the weeks covered by the week ending dates listed.

3. THE CERTIFICATION SHOULD BE MAILED ON THE DATE TO MAIL, OR BROUGHT INTO THE OFFICE AS SOON AS POSSIBLE AFTER THE DATE TO MAIL. Complete and <u>MAIL THIS FORM</u> to your local office <u>ON THE DATE TO MAIL SHOWN</u> not before.

4. ANSWER ALL QUESTIONS (A through L) completely and accurately by marking the corresponding "yes" or "no" box, and/or giving other information when appropriate. Failure to do so may result in a delay in your payment. <u>LIST YOUR WORK SEARCH IN THE SPACE PROVIDED.</u>

   A/B. You should answer "YES" to this question if, for the two weeks covered by this certification, you made an active search for work, were on a temporary layoff of four weeks or less with a definite return to work date, or you are a member in good standing of a union, approved by this Agency, which requires you to obtain all your work through its hiring hall. You are a member of an "approved" union if you were issued a Ill N 400 card, Report of Union Registration, when you filed your claim. If your union is not approved, you must look for work on your own. LIST YOUR EMPLOYER CONTACTS, TEMPORARY LAY OFF STATUS OR APPROVED UNION MEMBERSHIP INFORMATION IN THE WORK SEARCH AREA PROVIDED ON THIS FORM. (See 56 Illinois Administrative Code, Section 2720.125 for active search for work requirements.)

   C. If you were offered a job and refused it, answer this question yes.

   D/E. If you worked during the week(s) listed on the certification form you must report the date you started, <u>your gross earnings for the period you worked regardless of actual payment date,</u> employer's name and address, your last day worked, if applicable, and the number of days you worked. The STATUS OF JOBS held requires you to write the letter which corresponds to the status of your current employment

       R Returned to full time work,   S Still working,   P Part time employment,   L Laid off,   Q Quit,   or   F Fired.

   F. If you were unable to or unavailable for work on a normal work day during the weeks listed on the certification form, enter the total number of days in the proper column.

   EXAMPLE: You were in the hospital for three work days in the week ending 11-03-90 (unable to work) and were visiting relatives in Ohio for four work days the week ending 11-10-90 (unavailable for work). You would show in the space provided:

	WEEK ENDING	
	1	2
	11-03-90	11-10-90
	3	4

   G/H. If you earned holiday/vacation pay, enter the gross amount in the proper week ending date column to the left.

   EXAMPLE: If you earned holiday/vacation pay in the amount of $50.00 for 1-1-90, New Years Day, and you received it on 1-12-90, you would place the amount in the box under the week ending 1-6-90, the week in which the holiday/vacation occurred, not when the payment occurred.

   I. No specific instructions.

   J. No specific instructions.

   K. No specific instructions.

   L. To claim your non-working spouse as a dependent, report to your Local Office with his/her social security number. You should also report any change in your spouse's employment. If a child is to be added as a dependent, bring in the child's full name and date of birth. <u>Also, you must notify your Local Office when your dependent child reaches the age of 18.</u>

5. READ THE CERTIFICATION STATEMENT. Please note that you can be fined or imprisoned for giving false or misleading information on your form. Sign and date the form. Write your name, do not print.

6. BEFORE SEALING THE ENVELOPE, CHECK TO BE CERTAIN THE LOCAL OFFICE ADDRESS IS CLEARLY SHOWN IN THE ENVELOPE WINDOW. Place a stamp on the envelope and mail.

IMPORTANT

1. Continue to mail in certifications if you filed an appeal, even though you may not receive benefits until the appeal is decided.

2. If you fail to receive another mail certification form within two weeks from the date you mailed your last certification, report to your Local Office immediately.

3. Put your Social Security number on any correspondence sent to your Local Office.

4. If you are eligbile, you will receive benefits for the weeks claimed. If there is a question about your claim, you will receive a Claimant Notice of Possible Ineligibility in the mail. This notice will indicate the questions involved and what action is requested by you. If you disagree with the reasons given or if corrections or explanations are needed, report to your Local Office at once.

Your Rights As a Claimant

1. Your unemployment insurance benefits will not be suspended or terminated until a fact finding interview has been conducted and a written decision has been mailed to you. If the decision is favorable to you, your benefits will not be suspended or terminated. If the decision is made against you, your benefits will be suspended or terminated in accordance with the provisions of the Illinois Unemployment Insurance Act. However, should you receive a determination of ineligibility for benefits for any period, you will have the right to appeal to the Referee. The determination you receive will explain how to file such an appeal.

2. If the Claims Adjudicator determines that you are ineligible for benefits which you have already received, a recoupment decision will be issued in accordance with Section 900 of the Illinois Unemployment Insurance Act. No benefits will be recouped until the expiration of the time for filing an appeal or, if an appeal has been filed, until the decision of a Referee has been made affirming the determination of the Claims Adjudicator.

3. You may be represented by an attorney or a legal representative during your interview. A friend or other person may also help you present the facts. If you cannot afford a lawyer, you may contact your local legal aid society or legal assistance program for help.

4. In order that you have sufficient time to prepare your case, this interview has been scheduled at least seven days from the date of this notice.

5. At the beginning of the interview, the Claims Adjudicator will read to you the contents of your file which are relevant to your eligibility for benefits. You will have an opportunity to comment upon that information.

6. You have the right to have witnesses present at your interview. If your witnesses cannot appear in person or by telephone, you may submit statements from them in writing.

7. Any adverse information offered over the telephone by your former employer or his employees must be confirmed by the employer or his employees in writing if it is to be considered.

8. If you choose to report in person rather than by telephone: you will have an opportunity to inspect, first hand, the contents of your file; you may inspect any written information obtained from the employer or other witnesses; and, at the conclusion of the interview, you will have an opportunity to sign a statement verifying the accuracy of the information obtained from you.

9. At the interview, you may request the Claims Adjudicator to have your former employer produce any documents which relate to your eligibility for benefits and which will substantiate your claim for benefits. You may also request the Claims Adjudicator to ask your employer for any information which will support your benefit claim.

10. If any adverse information is obtained by the Claims Adjudicator after the interview, you will be notified and given the opportunity for another interview before a determination is made.

WARNING: The Illinois Unemployment Insurance Act provides for disqualification, fines, imprisonment and the recovery of benefits from persons who knowingly make false statements or knowingly fail to disclose a material fact for the purpose of obtaining unemployment insurance benefits.

State Employment Security Agency Addresses

Alabama
Industrial Relations Department
Employment Security Administration
649 Monroe Street
Montgomery, AL 36131

Alaska
Labor Department
Employment Security Division
1111 W. Eighth Street
P.O. Box 3-7000
Juneau, AK 99802-1218

Arizona
Economic Security Department
1717 West Jefferson
Phoenix, AZ 85007

Arkansas
Labor Department
Employment Security Division
10421 West Markham
Little Rock, AR 72205

California
Employment Development Department
800 Capitol Mall
Room 5000
P.O. Box 826880
Sacramento, CA 94280-0001

Colorado
Labor and Employment Department
600 Grant Street
Suite 900
Denver, CO 80203-3528

Connecticut
Labor Department
200 Folly Brook Boulevard
Wethersfield, CT 06109-1114

Delaware
Labor Department
Employment and Training Division
Stockton Building
University Office Plaza
Newark, DE 19714-9029

District of Columbia
Employment Services Department
500 C Street, N.W.
Washington, D.C. 20001

Florida
Labor and Employment Security
Department
303 Hartman Building
2012 Capitol Circle S.E.
Tallahassee, FL 32399-2152

Georgia
Labor Department
148 International Boulevard N.E.
Atlanta, GA 30303-1751

Hawaii
Labor and Industrial Relations
Department
Employment and Training Office
830 Punchbowl Street
Honolulu, HI 96813

Idaho
Employment Department
317 Main Street
Boise, ID 83735-0001

Illinois
Employment Security Department
401 South State Street, 6th Floor
Chicago, IL 60605

Indiana
Employment and Training Service
Department
10 North Senate Avenue
Room 331
Indianapolis, IN 46204

Iowa
Employment Services Department
1000 East Grand Avenue
Des Moines, IA 50319

Kansas
Human Resources Department
Employment Security Division
401 S.W. Topeka Boulevard
Topeka, KS 66603-3182

Kentucky
Human Resources Cabinet
Employment Services Department
275 East Main Street
Frankfort, KY 40621-0001

Louisiana
Employment and Training Department
Employment Security Office
P.O. Box 94094
Baton Rouge, LA 70804-9094

Maine
Labor Department
Employment Security Bureau
P.O. Box 309
Augusta, ME 04332-0309

Maryland
Human Resources Department
311 West Saratoga Street
Baltimore, MD 21201

Massachusetts
Employment and Training Department
Hurley Building
Government Center
Boston, MA 02114

Michigan
Michigan Employment Security
   Commission
Department of Labor Building
7310 Woodward Avenue
Detroit, MI 48202

Minnesota
Jobs and Training Department
Job Opportunities and Insurance Division
390 North Robert Street
St. Paul, MN 55101

Mississippi
Employment Security Commission
1520 West Capitol
P.O. Box 1699
Jackson, MS 39215-1699

Missouri
Labor and Industrial Relations
   Department
Employment Security Division
3315 West Truman Boulevard
Jefferson City, MO 65109

Montana
Labor and Industry Department
Unemployment Insurance Division
P.O. Box 1728
Helena, MT 59624-1728

Nebraska
Labor Department
Unemployment Insurance Division
P.O. Box 94600
Lincoln, NE 68509

Nevada
Employment Security Department
500 East Third Street
Cannon City, NV 89713

New Hampshire
Employment Security Department
32 South Main Street
Concord, NH 03301-4857

New Jersey
Labor Department
Employment Security and Job Training
John Fitch Plaza
CN110
Trenton, NJ 08625

New Mexico
Labor Department
Employment Security Division
P.O. Box 1928
Albuquerque, NM 87103

New York
Labor Department
Employment and Training Department
Unemployment Insurance Division
W. A. Harriman Campus
Building 12
Albany, NY 12240

North Carolina
Employment Security Commission
700 Wade Avenue
P.O. Box 25903
Raleigh, NC 27611

North Dakota
Job Service
Job Insurance Division
P.O. Box 1537
Bismarck, ND 58502

Ohio
Employment Services Bureau
145 South Front Street
Columbus, OH 43215

Oklahoma
Employment Security Commission
Unemployment Insurance Division
212 Will Roberts Memorial Building
Oklahoma City, OK 73105

Oregon
Human Resources Department
Employment Division
875 Union Street N.E.
Salem, OR 97311

Pennsylvania
Labor and Industry Department
Employment Security and Job Training
  Division
Seventh and Forster Streets
Harrisburg, PA 17120

Rhode Island
Employment and Training Department
101 Friendship Street
Providence, RI 02903-3740

South Carolina
Employment Security Commission
P.O. Box 995
Columbia, SC 29202

South Dakota
Labor Department
700 Governors Drive
Pierre, SD 57501-2291

Tennessee
Employment Security Department
Volunteer Plaza Building
500 James Robertson Parkway
Nashville, TN 37245

Texas
Employment Commission
Unemployment Insurance Division
101 East 15th Street
Austin, TX 78778

Utah
Industrial Commission
Employment Security Department
160 East 300 South, 3rd Floor
P.O. Box 510910
Salt Lake City, UT 84151-0910

Vermont
Employment and Training Department
Green Mountain Drive
P.O. Box 488
Montpelier, VT 05602

Virginia
Employment Commission
Unemployment Insurance Division
703 East Main Street
Richmond, VA 23219

Washington
Employment Security Department
Unemployment Insurance Division
212 Maple Park
Olympia, WA 98504

West Virginia
Employment Programs Bureau
112 California Avenue
Charleston, WV 25305-0112

Wisconsin
Industry, Labor and Human Relations
   Department
Unemployment Compensation Division
P.O. Box 7946
Madison, WI 53707

Wyoming
Employment Department
Unemployment Insurance Division
Herschler Building, 2nd Floor East
122 West 25th Street
Cheyenne, WY 82002

Making the Most of Government Support

This chapter will introduce you to available sources of financial aid. This assistance, plus your unemployment compensation benefits, will provide you with the essentials to live as you search for employment.

By now you have wrestled with and are streamlining your Survival Budget. Perhaps you are also waiting for the mail carrier to deliver your first unemployment check. This income, on which you pay taxes, will help you meet your daily living expenses. The assistance discussed in this chapter is non-taxable and is available to help you satisfy your basic human needs; it will complete your survival package. Your basic survival needs include:

- Food

- Medical needs

- Shelter

- Utilities

- Legal assistance

Fortunately, when most people combine their unemployment compensation and severance pay, they have enough to enable them to survive a period of unemployment.

Others are not as fortunate. You need to know what options are available if you have used up your assets or have exhausted your unemployment compensation.

You will need at least as much stamina to work with government personnel as you needed at the unemployment office. These financial assistance programs not only help the legions of the unemployed, but also help the poorest people in our society who need assistance on a variety of fronts.

- Expect long waits.

- Accept the fact that you might have to visit several different agencies to qualify for all of these benefits. *Government agencies are not supermarkets.* You will not find everything you need under one roof.

- Adopt a survival mindset: "I need these benefits and I will endure the lines and the time it takes to get them."

Remember: Most government agencies do not communicate with each other. Each has its own set of requirements, documents, and lists of information that you need to bring with you when you apply.

Psychologically Preparing Yourself to Accept Government Aid

For many of us, accepting government aid is something we thought we would never do. It cuts too deeply against our grain of self-reliance. I felt uneasy about applying for government help. I have worked all of my life. I entered the working world mowing yards at the age of nine. I worked as a grocery stockboy during high school. In college and again as a graduate student I held a variety of jobs. These included operating a ten-ton cold extrusion press which made alternator parts for Plymouths, driving Jeeps as a tour guide in Colorado, and negotiating contracts as a purchasing agent for a public utility. I have spent most of my adult years working in the financial services industry. I needed to overcome my feelings about accepting government aid. I want to share some facts with you that helped me do this.

It helps to know that our government makes a distinction, both philosophically and financially, between unemployment benefits and entitlements. Unemployment benefits are taxable, while government aid is tax-free. Unemployment compensation funds come from taxes paid by your employer to your state's unemployment insurance fund, while aid moneys are allocated from government funds obtained through public taxation—yours and mine. In a sense, both are part of your compensation. You *earned* the right to receive benefits by working. If these benefits did not exist, your employer would be paying you a higher wage and you would be paying lower taxes. These are your resources. You are entitled to use them.

The thought of becoming dependent upon a bureaucracy as the sole provider of your financial and vocational support can create an image of a dehumanizing experience. All too many of us—those of us who work with our hands and those of us in white-collar or managerial positions—seem to be saddled with a nearly Puritanical sense of guilt. We remember Benjamin Franklin's admonishments that "A penny saved is a penny earned" and "Never borrower nor lender be." Another platitude of that era was "Do a good day's work and ye shall be blessed." In the late eighteenth century those who couldn't pay their bills were incarcerated in debtors' prisons. The nineteenth century was no easier on those in debt. The philosophy regarding people in need tended to be "Charity begins at home." Those who had no family to help them lived on "poor farms."

America has always known unemployment. Most of the "Panics" during the last century resulted from economic busts fueled by speculation and excess in which many people lost their jobs through no fault of their own. Examples include the over-building of canals during the 1830s and 1840s, the collapse of the stock market in 1869 (caused by Jay Gould trying to corner the gold market) and the brutal antics of the robber barons of the 1880s and 1890s. The Great Depression of the 1930s was caused in part by financial speculation during the 1920s, which caused the market crash of 1929 and led to the failures of many banks.

In 1938, after the Great Depression, the U.S. Congress enacted the Unemployment Insurance programs with these objectives:

- Alleviate the hardships due to loss of wages of eligible, unemployed workers in a manner to preserve their dignity and self-respect

- Promote the purchasing power of the community (unemployment benefits are spent and this keeps others employed)

- Prevent the dispersal of an employer's labor force during temporary layoffs

- Maintain reserves built up during times of expanding economic activity to be paid out during periods of economic contraction

- Provide for equitable distribution of the costs of unemployment among employers

- Prevent the deterioration of wage levels

Your job search won't last forever, but you need to learn about government assistance programs.

Federal and State Assistance Programs

Food stamps

In 1964 Congress mandated that every American is entitled to an adequate, nutritional diet. To help attain this goal, Congress established the Food Stamp Program and gave the Department of Agriculture the responsibility for its administration.

How to enroll for food stamps. You can request an application for food stamps by phoning or going in person to your state's Department of Public Aid or Social Services office that is located nearest where you live. After the department receives your completed application, a representative will interview you confidentially, either in person or by phone. In a few days, the department will mail you a notice that explains the amount of your monthly allocation and where you can pick up your food stamps. You will receive your stamps within 30 days after you file your application. If you are desperate, the department will make an emergency allotment available to you.

Important Tip: Even if you believe you are not eligible— apply anyway. Your unique set of circumstances may qualify you for at least the minimum dollar amount.

Under the program's direction, those eligible receive food stamps to purchase food at authorized retail stores. Food stamps can only be used to purchase food and plants or seeds to grow food for your household. You cannot use food stamps to buy alcohol, tobacco, or prepared meals.

How to qualify for food stamps: Federal guidelines determine your household's eligibility for the Food Stamp Program by measuring the worth of your assets and your gross monthly income against certain dollar limits.

Your household's assets are categorized as *exempt* or as *countable*. These assets are typically considered for the purpose of determining eligibility:

Exempt	Countable
• Family home	Stocks
• Household goods and clothing	Bonds
• One car*	Vacation homes
• Wedding and engagement rings	Certificates of deposit
• Some life insurance	Bank accounts
• Burial plots	Individual Retirement Accounts
• Pension plans (except IRAs and Keogh plans, unless they are owned jointly with someone who is not a member of the same household)	

* Your car cannot have a wholesale market value of over $4,500.

Your household can own up to $2,000 worth of assets in addition to the exempt assets and still qualify. If at least one person living in your household is 60 or over, your household can have assets up to $3,000.

Your household income consists of all money earned by the members of the household, except students under 18 years, and includes the following:

- Wages and unemployment compensation

- Public assistance

- Old age benefits

- Survivors' benefits

- Strike benefits*

- Support payments

- Alimony

- Scholarships

- Educational grants

- Fellowships and veterans educational benefits

- Dividends

- Interest

1995 income limits and food stamp allotments*

Your household must meet federal monthly gross income and net income standards, which vary with household size.

* Households with striking members are ineligible for food stamps unless on the day *before* the strike the household was eligible for benefits or the striker was exempt from work registration requirements.
**From 10/94 through 9/95.

	Maximum food stamp allotment	Gross income limit	Net income limit
1	$115	$ 798	$ 614
2	$212	$1066	$ 820
3	$304	$1335	$1027
4	$386	$1604	$1234
5	$459	$1872	$1440
6	$550	$2141	$1647
7	$608	$2410	$1854
8	$695	$2678	$2060
9	$782	$2947	$2267
10	$869	$3216	$2474
For each additional member:	+$83	+$258	+$207

The following information will help you learn how your food stamp allotment is calculated. The allowable deductions and deduction amounts may vary from state to state. The following example (from Illinois) details some of the information your caseworker will use as he or she determines your allotment amount.

Net income equals gross income minus your allowable deductions. They are:

1. Twenty percent of total earned household income, including unemployment compensation

2. A $134 standard deduction

3. Up to $160 dependent care costs for each dependent household member

4. Up to $231 "excess shelter costs" or the amount of excess shelter costs for a household with a person who is elderly or has a disability

5. Non-reimbursable medical expenses exceeding $35 incurred by household members over 60 years old or who receive certain disability benefits

Now let's examine how your caseworker would figure your household's food stamp allotment. In Illinois a household of three with an unemployed spouse and one dependent child under age 18 receives approximately

$1,200 in unemployment compensation benefits each month. The household meets other food stamp eligibility requirements and has no other source of earned income.

Unemployment compensation		$1200
Less:		
20 percent of total earned income	$240	
Standard deduction	134	
Dependent care costs*	320	
Excess shelter costs*	209	
	$903	903
		$297

Multiply $297 by 30 percent ($297 × .3 = $89.00) and subtract this amount from your maximum food stamp allotment. Your net income for an allotment falls under the net income limit for a household of three.

Maximum allotment for a household of three	$304
	−89
Household monthly food stamp eligibility	$215

Even if you don't think you qualify for the Food Stamp program, apply anyway. Your personal situation may involve special circumstances that would qualify you for some amount of assistance. Medical and utility expenses can help you meet your net income limit. You need to bring the following information when you apply:

- Proof of gross income including unemployment compensation

- Citizenship or alien status

- Medical expenses, if eligible to claim

- Housing costs

- Utility expenses—the state utility standard is $209, but you can request the use of actual utility expenses

- Social Security numbers for all household members

- Proof of residency in the county or district of application

*Assumes the maximum.

- Proof of all assets

- Proof of all moneys received as loans

- Any other questionable information

After you have completed your interview and submitted your application, your Department of Public Aid will determine your eligibility. If you are eligible, you can pick up your food stamps within 30 days at a convenient location. If you have an immediate need, tell your caseworker and he or she will arrange for you to pick up your food stamps in just a few days.

What to do if you are denied food stamps. If you are denied food stamps and do not agree with the decision, you may ask for a fair hearing at any time within 90 days from the date of your denial. You may bring another person to the hearing to assist you, such as a lawyer, friend, or relative. You may re-apply for food stamps any time you think you may be considered eligible.

Medicaid

The Medicaid program was approved by Congress in 1965 and is jointly financed by federal and state tax revenues. It is designed to cover the costs of medical care for persons who do not have the income to pay for adequate medical treatment. You apply for medical benefits at the local office of your state's departments of Public Aid or Social Services. If you qualify for food stamps, you will automatically qualify for medical assistance, as they have the same asset and income limits.

Medicaid pays for these services in most states:

- Hospital care

- Intermediate and skilled nursing care

- Home and special nursing care

- Doctors' services

- Care at clinics

- Help for rehabilitation (physical therapy)

- Laboratory tests and X-rays

- Podiatry (foot care)

- Treatment for alcohol and substance abuse

- Dental care

- Psychiatric care

- Chiropractic care

- Prescription drugs

- Medical equipment and supplies

- Special appliances and devices

- Medical transportation

- Hospice care

- Second opinions regarding the need for surgery

- Renal dialysis

- Family planning

Who provides these medical services?

When you take part in the Medical Assistance Program, the doctors, hospitals, clinics, health maintenance organizations (HMOs), and others who give you care need to be approved by Public Aid. Depending upon where you live, Public Aid may provide for your health care through certain hospitals that take part in the Public Aid Hospital Services Program.

What is available if I do not qualify for Medicaid?

The Medical Assistance No Grant Program (MANG) or Spend-down Program is a catastrophic insurance program which many states offer as an addendum to Medicaid coverage. Many caseworkers call this program "Medicaid with a deductible." If your state's department of Public Aid or Social Services decides you have too much income or too many assets to qualify for Medicaid, but you meet other eligibility requirements, they will put you into their medical spend-down program. Public Aid will pay your medical expenses each month after you submit medical bills that equal your spend-down amount to your caseworker. You submit your household medical bills each month. If you meet your spend-down amount, a MediPlan card will be mailed to you in about a week.

Your caseworker determines your spend-down amount each month. To determine this amount he or she will consider your total assets, monthly income, employment or day care expenses, minus any deductions and your household's Monthly Income Standard (a dollar amount that is determined by your state). Your spend-down amount will be the total of your monthly income in excess of your state's standard, plus your monthly excess resource spend-down.

This is less complicated than it sounds. Let's consider how the Addams family made use of MANG.

> Joe and Mary Addams have a five-year old daughter, Kimberly. Three years ago Mary contracted bone cancer. Since then she has undergone three bone marrow transplants and has been hospitalized several times. Joe, an accountant, earns $45,000 a year and has a $500,000 per illness limit on his company health-care insurance policy. The family owes $15,000 in outstanding unpaid family medical bills, and they are approaching their per illness insurance limit. Their family spend-down amount is $2900 each month. Joe may use his unpaid bills *in addition to* his current medical expenses to meet his monthly spend-down amount. Medicaid will pay his family's medical bills above his spend-down amount. Each month Joe mails his bills to his caseworker. He presents his MediPlan card to the doctor's billing person and the doctor bills Medicaid. Joe understands that Medicaid is not his primary health insurance carrier. Medicaid pays *after* all other insurance carriers have paid. As we learn from the Addams family example, you can take advantage of spend-down if you're employed or unemployed.

What kinds of medical expenses can be used to meet your spend-down?

Bills and receipts for medical services and supplies can be used to meet your spend-down amount. These include:

- Doctor services

- Hospital services

- Nursing home services

- Clinic services

- Dentist services

- Podiatrist services

- Chiropractor services

- Prescription eyeglasses

- Medicines, medical supplies and equipment prescribed by your doctor

- Medical or personal care in your home

- Health insurance premiums, including Medicare premiums

- Transportation to and from medical care

- Any co-payments or deductibles on your medical care

Medicaid will pay for your household's medical care for the three months before you applied for benefits if you met your monthly spend-down for those months. You may use both paid and unpaid bills to meet your spend-down amount.

You can use unpaid medical bills to meet your spend-down amount as long as you received the bill no more than *six months* before you applied for Medicaid. Your paid bills can be used to meet your spend-down amount during any of the six months after you become eligible for benefits.

Aid For Dependent Children

The *Aid For Dependent Children* (AFDC Program) was established by Congress and is designed to provide the essentials of life for dependent children. The asset test for eligibility is stricter than for food stamps and Medicaid. Benefits available under AFDC are based on a "Standard of Need" (the amount of money your family size needs to meet living expenses) and vary significantly from state to state and even within states. Your caseworker will help you determine whether you are eligible. Even if you don't qualify, you may be able to receive Medicaid coverage and food stamps for up to 12 months.

Subsidized rent payments

If you have to give up your home or can no longer afford to pay your current apartment rent, you and your family can obtain decent, sanitary, and safe rental housing. The Department of Housing and Urban Development (HUD) operates two major programs to help low-income families with their rental expenses. These federal programs are administered through local city or county housing authorities and are listed in the Yellow Pages. Under Section 8 of the Rental Assistance Program, you pay at least 15 percent but not over 30 percent of your monthly income for rent expenses. To be eligible you must fall within certain income and asset limits that vary with geographic location. One prime qualification is that you currently are paying more than 50 percent of your annual gross income for rent.

After being certified you have 60 days to find a home or apartment to rent. Your local housing authority will give you a list of available apartment buildings and houses and their income and rent maximums. You are free to find any rental accommodations as long as they meet the standards set by HUD. The maximum rent you are allowed to pay is based upon "fair market rent" standards established for the county and metropolitan area as well as on the size and composition of your family. HUD pays a share of your rent directly to your landlord.

Section 236 of the Program allows low and moderate income families to rent upscale housing at prices substantially lower than similar accommodations in the same area. You must meet certain annual income and other requirements (see HUD Overview of Eligibility Criteria in the addenda to Chapter 5), but there is *no limitation on the amount of assets you can own.*

HUD is able to reduce their borrowing costs to build housing because they can use tax-exempt financing. Developers can use favorable depreciation schedules. Although the program is now inactive (no new projects are being built), applicants can continue to apply for housing in existing buildings.

Legal Aid

If you believe you were wrongly denied benefits in any of the programs discussed in this chapter, you may request a fair hearing in order to file an appeal with the agency that administers the particular program. Free legal assistance is available to you through your local Legal Aid Society. In 1974 Congress established the Legal Services Corporation to provide free legal services in all civil matters to individuals who cannot afford to pay for private legal counsel. To qualify for legal aid, you must fall below certain income requirements. If you need legal help with any civil matter, contact your local Legal Aid Foundation (listed in the Yellow Pages) and explore whether you are eligible for free legal assistance.

Help Right in Your Own Backyard

We've covered the highlights of the major federal and state assistance programs, which are administered at the local branch offices of your state's Departments of Employment Security, Public Aid, and HUD. There is also help available at the county, township, and community level for persons experiencing financial crisis.

General Assistance

Many counties fund a General Assistance program that provides financial assistance to single people and couples without children who desperately need money. The applicant usually cannot have more cash on hand than the monthly benefit. Your township might also offer General Assistance which is funded through local tax levies. Eligibility and benefit amounts vary with each governmental unit.

Energy Assistance programs

Local low-income and state Energy Assistance programs are available through the winter months (usually beginning November 1 and lasting through April 1) to help income-eligible households pay their gas and electric bills. This assistance normally falls into two categories:

- Locally sponsored programs that pay a "lump sum" directly to your gas and electric utilities. To qualify, your household's gross earned income plus unemployment compensation for the past 30 days must fall within certain income limits. Limits are determined by where you live.

- Residential Energy Assistance Partnership Programs that allow your household to pay a certain percentage of your household's 90-day gross income to your primary utility (energy) and to your secondary utility (electric). For example, Illinois has a 12 percent payment plan which lets you pay 8 percent of your 90-day gross income to your primary utility and 4 percent to your secondary utility. Your household's 90-day gross earnings including unemployment compensation must fall within your state's maximum income level guidelines.

Most townships have Social Service administrations who inform people in need about local food pantries, churches, and civic organizations that serve nutritious midday and evening meals.

Funds permitting, many townships offer assistance to pay for one month's rent or mortgage payment up to a determined amount. This assistance is available to households that experience a sudden reduction in income due to conditions beyond their control. To qualify, you must have a foreclosure or eviction notice and be able to show how you will be able to maintain the payments after receiving your assistance. You can use this assistance to pay for shelter while you are looking for appropriate Section 8 rent-subsidized housing.

Local charities

Local charities offer financial as well as emotional help to families who are in the midst of a crisis. Your public library or chamber of commerce will have literature describing the local charities and how they can help you.

Now you know something about the survival threads offered by assistance programs. Weave them into a survival net that meets your needs.

Addenda to Chapter 5

HUD Eligibility Criteria

OVERVIEW OF ELIGIBILITY CRITERIA. A household may be assisted under the Rent Supplement, RAP or Section 8 programs or pay less than the BMIR or Section 236 Market Rent ONLY IF:

a. The household is: (1) a family; or (2) a single person who is eligible under Paragraph 2–3.

b. The household's annual income does not exceed the limits in Section 2 of this chapter.

c. The owner and the tenant comply with the unit size standards in Section 3 of this chapter.

d. The applicant agrees to pay the rent required by the subsidy program under which the applicant will be admitted. (See Chapter 3, Section 4.)

e. The unit will be the family's only residence.

DEFINITIONS. Owners must use the following definitions.

a. Elderly Person - one who is at least 62 years old.

b. Elderly Household - a household whose head or spouse is elderly, handicapped or disabled. The household may be two or more elderly, handicapped or disabled persons who are not related, or one or more such persons living with someone essential to their care or well-being.

   NOTE: A household may NOT designate a family member as head of household solely to qualify the family as an elderly household.

c. Live-In Aide/Attendant. A person who lives with an elderly, disabled or handicapped individual(s) and is essential to that individual's care and well-being, not obligated for the individual's support and would not be living in the unit except to provide the support services. While a relative may be considered to be a live-in aide/attendant, they must meet the above requirements, especially the last. The live-in qualifies for occupancy only as long as the individual needing supportive services does and may not qualify for continued occupancy as a remaining family member.

d. Handicapped - a person with a physical or mental impairment that:

   (1) is expected to be of long-continued and indefinite duration;

   (2) substantially impedes the person's ability to live independently; and

   (3) is such that the person's ability to live independently could be improved by more suitable housing conditions.

e. Disabled - When determining eligibility for admission to a Section 202 project, persons are considered "disabled" ONLY if they meet the criteria in paragraph e(2) below. For all other purposes, persons are considered disabled if they meet the criteria in either paragraph e(1) or e(2).

   (1) The person has a disability, as defined in Section 223 of the Social Security Act: an inability to engage in any substantial gainful activity because of any physical or mental impairment that is expected to result in death or has lasted or can be expected to last continuously for at least 12 months; or, for a blind person at least 55 years old, inability because of blindness to engage in any substantial gainful activities comparable to those in which the person was previously engaged with some regularity and over a substantial period.

   NOTE: Owners must determine if a disability meets this definition. Receipt of veteran's disability benefits does not automatically qualify a person as disabled, because the Veterans Administration and Social Security Administration define disabled differently. Except in 202 projects, applicants who meet Social Security's definition of disabled are eligible even if they do not receive social security benefits.

(2) The person has a developmental disability as defined in 42 USC § 6001(7): a severe, chronic disability which:

    (a) is attributable to a mental and/or physical impairment;

    (b) was manifested before age 22;

    (c) is likely to continue indefinitely;

    (d) results in substantial functional limitations in 3 or more of the following areas: capacity for independent living; self-care; receptive and expressive language; learning; mobility; self-direction; and economic self-sufficiency;

                             AND

    (e) requires special, interdisciplinary, or generic care, treatment, or other services which are of lifelong or extended duration and are individually planned and coordinated.

f.   Displaced - a person who: (1) is displaced by government action; or (2) lives in a residence that is uninhabitable due to a disaster declared or formally recognized by the Federal Government.

g.   Single person - one who intends to live alone.

h.   Substandard - housing which is dilapidated, because it does not have operable indoor plumbing, does not have a useable flush toilet, bathtub or shower inside the unit for the exclusive use of a family; does not have electricity; has inadequate or unsafe electrical service; has no safe or adequate source of heat; should, but does not, have a kitchen, or has been declared unfit for habitation by an agency or unit of government.

A dilapidated unit does not provide safe and adequate shelter and, in its present condition, endangers the health, safety, or well-being of a family, or it has one or more critical defects, or a combination of intermediate defects in sufficient number or extent to require considerable repair or rebuilding. (The defects may involve original construction, or they may result from continued neglect or lack of repair or from serious damage to the structure.)

(1) "Homeless family" - individual/family who lacks a fixed, regular and adequate night time residence <u>and</u> has a primary night time residence which is—a supervised publicly/privately operated shelter designed to provide temporary living arrangements (welfare hotels, congregate shelters, and transitional housing for the mentally ill); an institution that provides temporary residence for individuals intended to be institutionalized, or public/private place not designed for, or ordinarily used as, a regular sleeping accommodation for human beings.

A "homeless family" does not include an individual imprisoned or otherwise detained pursuant to an Act of Congress or a State law.

(2) "Single room occupancy" housing is not substandard solely because it does not contain sanitary or food preparation facilities (or both).

i.   Involuntary displacement - an applicant is or will be considered involuntarily displaced if he has vacated or will have to vacate the housing unit as a result of one or more of these actions:

(1) A natural disaster (fire, flood, etc.) that results in the unit being uninhabitable;

(2) Activity by a U.S. agency or State or local governmental body or agency for code enforcement or public improvement or development program;

(3) Action by an owner resulting in the applicant having to vacate the unit when the owner's action is beyond the applicant's ability to control or prevent; the action is despite the applicant having met all previously imposed occupancy conditions and the action is other than a rent increase;

Having to vacate includes—unit conversion to non-rental or nonresidential use; rehabilitation, owner desires unit for personal/family use or occupancy; unit sale where applicant's agreement is the unit is vacant when possession is transferred; or other legally authorized act resulting in unit being withdrawn from rental market. Do not include tenant's refusal to (1) comply with overcrowded/underoccupied units, or (2) accept transfer under HUD-approved desegregation plan.

(4) The applicant has vacated unit as a result of actual or threatened physical violence by a spouse or other member against the applicant or a member of the family; or lives with an individual who engages in such violence. Such violence must have occurred recently or be of a continuing nature.

j. <u>Paying more than 50 percent of family income for rent</u>. For purposes of this definition, family income is one-twelfth of annual gross income. In making this determination, rent is the actual amount due monthly under a lease or occupancy agreement. The amount of tenant-paid utilities may be determined by using the utility allowances established by the local PHA for its Section 8 Existing program. The family may choose to document the actual average monthly utilities for the past 12 months (or for an appropriate recent period if a full 12 months of information is not attainable). For applicants who own a manufactured home, but rent the space for the home, rent includes the monthly amortized price. Rent excludes energy assistance amounts paid to or on behalf of a family to the extent they are not included in income.

Unemployable? No Way!

In this chapter you will learn about the government programs that can help you:

- Upgrade your career skills

- Retool for a new career

- Start your own business

No one wants to lose their job, but when it happens, it can provide a catalyst for change. It forces us to take a good look at our lives and pursue personal growth. You need to draw upon your reserves of skills, talents, and interests that you have developed during your lifetime, both in and out of your work environment.

The organizations that can help you get a fresh start include:

- Agencies in your community with programs to help you evaluate your talents, pay tuition for continuing education, and retool or launch your own business

- The Small Business Administration, which can provide you with invaluable information you need to consider before you go into business for yourself, including how to obtain financing for your new venture

- Government foundations and programs that offer grants and cash stipends to those who create projects that mesh with their cultural and scientific interests and abilities

Programs Available in Your Community

The Economic Dislocation and Worker Adjustment Act (EDWAA) was created by Congress to ease the disruption of employees, employers, and the community when faced with a plant closing or mass layoffs. EDWAA defines dislocated workers as individuals who:

- Have been laid off or unemployed or have received notice of layoff or termination due to a plant closure or mass layoff

- Are unemployed through no fault of their own, are eligible for or have exhausted their unemployment compensation, and are unlikely to return to their previous occupation

- Are long-term unemployed and have limited opportunities for employment or re-employment in the same or similar occupation

- Were self-employed (including farmers and ranchers) and are unemployed as a result of general economic conditions in their community

The Department of Commerce and Community Affairs has the primary responsibility for administering the Job

Partnership Training Act (JPTA) in each state. These services are offered through agencies called Private Industry Councils (PICs), Dislocated Worker Centers, or your county's JPTA or Office of Employment and Human Resources. Over 1100 PICs are located throughout the United States and its territories.

Most of the Private Industry Councils have established programs that provide dislocated workers with:

- Pre-layoff assistance

- On-the-job training

- Assessment of job-related skills and interests

- Résumé preparation

- Job search and placement assistance

- Career exploration

- Vocational training

- Classroom training

Your PIC coordinates its services with your unemployment office. You will receive your benefit checks while you participate in one of their programs.

These excellent training and employment services programs help you develop new job skills to keep up with the changing technology in a wide variety of careers. If you want to attend college or vocational school to learn a new trade or to upgrade your existing skills, your PIC will pay for your tuition, fees, and books.

PIC training programs are rigorous and usually last from six to eight weeks. You meet twice a week with your instructor in small classes (there are usually less than 10 students). You will have plenty of homework which you are required to complete before each class. Those who don't do their homework or show up for class are dropped from the program.

Your PIC has a program, called the Seed Program, that will provide you with technical assistance and guidance to help you start your own business. If you decide to become an entrepreneur—to start your own business—you will need seed money and ongoing financing. Your PIC training will teach you to calculate how much start-up capital you will need. You will also learn how to borrow money for working capital as your new venture matures. These topics are well covered in the two informative Small Business Administration pamphlets "Checklist for Going into Business" and "The ABC's of Borrowing," which are reprinted in the addenda to this chapter.

In the course of giving seminars on financial survival and counseling many people who have lost their jobs because of corporate downsizing, I've come to believe that many of us will never find a job that duplicates exactly what we did on our last job. The PIC programs are a golden opportunity to make yourself employable in a new career that you will really enjoy. Call your local PIC, arrange for an interview, and sign up for a program! My successful consulting practice and this book itself are a direct result of what I learned from my own PIC project.

Government Grants and Stipends

There are scores of government grants and stipends available to help you enhance your job skills and pursue new career interests.

The *Catalog of Federal Domestic Assistance* is published by the government and is released in June each year. The catalog describes 1,226 assistance programs that are administered by 50 federal agencies.

It is a government-wide compendium of many federal projects, programs, services, and activities that provide benefits to the American public. The Government Services Administration distributes this catalog to agencies at the federal, state, and local level, and it is available at most large public libraries.

There are government programs covering almost every imaginable area—aging, education, the humanities, scientific pursuits, vocational rehabilitation and more. Although the majority of these programs provide assistance to other government agencies, universities, and not-for-profit organizations, many offer assistance in grants and aid to individuals. The catalog describes:

- Programs

- Objectives

- Types of assistance

- Uses and restrictions

- Applicant eligibility

- Beneficiary eligibility

- Credentials/documentation required with your application

- Application and award procedures

- Deadlines and length of approval time

Programs

Examples of some programs that could mesh with your interests and abilities can be found in the addenda to this chapter. These examples will familiarize you with how the programs are presented in the catalog. You will also find instructions for using the catalog as well as information on developing and writing grant proposals. If you are interested in applying for a grant, contact the government foundation or agency that administers the program to learn about any current details or changes.

Addenda to
Chapter 6

Small Business Administration Pamphlet:
"Checklist for Going into Business"

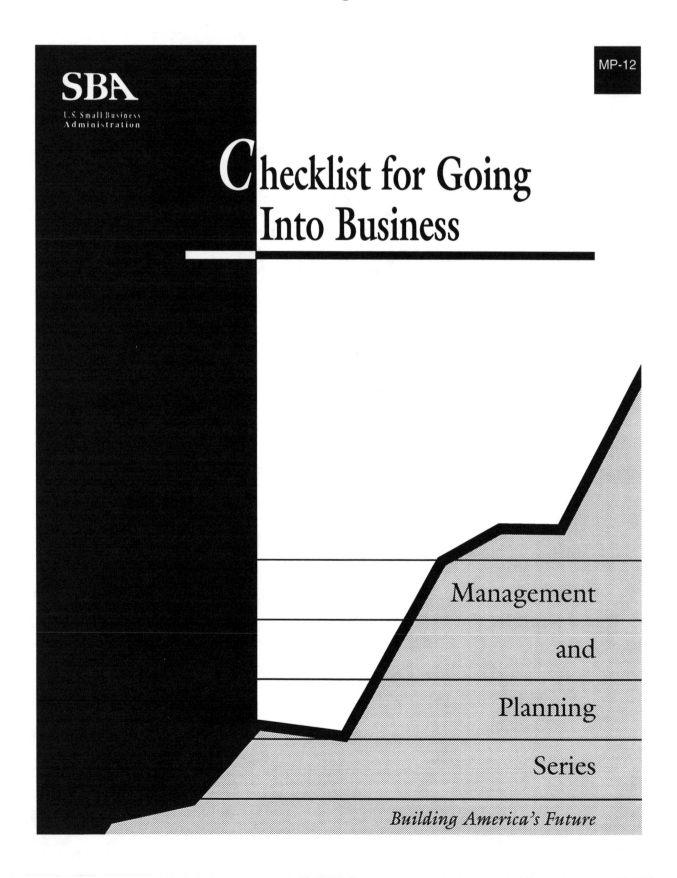

TABLE OF CONTENTS

INTRODUCTION

Owning a business is the dream of many Americans . . . starting that business converts your dream into reality. But there is a gap between your dream and reality that can only be filled with careful planning. As a business owner, you will need a plan to avoid pitfalls, to achieve your goals and to build a profitable business.

The "Checklist for Going into Business" is a guide to help you prepare a comprehensive business plan and determine if your idea is feasible, to identify questions and problems you will face in converting your idea into reality and to prepare for starting your business.

Operating a successful small business will depend on

- a practical plan with a solid foundation;

- dedication and willingness to sacrifice to reach your goal;

- technical skills; and

- basic knowledge of management, finance, record keeping and market analysis.

As a new owner, you will need to master these skills and techniques if your business is to be successful.

IDENTIFY YOUR REASONS

As a first and often overlooked step, ask yourself why you want to own your own business. Check the reasons that apply to you.

	YES
1. Freedom from the 9–5 daily work routine.	_____
2. Being your own boss.	_____
3. Doing what you want when you want to do it.	_____

	YES
4. Improving your standard of living.	_____
5. Boredom with your present job.	_____
6. Having a product or service for which you feel there is a demand.	_____

Some reasons are better than others, none are wrong; however, be aware that there are tradeoffs. For example, you can escape the 9–5 daily routine, but you may replace it with a 6 a.m. to 10 p.m. routine.

A SELF-ANALYSIS

Going into business requires certain personal characteristics. This portion of the checklist deals with you, the individual. These questions require serious thought. Try to be objective. Remember, it is your future that is at stake!

Personal Characteristics

	YES	NO
1. Are you a leader?	_____	_____
2. Do you like to make your own decisions?	_____	_____

	YES	NO
3. Do others turn to you for help in making decisions?	_____	_____
4. Do you enjoy competition?	_____	_____
5. Do you have will power and self discipline?	_____	_____
6. Do you plan ahead?	_____	_____
7. Do you like people?	_____	_____
8. Do you get along well with others?	_____	_____

Personal Conditions

This next group of questions, though brief, is vitally important to the success of your plan. It covers the physical, emotional and financial strains you will encounter in starting a new business.

	YES	NO
1. Are you aware that running your own business may require working 12–16 hours a day, six days a week, and maybe even Sundays and holidays?	_____	_____
2. Do you have the physical stamina to handle the workload and schedule?	_____	_____
3. Do you have the emotional strength to withstand the strain?	_____	_____
4. Are you prepared, if needed, to temporarily lower your standard of living until your business is firmly established?	_____	_____
5. Is your family prepared to go along with the strains they, too, must bear?	_____	_____
6. Are you prepared to lose your savings?	_____	_____

PERSONAL SKILLS AND EXPERIENCE

Certain skills and experience are critical to the success of a business. Since it is unlikely that you possess **all** the skills and experience needed, you'll need to hire personnel to supply those you lack. There are some basic and special skills you will need for your particular business.

By answering the following questions, you can identify the skills you possess and those you lack (your strengths and weaknesses).

	YES	NO
1. Do you know what basic skills you will need in order to have a successful business?	_____	_____
2. Do you possess those skills?	_____	_____
3. When hiring personnel, will you be able to determine if the applicants' skills meet the requirements for the positions you are filling?	_____	_____
4. Have you ever worked in a managerial or supervisory capacity?	_____	_____
5. Have you ever worked in a business similar to the one you want to start?	_____	_____
6. Have you had any business training in school?	_____	_____
7. If you discover you don't have the basic skills needed for your business, will you be willing to delay your plans until you've acquired the necessary skills?	_____	_____

FINDING A NICHE

Small businesses range in size from a manufacturer with many employees and millions of dollars in equipment to the lone window washer with a bucket and a sponge. Obviously, the knowledge and skills required for these two extremes are far apart, but, for success, they have one thing in common: each has found a business niche and is filling it.

The most critical problems you will face in your early planning will be to find your niche and determine the feasibility of your idea. "Get into the right business at the right time" is very good advice but following that advice may be difficult. Many entrepreneurs plunge into a business venture so blinded by the dream that they fail to thoroughly evaluate its potential.

Before you invest time, effort and money, the following exercise will help you separate sound ideas from those bearing a high potential for failure.

IS YOUR IDEA FEASIBLE?

1. Identify and briefly describe the business you plan to start.

   _____
   _____
   _____
   _____

2. Identify the product or service you plan to sell.

   _____

3. Does your product or service satisfy an unfilled need?   Yes _____   No _____

4. Will your product or service serve an existing market in which demand exceeds supply?   Yes _____   No _____

5. Will your product or service be competitive based on its quality, selection, price or location?   Yes _____   No _____

Answering yes to any of these questions means you are on the right track; a negative answer means the road ahead could be rough.

MARKET ANALYSIS

For a small business to be successful, the owner must know the market. To learn the market, you must analyze it, a process that takes time and effort. You don't have to be a trained statistician to analyze the marketplace, nor does the analysis have to be costly.

Analyzing the market is a way to gather facts about potential customers and to determine the demand for your product or service. The more information you gather, the greater your chances of capturing a segment of the market. Know the market before investing your time and money in any business venture.

These questions will help you collect the information necessary to analyze your market and determine if your product or service will sell.

	YES	NO
1. Do you know who your customers will be?	_____	_____
2. Do you understand their needs and desires?	_____	_____
3. Do you know where they live?	_____	_____
4. Will you be offering the kind of products or services that they will buy?	_____	_____
5. Will your prices be competitive in quality and value?	_____	_____

	YES	NO
6. Will your promotional program be effective?	_____	_____
7. Do you understand how your business compares with your competitors?	_____	_____
8. Will your business be conveniently located for the people you plan to serve?	_____	_____

	YES	NO
9. Will there be adequate parking facilities for the people you plan to serve?	_____	_____

This brief exercise will give you a good idea of the kind of market planning you need to do. An answer of "no" indicates a weakness in your plan, so do your research until you can answer each question with a "yes."

PLANNING YOUR START-UP

So far, this checklist has helped you identify questions and problems you will face converting your idea into reality and determining if your idea is feasible. Through self-analysis you have learned of your personal qualifications and deficiencies, and through market analysis you have learned if there is a demand for your product or service.

The following questions are grouped according to function. They are designed to help you prepare for "Opening Day."

Name and Legal Structure

	YES	NO
1. Have you chosen a name for your business?	_____	_____
2. Have you chosen to operate as sole proprietorship, partnership or corporation?	_____	_____

Your Business and the Law

A person in business is not expected to be a lawyer, but each business owner should have a basic knowledge of laws affecting the business. Here are some of the legal matters you should be acquainted with:

	YES	NO
1. Do you know which licenses and permits you may need to operate your business?	_____	_____
2. Do you know the business laws you will have to obey?	_____	_____

	YES	NO
3. Do you have a lawyer who can advise you and help you with legal papers?	_____	_____
4. Are you aware of		
• Occupational Safety and Health Administration (OSHA) requirements?	_____	_____
• Regulations covering hazardous material?	_____	_____
• Local ordinances covering signs, snow removal, etc.?	_____	_____
• Federal Tax Code provisions pertaining to small business?	_____	_____
• Federal regulations on withholding taxes and Social Security?	_____	_____
• State Workmen's Compensation laws?	_____	_____

Protecting Your Business

It is becoming increasingly important that attention be given to security and insurance protection for your business. There are several areas that should be covered. Have you examined the following categories of risk protection?

	YES	NO
• Fire	_____	_____
• Theft	_____	_____
• Robbery	_____	_____
• Vandalism	_____	_____
• Accident liability	_____	_____

Discuss the types of coverage you will need and make a careful comparison of the rates and coverage with several insurance agents before making a final decision.

Business Premises and Location

	YES	NO
1. Have you found a suitable building in a location convenient for your customers?	_____	_____
2. Can the building be modified for your needs at a reasonable cost?	_____	_____
3. Have you considered renting or leasing with an option to buy?	_____	_____
4. Will you have a lawyer check the zoning regulations and lease?	_____	_____

Merchandise

	YES	NO
1. Have you decided what items you will sell or produce, or what service(s) you will provide?	_____	_____
2. Have you made a merchandise plan based upon estimated sales, to determine the amount of inventory you will need to control purchases?	_____	_____
3. Have you found reliable suppliers who will assist you in the start-up?	_____	_____
4. Have you compared the prices, quality and credit terms of suppliers?	_____	_____

Business Records

	YES	NO
1. Are you prepared to maintain complete records of sales, income and expenses, accounts payable and receivables?	_____	_____
2. Have you determined how to handle payroll records, tax reports and payments?	_____	_____
3. Do you know what financial reports should be prepared and how to prepare them?	_____	_____

FINANCES

A large number of small businesses fail each year. There are a number of reasons for these failures, but one of the main reasons is insufficient funds. Too many entrepreneurs try to start and operate a business without sufficient capital (money). To avoid this dilemma, you can review your situation by analyzing these three questions:

1. How much money do you have?
2. How much money will you need to start your business?
3. How much money will you need to stay in business?

Use the following chart to answer the first question:

```
┌─────────────────────────────────────────────┐
│           CHART 1 – PERSONAL                  │
│           FINANCIAL STATEMENT                 │
│           _____ , 19 _____              │
│                                               │
│        ASSETS              LIABILITIES        │
│                                               │
│  Cash on hand      ____  Accounts payable  ___│
│  Savings account   ____  Notes payable     ___│
│  Stocks, bonds,          Contracts            │
│    securities      ____    payable         ___│
│  Accounts/notes          Taxes             ___│
│    receivable      ____  Real estate loans ___│
│  Real estate       ____  Other liabilities ___│
│  Life insurance                               │
│    (cash value)    ____                       │
│  Automobile/other                             │
│    vehicles        ____                       │
│  Other liquid assets ___                      │
│                                               │
│  TOTAL                   TOTAL                 │
│  ASSETS            ____  LIABILITIES       ___│
│                                               │
│  NET WORTH (ASSETS MINUS LIABILITIES) ___     │
└─────────────────────────────────────────────┘
```

Chart 2 will help you answer the second question: How much money will you need to start your business? The chart is for a retail business; items will vary for service, construction and manufacturing firms.

The answer to the third question (How much money will you need to stay in business?) must be divided into two parts: immediate costs and future costs.

```
┌─────────────────────────────────────────────┐
│      CHART 2 – START-UP COST ESTIMATES        │
│                                               │
│  Decorating, remodeling             _____    │
│  Fixtures, equipment                _____    │
│  Installing fixtures, equipment     _____    │
│  Services, supplies                 _____    │
│  Beginning inventory cost           _____    │
│  Legal, professional fees           _____    │
│  Licenses, permits                  _____    │
│  Telephone utility deposits         _____    │
│  Insurance                          _____    │
│  Signs                              _____    │
│  Advertising for opening            _____    │
│  Unanticipated expenses             _____    │
│                                               │
│                                               │
│  TOTAL START-UP COSTS               _____    │
└─────────────────────────────────────────────┘
```

From the moment the door to your new business opens, a certain amount of income will undoubtedly come in. However, this income should not be projected in your operating expenses. You will need enough money available to cover costs for at least the first three months of operation. Chart 3 will help you project your operating expenses on a monthly basis.

Now multiply the total of Chart 3 by three. This is the amount of cash you will need to cover operating expenses for three months. Deposit this amount in a savings

```
┌─────────────────────────────────────────────┐
│      CHART 3 – EXPENSES FOR ONE MONTH         │
│                                               │
│  Your living costs                  _____    │
│  Employee wages                     _____    │
│  Rent                               _____    │
│  Advertising                        _____    │
│  Supplies                           _____    │
│  Utilities                          _____    │
│  Insurance                          _____    │
│  Taxes                              _____    │
│  Maintenance                        _____    │
│  Delivery/transportation            _____    │
│  Miscellaneous                      _____    │
│                                               │
│  TOTAL EXPENSES                     _____    │
└─────────────────────────────────────────────┘
```

account before opening your business. Use it only for those purposes listed in the above chart, because this money will ensure that you will be able to continue in business during the crucial early stages.

By adding the total start-up costs (Chart 2) to the total expenses for three months (three times the total cost on Chart 3), you can learn what the estimated costs will be to start and operate your business for three months. By subtracting the totals of Charts 2 and 3 from the cash available (Chart 1), you can determine the amount of additional financing you may need, if any. Now you will need to estimate your operating expenses for the first year after start-up. Use the Income Projection Statement (Appendix A) for this estimate.

The first step in determining your annual expenses is to estimate your sales volume month by month. Be sure to consider seasonal trends that may affect your business. Information on seasonal sales patterns and typical operating ratios can be secured from your trade associations.

(NOTE: The relationships among amounts of capital that you invest, levels of sales, each of the cost categories, the number of times that you will sell your inventory (turnover) and many other items form "financial ratios." These ratios provide you with extremely valuable checkpoints before it's too late to make adjustments. In the reference section of your local library are publications, such as "The Almanac of Business and Industrial Financial Ratios," to compare your performance with that of other, similar businesses. For thorough explanations of these ratios and how to use them, follow up on the sources of help and information mentioned at the end of this publication.)

Next, determine the cost of sales. The cost of sales is expressed in dollars. Fill out each month's column in dollars, total them in the annual total column and then divide each item into the total net sales to produce the annual percentages. Examples of operating ratios include cost of sales to sales and rent to sales.

AFTER START-UP

The primary source of revenue in your business will be from sales, but your sales will vary from month to month because of seasonal patterns and other factors. It is important to determine if your monthly sales will produce enough income to pay each month's bills.

An estimated cash flow projection (Chart 4) will show if the monthly cash balance is going to be subject to such factors as

- Failure to recognize seasonal trends;

- Excessive cash taken from the business for living expenses;

- Too rapid expansion; and

- Slow collection of accounts if credit is extended to customers.

Use the following chart to build a worksheet to help you with this problem. In this example, all sales are made for cash.

CHART 4 – ESTIMATED CASH FLOW FORECAST

	Jan.	Feb.	Mar.	Apr.	May	Jun.	(etc.)
Cash in bank (1st of month)	___	___	___	___	___	___	___
Petty cash (1st of month)	___	___	___	___	___	___	___
Total cash (1st of month)	___	___	___	___	___	___	___
Anticipated cash sales	___	___	___	___	___	___	___
Total receipts	___	___	___	___	___	___	___
Total cash & receipts	___	___	___	___	___	___	___
Disbursements for month (rent, loan payments, utilities, wages, etc.)	___	___	___	___	___	___	___
Cash balance (end of month)	___	___	___	___	___	___	___

CONCLUSION

Beyond a doubt, preparing an adequate business plan is the most important step in starting a new business. A comprehensive business plan will be your guide to managing a successful business. **The business plan is paramount to your success.** It must contain all the pertinent information about your business; it must be well written, factual and organized in a logical sequence. Moreover, it should not contain any statements that cannot be supported.

If you have carefully answered all the questions on this checklist and completed all the worksheets, you have seriously thought about your goal. But . . . there may be some things you may feel you need to know more about.

Owning and running a business is a continuous learning process. Research your idea and do as much as you can yourself, but don't hesitate to seek help from people who can tell you what you need to know.

APPENDIX A: INCOME PROJECTION STATEMENT

	Industry %	J	F	M	A	M	J	J	A	S	O	N	D	Annual total	Annual %
Total net sales (revenues)															
Cost of sales															
Gross profit															
Gross profit margin															
Controllable expenses															
Salaries/wages															
Payroll expenses															
Legal/accounting															
Advertising															
Automobile															
Office supplies															
Dues/subscriptions															
Utilities															
Miscellaneous															
Total controllable expenses															
Fixed expenses															
Rent															
Depreciation															
Utilities															
Insurance															
Licenses/permits															
Loan payments															
Miscellaneous															
Total fixed expenses															
Total expenses															
Net profit (loss) before taxes															
Taxes															
Net profit (loss) after taxes															

INSTRUCTIONS FOR INCOME PROJECTION STATEMENT

The income projection (profit and loss) statement is valuable as both a planning tool and a key management tool to help control business operations. It enables the owner-manager to develop a preview of the amount of income generated each month and for the business year, based on reasonable predictions of monthly levels of sales, costs and expenses.

As monthly projections are developed and entered into the income projection statement, they can serve as definite goals for controlling the business operation. As actual operating results become known each month, they should be recorded for comparison with the monthly projections. A completed income statement allows the owner-manager to compare actual figures with monthly projections and to take steps to correct any problems.

Industry Percentage

In the industry percentage column, enter the percentages of total sales (revenues) that are standard for your industry, which are derived by dividing

$$\frac{\text{cost/expense items}}{\text{total net sales}} \times 100\%$$

These percentages can be obtained from various sources, such as trade associations, accountants or banks. The reference librarian in your nearest public library can refer you to documents that contain the percentage figures, for example, Robert Morris Associates' *Annual Statement Studies* (One Liberty Place, Philadelphia, PA 19103).

Industry figures serve as a useful benchmark against which to compare cost and expense estimates that you develop for your firm. Compare the figures in the industry percentage column to those in the annual percentage column.

Total Net Sales (Revenues)

Determine the total number of units of products or services you realistically expect to sell each month in each department at the prices you expect to get. Use this step to create the projection to review your pricing practices.

- What returns, allowances and markdowns can be expected?

- Exclude any revenue that is not strictly related to the business.

Cost of Sales

The key to calculating your cost of sales is that you do not overlook any costs that you have incurred. Calculate cost of sales for all products and services used to determine total net sales. Where inventory is involved, do not overlook transportation costs. Also include any direct labor.

Gross Profit

Subtract the total cost of sales from the total net sales to obtain gross profit.

Gross Profit Margin

The gross profit is expressed as a percentage of total sales (revenues). It is calculated by dividing

$$\frac{\text{gross profits}}{\text{total net sales}}$$

Controllable Expenses

- *Salary expenses*—Base pay plus overtime.

- *Payroll expenses*—Include paid vacations, sick leave, health insurance, unemployment insurance and social security taxes.

- *Outside services*—Include costs of subcontracts, overflow work and special or one-time services.

- *Supplies*—Services and items purchased for use in the business.

- *Repairs and maintenance*—Regular maintenance and repair, including periodic large expenditures such as painting.

- *Advertising*—Include desired sales volume and classified directory advertising expenses.

- *Car, delivery and travel*—Include charges if personal car is used in business, including parking, tolls, buying trips, etc.

- *Accounting and legal*—Outside professional services.

Fixed Expenses

- *Rent*—List only real estate used in the business.

- *Depreciation*—Amortization of capital assets.

- *Utilities*—Water, heat, light, etc.

- *Insurance*—Fire or liability on property or products. Include workers' compensation.

- *Loan repayments*—Interest on outstanding loans.

- *Miscellaneous*—Unspecified; small expenditures without separate accounts.

Net Profit (loss) (before taxes)	•	Subtract total expenses from gross profit.
Taxes	•	Include inventory and sales taxes, excise tax, real estate tax, etc.
Net Profit (loss) (after taxes)	•	Subtract taxes from net profit (before taxes).
Annual Total	•	For each of the sales and expense items in your income projection statement, add all the monthly figures across the table and put the result in the annual total column.
Annual Percentage	•	Calculate the annual percentage by dividing

$$\frac{\text{annual total}}{\text{total net sales}} \times 100\%$$

- Compare this figure to the industry percentage in the first column.

APPENDIX B: INFORMATION RESOURCES

U.S. Small Business Administration (SBA)

The SBA offers an extensive selection of information on most business management topics, from how to start a business to exporting your products.

This information is listed in *The Small Business Directory*. For a free copy write to: SBA Publications, P.O. Box 1000, Fort Worth, TX 76119.

SBA has offices throughout the country. Consult the U.S. Government section in your telephone directory for the office nearest you. SBA offers a number of programs and services, including training and educational programs, counseling services, financial programs and contract assistance. Ask about

- **Service Corps of Retired Executives (SCORE),** a national organization sponsored by SBA of over 13,000 volunteer business executives who provide free counseling, workshops and seminars to prospective and existing small business people.

- **Small Business Development Centers (SBDCs),** sponsored by the SBA in partnership with state and local governments, the educational community and the private sector. They provide assistance, counseling and training to prospective and existing business people.

- **Small Business Institutes (SBIs),** organized through SBA on more than 500 college campuses nationwide. The institutes provide counseling by students and faculty to small business clients.

For more information about SBA business development programs and services call the SBA Small Business Answer Desk at **1-800-U-ASK-SBA (827-5722).**

Other U.S. Government Resources

Many publications on business management and other related topics are available from the Government Printing Office (GPO). GPO bookstores are located in 24 major cities and are listed in the Yellow Pages under the "bookstore" heading. You can request a *Subject Bibliography* by writing to **Government Printing Office,** Superintendent of Documents, Washington, DC 20402-9328.

Many federal agencies offer publications of interest to small businesses. There is a nominal fee for some, but most are free. Below is a selected list of government agencies that provide publications and other services targeted to small businesses. To get their publications, contact the regional offices listed in the telephone directory or write to the addresses below:

Consumer Information Center (CIC)
P.O. Box 100
Pueblo, CO 81002
The CIC offers a consumer information catalog of federal publications.

Consumer Product Safety Commission (CPSC)
Publications Request
Washington, DC 20207
The CPSC offers guidelines for product safety requirements.

U.S. Department of Agriculture (USDA)
12th Street and Independence Avenue, SW
Washington, DC 20250
The USDA offers publications on selling to the USDA. Publications and programs on entrepreneurship are also available through county extension offices nationwide.

U.S. Department of Commerce (DOC)
Office of Business Liaison
14th Street and Constitution Avenue, NW
Room 5898C
Washington, DC 20230
DOC's Business Assistance Center provides listings of business opportunities available in the federal government. This service also will refer businesses to different programs and services in the DOC and other federal agencies.

U.S. Department of Health and Human Services (HHS)
Public Health Service
Alcohol, Drug Abuse and Mental Health Administration
5600 Fishers Lane
Rockville, MD 20857
Drug Free Workplace Helpline: **1-800-843-4971.** Provides information on Employee Assistance Programs.
National Institute for Drug Abuse Hotline: **1-800-662-4357.** Provides information on preventing substance abuse in the workplace.
The National Clearinghouse for Alcohol and Drug Information: **1-800-729-6686** toll-free. Provides pamphlets and resource materials on substance abuse.

U.S. Department of Labor (DOL)
Employment Standards Administration
200 Constitution Avenue, NW
Washington, DC 20210
The DOL offers publications on compliance with
labor laws.

U.S. Department of Treasury
Internal Revenue Service (IRS)
P.O. Box 25866
Richmond, VA 23260
1-800-424-3676
The IRS offers information on tax requirements for small
businesses.

U.S. Environmental Protection Agency (EPA)
Small Business Ombudsman
401 M Street, SW (A-149C)
Washington, DC 20460
1-800-368-5888 except DC and VA
703-557-1938 in DC and VA
The EPA offers more than 100 publications designed to
help small businesses understand how they can comply
with EPA regulations.

U.S. Food and Drug Administration (FDA)
FDA Center for Food Safety and Applied Nutrition
200 Charles Street, SW
Washington, DC 20402
The FDA offers information on packaging and labeling
requirements for food and food-related products.

For More Information

A librarian can help you locate the specific information
you need in reference books. Most libraries have a variety
of directories, indexes and encyclopedias that cover many
business topics. They also have other resources, such as

- **Trade association information**
  Ask the librarian to show you a directory of trade
  associations. Associations provide a valuable
  network of resources to their members through
  publications and services such as newsletters,
  conferences and seminars.

- **Books**
  Many guidebooks, textbooks and manuals on
  small business are published annually. To find the
  names of books not in your local library check
  Books In Print, a directory of books currently
  available from publishers.

- **Magazine and newspaper articles**
  Business and professional magazines provide
  information that is more current than that found in
  books and textbooks. There are a number of
  indexes to help you find specific articles in
  periodicals.

In addition to books and magazines, many libraries offer
free workshops, lend skill-building tapes and have
catalogues and brochures describing continuing education
opportunities.

Small Business Administration Pamphlet:
"The ABCs of Borrowing"

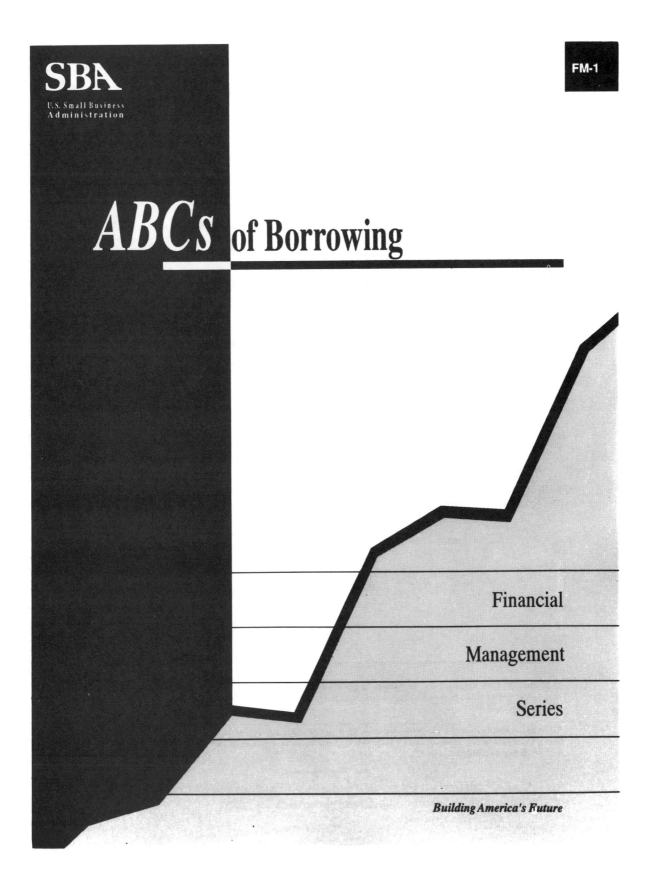

TABLE OF CONTENTS

INTRODUCTION

All businesses, no matter what size, will at some time need to raise more money. For small businesses, the owner may be able to dip into his or her personal savings, or friends may be able to lend the needed money. Usually, however, the owner will have to look to outside sources for financing.

IS YOUR FIRM CREDIT WORTHY?

Obtaining money when you need it is as necessary to the operation of your business as a good location or an adequate labor force. Before a bank will lend you money, the loan officer must feel satisfied with the answers to the following questions.

- What is your character—will you *want* to repay the loan? How capable are you in managing the business—will you be *able* to repay the loan?

- What is the specific purpose of the loan? Is it a short- or long-term need?

- Do you have a clear financial plan and forecast showing why you need the loan and how you will pay it back?

- Is the loan request large enough to cover any unexpected change in your situation, but not so large that its repayment will be a heavy burden?

- What is the general economic outlook for your business and industry?

- Do you have a reasonable amount at stake in the business?

- What collateral is available to secure the loan amount?

FINANCIAL INFORMATION REQUIRED BY LENDERS

The two basic financial documents that lenders require are the balance sheet and the income statement. The balance sheet is the major yardstick for solvency and the income statement is the common measure of profits. Using these and other sources, lenders ask the following questions.

General Questions

- Are the business's books and records up-to-date and in good condition?

- Does the business have a lawyer and/or accountant?

- Who are the customers and what percentage of total sales do the largest customers represent?

- Are all obligations paid promptly?

- What is the insurance coverage?

Accounts Receivable

- What is the quality of the accounts receivable?

- Have any been pledged to another creditor?

- Are customers paying you promptly?

- Is there an allowance for bad debts?

Inventory

- Can the merchandise be sold at full price?

- How much raw material is on hand?

- How much work is in progress?

- How much of production is finished goods?

- Is too much money tied up in inventory?

- Is the inventory turnover in line with industry norms?

Fixed Assets and Equipment

- What is the type, age and condition of the equipment?

- What are the depreciation schedules?

- What are the details of mortgages or leases?

- What are the future fixed asset and equipment needs for the company?

The lender scrutinizes the cash flow of the business to determine whether or not the owner-manager is providing sufficient cash to meet the firm's obligations. The lender also makes sure that cash needed for working capital is not being diverted to other areas, such as the acquisition of fixed assets, thereby reducing liquidity.

WHAT TYPE OF LOAN?

When you set out to borrow money for your firm, it is important to know the type of loan you want and its duration. There are two basic kinds of loans—lines of credit and installment loans—and two general categories of loan length—short-term and long-term.

The purpose for which the funds are to be used is a very important factor in deciding what kind of loan to request. There is also an important connection between the length of the loan and the source of repayment. Generally, short-term loans are repaid from the liquidation of the current assets (i.e., receivables, inventory) that are financed, while long-term loans are generally repaid from earnings.

Line of Credit

A line of credit is an arrangement in which the bank disburses funds as they are needed, up to a predetermined limit. The customer may borrow and repay repeatedly up to the limit within the approved time frame (usually one year).

Installment Loan

An installment loan is an agreement to provide a lump sum amount of money at the beginning of the loan. The loan is paid back in equal amounts over the course of a number of years.

Short-term loan

A short-term bank loan can be used for purposes such as financing a seasonal buildup in accounts receivable or inventory. Lenders usually expect these loans to be repaid after their purposes have been served: for example, accounts receivable loans when the outstanding accounts have been paid by the customers and inventory loans when the inventory has been sold and cash collected. Short-term loans are generally repaid in less than a year.

Long-term loan

A long-term loan is usually a formal agreement to provide funds for more than one year, and most are for an improvement that will benefit the company and increase earnings. An example is the purchase of a new building that will increase capacity or of a machine that will make the manufacturing process more efficient and less costly. Long-term loans are usually repaid from profits.

COLLATERAL

Sometimes your signature and general credit reputation are the only collateral the bank needs to make a loan. This type of loan is called unsecured. At other times, the bank requires a pledge of some or all of your assets as additional assurance that the loan will be repaid. This is called a secured loan. The kind and amount of collateral depends on the bank and on variables in the borrower's situation.

Many types of collateral can be pledged for a secured loan. The most common are endorser, warehouse receipts, floor planning, purchase money security interest (PMSI) in furniture and/or equipment, real estate, accounts receivable inventory, savings accounts, life insurance policies, and stocks and bonds.

Endorser, Co-maker, Guarantor

A borrower may ask another person to sign a note in order to augment his or her credit. This endorser is then liable for the note: if the borrower fails to pay, the bank expects the endorser to pay. Sometimes the endorser may also be asked to pledge assets.

A co-maker is an endorser who assumes an obligation jointly with the maker, or borrower. In this arrangement, the bank can collect directly from either maker or co-maker.

A guarantor is an endorser who guarantees the payment of a note if the borrower does not pay. Both private and government lenders often require guarantees from officers of corporations in order to assure continuity of effective management.

Warehouse Receipts

A bank may take commodities as collateral by lending money on a warehouse receipt. The receipt is usually delivered directly to the bank and shows that the merchandise has either been placed in a public warehouse or has been left on your premises under the control of one of your employees who is bonded. Such loans are generally made on staple or standard merchandise that can be readily marketed. The typical loan is for a percentage of the cost of the merchandise.

Floor Planning

Merchandise—such as automobiles, appliances and boats—must be displayed to be sold, but the only way many small marketers can afford displays is by borrowing

money. Such loans are often secured by a note and trust receipt. The trust receipt is used for serial numbered merchandise. It acknowledges receipt of the merchandise, shows agreement to keep the merchandise in trust for the bank and verifies the promise to pay the bank as the goods are sold.

Purchase Money Security Interest

If you buy expensive equipment, such as a cash register or a delivery truck, you may be able to get a loan using the equipment as collateral. (This kind of loan is also called a chattel mortgage.) The bank assesses the present and future market value of the equipment and makes sure it is adequately insured.

Real Estate

Real estate is another form of collateral, usually for long-term loans. In evaluating a real estate mortgage, the bank considers the market and foreclosure value of the property and its insurance coverage.

Accounts Receivable

Many banks lend money against accounts receivable; in effect, counting on your customers to pay your loan. The bank may take accounts receivable on a notification or nonnotification plan. Under the notification plan, the purchaser of the goods is informed by the bank that the account has been assigned and is asked to make payments directly to the bank. Under the nonnotification plan, customers continue to pay you and you pay the bank.

Inventory

Inventory is the merchandise, wares and any assets that can be liquidated of a retail, wholesale or manufacturing business that will provide a form of financial guarantee against the loan proceeds. Unless otherwise specified in the loan documents, plant and equipment (e.g., computers, cash registers, manufacturing equipment, telephones and other fixtures) can also be included as inventory to be held as collateral.

Savings Accounts and Certificates of Deposit

It is possible to get a loan by assigning a savings account to the bank. You assign the account and the bank keeps the passbook. If you assign an account at another bank as collateral, the lending bank asks the other bank to mark its records to show that the account is held as collateral.

Life Insurance

Another kind of collateral is the cash value of a life insurance policy, in which you assign the policy to the bank. Some people prefer to use life insurance as collateral rather than borrowing directly from the insurance company because a bank loan generally is easier to obtain and carries a lower interest rate.

Stocks and Bonds

Marketable stocks and bonds are also sources of collateral. Banks usually lend 75 percent or less on the value of high-grade stocks and up to 90 percent on government securities. The limits leave a cushion or margin for protection against declines. If the market value of the collateral does fall below a certain level, the bank may ask for additional collateral or a partial payment of the loan.

THE LOAN AGREEMENT

A loan agreement is a tailor-made document, fully stating all the terms and conditions of the loan. It gives the amount of the loan and terms of repayment, identifies the principle parties and lists any restrictions placed on the borrower.

Limitations

Banks often include limitations in a loan agreement that restrict what an owner can do. These limitations depend to a great extent on the company. If the company is a good risk, the limitations will be minimal. A higher risk company, on the other hand, will have greater limitations. The three principle limitations involve repayment terms, the use of collateral and periodic reporting. Limitations are spelled out in the covenant section.

Covenants—Negative and Positive

Negative covenants are restrictions placed on the borrower by the lender. Some examples are limitations on the borrower's total debt, agreement not to pledge assets to other creditors and limitations on the amount of dividends that may be issued.

Positive covenants are all actions the borrower must agree to. They include maintaining a minimum working capital, carrying adequate insurance, adhering to the repayment schedules and supplying the lender with regular financial statements and reports. Loan agreements can be amended from time to time and exceptions made. Certain provisions may be waived from year to year with the consent of the lender.

Negotiating with the Lender

Ask to see the papers before the loan closing. Reputable lenders will be glad to comply. While you're mulling over the terms you may want to get the advice of your associates and advisors. Discuss and negotiate the lending terms before you sign the loan agreement—it is good practice, no matter how much you need the money. Chances are the lender may be willing to "give" on some of the terms; try to get terms with which you know your company can live. Remember, though, that once the loan is made, you are bound by it.

THE LOAN APPLICATION

Banks and other lending institutions, including the SBA, require a loan application on which you list certain information about your business.

SBA Form 4 is an example of a loan application. It is more detailed than most bank forms, because the bank usually has the advantage of prior knowledge of the applicant and his or her activities, while SBA usually does not have such knowledge. Also, the longer maturities offered on SBA loans ordinarily require more information about the applicant.

Before you fill out a loan application, you should talk with an SBA representative, or your accountant or banker, to make sure that your business is eligible for an SBA loan. Because of public policy, SBA cannot make certain types of loans, nor can it make loans under certain conditions. For example, if you qualify for a loan on reasonable terms from a bank, SBA cannot lend you money. You also are not eligible for an SBA loan if you can get funds by selling assets that your company does not need in order to grow.

Most sections of the SBA loan application are self-explanatory; however, some applicants have trouble with certain sections because they do not know where to get the necessary information requested.

The collateral section is an example. Collateral is the borrower's assets that are pledged to the lender to guarantee the loan. Your company's books should show the market value of assets such as business real estate and business machinery and equipment. ("Market" means what you paid for such assets less depreciation.) If your records do not contain detailed information on these assets, the bank sometimes can get it from your federal income tax returns. Reviewing the depreciation that you have taken for tax purposes on such assets can help to ascertain their value.

If you are a good manager, you probably balance your books every month. Some businesses, however, prepare balance sheets less regularly. In filling out your "Balance Sheet as of _____, 19___, Fiscal Year Ends_____," remember that you must show the condition of your business within 60 days of the date on your loan application. It is best to get expert advice when working up this vital information. Your accountant or banker can help you.

Again, if your records do not show the details necessary for working up income (profit and loss) statements, your federal income tax returns may be useful in getting together facts for a loan application.

APPENDIX A: APPLICATION FOR BUSINESS LOAN

OMB Approval No. 3245-0016
Expiration Date: 10-31-93

U.S. Small Business Administration
APPLICATION FOR BUSINESS LOAN

Individual	Full Address

Name of Applicant Business	Tax I.D. No. or SSN

Full Street Address of Business	Tel. No. (inc. A/C)

City	County	State	Zip	Number of Employees (Including subsidiaries and affiliates)
Type of Business			Date Business Established	At Time of Application _____
Bank of Business Account and Address				If Loan is Approved _____
				Subsidiaries or Affiliates (Separate from above) _____

Use of Proceeds: (Enter Gross Dollar Amounts Rounded to the Nearest Hundreds)	Loan Requested		Loan Requested
Land Acquisition		Payoff SBA Loan	
New Construction/ Expansion Repair		Payoff Bank Loan (Non SBA Associated)	
Acquisition and/or Repair of Machinery and Equipment		Other Debt Payment (Non SBA Associated)	
Inventory Purchase		All Other	
Working Capital (Including Accounts Payable)		Total Loan Requested	
Acquisition of Existing Business		Term of Loan - (Requested Mat.)	_____ Yrs.

PREVIOUS SBA OR OTHER FEDERAL GOVERNMENT DEBT: If you or any principals or affiliates have 1) ever requested Government Financing or 2) are delinquent on the repayment of any Federal Debt complete the following:

Name of Agency	Original Amount of Loan	Date of Request	Approved or Declined	Balance	Current or Past Due
	$			$	
	$			$	

ASSISTANCE   List the names(s) and occupations of any who assisted in the preparation of this form, other than applicant.

Name and Occupation	Address	Total Fees Paid	Fees Due
Name and Occupation	Address	Total Fees Paid	Fees Due

PLEASE NOTE The estimated burden hours for the completion of this form is 19.8 hours per response If you have any questions or comments concerning this estimate or any other aspect of this information collection please contact Chief Administrative Information Branch, U.S. Small Business Administration, Washington, D.C. 20416 and Gary Waxman, Clearance Officer, Paperwork Reduction Project (3245-0016), Office of Management and Budget, Washington, D.C 20503

SBA Form 4 (5 92) Previous Edition is Obsolete   Page 1

ALL EXHIBITS MUST BE SIGNED AND DATED BY PERSON SIGNING THIS FORM

BUSINESS INDEBTEDNESS: Furnish the following information on all installment debts, contracts, notes, and mortgages payable. Indicate by an asterisk(*) items to be paid by loan proceeds and reason for paying same (present balance should agree with the latest balance sheet submitted).

To Whom Payable	Original Amount	Original Date	Present Balance	Rate of Interest	Maturity Date	Monthly Payment	Security	Current or Past Due
Acct. #	$		$			$		
Acct. #	$		$			$		
Acct. #	$		$			$		
Acct. #	$		$			$		

MANAGEMENT (Proprietor, partners, officers, directors all holders of outstanding stock - <u>100% of ownership must be shown</u>). Use separate sheet if necessary.

Name and Social Security Number and Position Title	Complete Address	% Owned	*Military Service From	To	*Race	*Sex

*This data is collected for statistical purpose only. It has no bearing on the credit decision to approve or decline this application.

THE FOLLOWING EXHIBITS MUST BE COMPLETED WHERE APPLICABLE . ALL QUESTIONS ANSWERED ARE MADE A PART OF THE APPLICATION.

For Guaranty Loans please provide an original and one copy (Photocopy is Acceptable) of the Application Form, and all Exhibits to the participating lender. For Direct Loans submit one original copy of the application and Exhibits to SBA.

1. Submit SBA Form 912 (Personal History Statement) for each person e g owners, partners, officers, directors, major stockholders, etc ; the instructions are on SBA Form 912.

2. If your collateral consists of (A) Land and Building, (B) Machinery and Equipment, (C)Furniture and Fixtures, (D) Accounts Receivable (E) Inventory, (F) Other, please provide an itemized list (labeled Exhibit A) that contains serial and identification numbers for all articles that had an original value greater than $500 Include a legal description of Real Estate offered as collateral

3. Furnish a signed current personal balance sheet (SBA Form 413 may be used for this purpose) for each stockholder (with 20% or greater ownership), partner, officer, and owner Social Security number should be included on personal financial statement It should be as of the same date as the most recent business financial statements Label this Exhibit B

4. Include the statements listed below: 1,2,3 for the last three years; also 1,2,3, 4 as of the same date, which are current within 90 days of filing the application; and statement 5, if applicable. This is Exhibit C (SBA has Management Aids that help in the preparation of financial statements.) All information must be **signed and dated**.

1. Balance Sheet   2. Profit and Loss Statement
3. Reconciliation of Net Worth
4. Aging of Accounts Receivable and Payable
5. Earnings projects for a least one year where financial statements for the last three years are unavailable or where requested by District Office.
    (If Profit and Loss Statement is not available, explain why and substitute Federal Income Tax Forms)

5. Provide a brief history of your company and a paragraph describing the expected benefits it will receive from the loan. Label it Exhibit D

6. Provide a brief description similar to a resume of the education, technical and business background for all the people listed under Management Please mark it Exhibit E

SBA Form 4 (5-92) Previous Edition is Obsolete   Page 2

ALL EXHIBITS MUST BE SIGNED AND DATED BY PERSON SIGNING THIS FORM

7. Do you have any co-signers and/or guarantors for this loan? If so, please submit their names, addresses, tax Id Numbers, and current personal balance sheet(s) as Exhibit F.

8. Are you buying machinery or equipment with your loan money? If so, you must include a list of equipment and cost as quoted by the seller and his name and address. This is Exhibit G.

9. Have you or any officer of your company ever been involved in bankruptcy or insolvency proceedings? If so, please provide the details as Exhibit H. If none, check here: [Yes] [No]

10. Are you or your business involved in any pending lawsuits? If yes, provide the details as Exhibit I. If none, check here: [Yes] [No]

11. Do you or your spouse or any member of your household, or anyone who owns, manages, or directs your business or their spouses or members of their households work for the Small Business Administration, Small Business Advisory Council, SCORE or ACE, any Federal Agency, or the participating lender? If so, please provide the name and address of the person and the office where employed. Label this Exhibit J. If none, check here: [Yes] [No]

12. Does your business, its owners or majority stockholders own or have a controlling interest in other businesses? If yes, please provide their names and the relationship with your company along with a current balance sheet and operating statement for each. This should be Exhibit K.

13. Do you buy from, sell to, or use the services of any concern in which someone in your company has a significant financial interest? If yes, provide details on a separate sheet of paper labeled Exhibit L.

14. If your business is a franchise, include a copy of the franchise agreement and a copy of the FTC disclosure statement supplied to you by the Franchisor. Please include it as Exhibit M.

CONSTRUCTION LOANS ONLY

15. Include a separate exhibit (Exhibit N) the estimated cost of the project and a statement of the source of any additional funds.

16. Provide copies of preliminary construction plans and specifications. Include them as Exhibit O. Final plans will be required prior to disbursement.

DIRECT LOANS ONLY

17. Include two bank declination letters with your application. (In cities with 200,000 people or less, one letter will be sufficient.) These letters should include the name and telephone number of the persons contacted at the banks, the amount and terms of the loan, the reason for decline and whether or not the bank will participate with SBA.

EXPORT LOANS

18. Does your business presently engage in Export Trade? Check here: [Yes] [No]

19. Do you have plans to begin exporting as a result of this loan? Check here: [Yes] [No]

20. Would you like information on Exporting? Check here: [Yes] [No]

AGREEMENTS AND CERTIFICATIONS

Agreements of non-employment of SBA Personnel: I agree that if SBA approves this loan application I will not, for at least two years, hire as an employee or consultant anyone that was employed by the SBA during the one year period prior to the disbursement of the loan.

Certification: I certify: (a) I have not paid anyone connected with the Federal Government for help in getting this loan. I also agree to report to the SBA office of the Inspector General, Washington, D.C. 20416 any Federal Government employee who offers, in return for any type of compensation, to help get this loan approved.

(b) All information in this application and the Exhibits are true and complete to the best of my knowledge and are submitted to SBA so SBA can decide whether to grant a loan or participate with a lending institution in a loan to me. I agree to pay for or reimburse SBA for the cost of any surveys, title or mortgage examinations, appraisals credit reports, etc., performed by non-SBA personnel provided I have given my consent.

(c) I understand that I need not pay anybody to deal with SBA. I have read and understand SBA Form 159 which explains SBA policy on representatives and their fees.

(d) As consideration for any Management, Technical, and Business Development Assistance that may be provided, I waive all claims against SBA and its consultants.

If you make a statement that you know to be false or if you over value a security in order to help obtain a loan under the provisions of the Small Business Act, you can be fined up to $5,000 or be put in jail for up to two years, or both.

If Applicant is a proprietor or general partner, sign below.

By: _____ Date _____

If Applicant is a Corporation, sign below:

Corporate Name and Seal _____ Date _____

By: _____
Signature of President

Attested by: _____
Signature of Corporate Secretary

SBA Form 4 (5-92) Previous Edition is Obsolete   Page 3

APPLICANT'S CERTIFICATION

By my signature I certify that I have read and received a copy of the "STATEMENTS REQUIRED BY LAW AND EXECUTIVE ORDER" which was attached to this application. My signature represents my agreement to comply with the approval of my loan request and to comply, whenever applicable, with the hazard insurance, lead-based paint, civil rights or other limitations in this notice.

Each Proprietor, each General Partner, each Limited Partner or Stockholder owning 20% or more, and each Guarantor must sign. Each person should sign only once.

Business Name _____

_____ By _____
Date   Signature and Title

_____
Date   Signature

_____
Date   Signature

_____
Date   Signature

_____
Date   Signature

SBA Form 4 (5-92) Previous Edition is Obsolete   *U.S. Government Printing Office: 1992 — 323-043/69067   Page 4

APPENDIX B: CASH BUDGET

(For three months, ending March 31, 19_____)

	January budget	Actual	February budget	Actual	March budget	Actual
Expected cash receipts:						
1. Cash sales	_____	_____	_____	_____	_____	_____
2. Collections on accounts receivable	_____	_____	_____	_____	_____	_____
3. Other income	_____	_____	_____	_____	_____	_____
4. Total cash receipts						
Expected cash payments:						
5. Raw materials	_____	_____	_____	_____	_____	_____
6. Payroll	_____	_____	_____	_____	_____	_____
7. Other factory expenses (including maintenance)	_____	_____	_____	_____	_____	_____
8. Advertising	_____	_____	_____	_____	_____	_____
9. Selling expense	_____	_____	_____	_____	_____	_____
10. Administrative expense (including salary of owner-manager)	_____	_____	_____	_____	_____	_____
11. New plant and equipment	_____	_____	_____	_____	_____	_____
12. Other payments (taxes, including estimated income tax; repayment of loans; interest; etc.)	_____	_____	_____	_____	_____	_____
13. Total cash payments	_____	_____	_____	_____	_____	_____
14. Expected cash balance at beginning of the month	_____	_____	_____	_____	_____	_____
15. Cash increase or decrease (item 4 minus item 13)	_____	_____	_____	_____	_____	_____
16. Expected cash balance at end of month (item 14 plus item 15)	_____	_____	_____	_____	_____	_____
17. Desired working cash balance	_____	_____	_____	_____	_____	_____
18. Short-term loans needed (item 17 minus item 16, if item 17 is larger)	_____	_____	_____	_____	_____	_____
19. Cash available for dividends, capital cash expenditures, and/or short investments (item 16 minus item 17, if item 16 is larger)	_____	_____	_____	_____	_____	_____
Capital cash:						
20. Cash available (item 19 after deducting dividends, etc.)	_____	_____	_____	_____	_____	_____
21. Desired capital cash (item 11, new plant equipment)	_____	_____	_____	_____	_____	_____
22. Long-term loans needed (item 21 less item 20, if item 21 is larger)	_____	_____	_____	_____	_____	_____

APPENDIX C: GLOSSARY

Accounts receivable	Money your customers owe you that you have sent them a bill for.
Bad debt	Money owed to you that is not repaid.
Cash flow	The movement of money into and out of your business.
Collateral	Item (equipment, property, etc.) that is pledged to guarantee a loan.
Covenant	Prescription for action in a loan agreement.
Current assets	Money, inventory and equipment that will be used up in the short term (usually within one year).
Depreciation schedule	Accounting procedure for determining the amount of value left in a piece of equipment.
Financial forecast	Projection of revenues and expenses for the next one to five years.
Financial plan	Outline for how to use the money (capital) you have and how to raise the money you will need.
Fixed assets	Equipment, buildings, etc., that are purchased and used for long-term purposes.
Inventory	Merchandise that is purchased and/or produced and stored for eventual sale.
Inventory turnover	How often the inventory is sold and replenished in one year.
Liquidation	Sale of products or merchandise.
Long term	Period usually greater than one year.
Obligation	Money, merchandise or service owed to someone. Another term for debt.
Short term	Period usually one year or less.
Solvency	The ability to continue business.
Working capital	Cash and short-term assets that can be used for current needs (bills, etc.).

APPENDIX D: INFORMATION RESOURCES

U.S. Small Business Administration (SBA)

The SBA offers an extensive selection of information on most business management topics, from how to start a business to exporting your products.

This information is listed in *The Small Business Directory*. For a free copy write to: SBA Publications, P.O. Box 1000, Fort Worth, TX 76119.

SBA has offices throughout the country. Consult the U.S. Government section in your telephone directory for the office nearest you. SBA offers a number of programs and services, including training and educational programs, counseling services, financial programs and contract assistance. Ask about

- **Service Corps of Retired Executives (SCORE),** a national organization sponsored by SBA of over 13,000 volunteer business executives who provide free counseling, workshops and seminars to prospective and existing small business people.

- **Small Business Development Centers (SBDCs),** sponsored by the SBA in partnership with state and local governments, the educational community and the private sector. They provide assistance, counseling and training to prospective and existing business people.

- **Small Business Institutes (SBIs),** organized through SBA on more than 500 college campuses nationwide. The institutes provide counseling by students and faculty to small business clients.

For more information about SBA business development programs and services call the SBA Small Business Answer Desk at **1-800-U-ASK-SBA (827-5722).**

Other U.S. Government Resources

Many publications on business management and other related topics are available from the Government Printing Office (GPO). GPO bookstores are located in 24 major cities and are listed in the Yellow Pages under the "bookstore" heading. You can request a *Subject Bibliography* by writing to **Government Printing Office**, Superintendent of Documents, Washington, DC 20402-9328.

Many federal agencies offer publications of interest to small businesses. There is a nominal fee for some, but most are free. Below is a selected list of government agencies that provide publications and other services targeted to small businesses. To get their publications, contact the regional offices listed in the telephone directory or write to the addresses below:

Consumer Information Center (CIC)
P.O. Box 100
Pueblo, CO 81002
The CIC offers a consumer information catalog of federal publications.

Consumer Product Safety Commission (CPSC)
Publications Request
Washington, DC 20207
The CPSC offers guidelines for product safety requirements.

U.S. Department of Agriculture (USDA)
12th Street and Independence Avenue, SW
Washington, DC 20250
The USDA offers publications on selling to the USDA. Publications and programs on entrepreneurship are also available through county extension offices nationwide.

U.S. Department of Commerce (DOC)
Office of Business Liaison
14th Street and Constitution Avenue, NW
Room 5898C
Washington, DC 20230
DOC's Business Assistance Center provides listings of business opportunities available in the federal government. This service also will refer businesses to different programs and services in the DOC and other federal agencies.

U.S. Department of Health and Human Services (HHS)
Public Health Service
Alcohol, Drug Abuse and Mental Health
   Administration
5600 Fishers Lane
Rockville, MD 20857
Drug Free Workplace Helpline: **1-800-843-4971.** Provides information on Employee Assistance Programs.
National Institute for Drug Abuse Hotline: **1-800-662-4357.** Provides information on preventing substance abuse in the workplace.
The National Clearinghouse for Alcohol and Drug Information: **1-800-729-6686** toll-free. Provides pamphlets and resource materials on substance abuse.

U.S. Department of Labor (DOL)
Employment Standards Administration
200 Constitution Avenue, NW
Washington, DC 20210
The DOL offers publications on compliance with
labor laws.

U.S. Department of Treasury
Internal Revenue Service (IRS)
P.O. Box 25866
Richmond, VA 23260
1-800-424-3676
The IRS offers information on tax requirements for small
businesses.

U.S. Environmental Protection Agency (EPA)
Small Business Ombudsman
401 M Street, SW (A-149C)
Washington, DC 20460
1-800-368-5888 except DC and VA
703-557-1938 in DC and VA
The EPA offers more than 100 publications designed to
help small businesses understand how they can comply
with EPA regulations.

U.S. Food and Drug Administration (FDA)
FDA Center for Food Safety and Applied Nutrition
200 Charles Street, SW
Washington, DC 20402
The FDA offers information on packaging and labeling
requirements for food and food-related products.

For More Information

A librarian can help you locate the specific information
you need in reference books. Most libraries have a variety
of directories, indexes and encyclopedias that cover many
business topics. They also have other resources, such as

- **Trade association information**
  Ask the librarian to show you a directory of trade
  associations. Associations provide a valuable
  network of resources to their members through
  publications and services such as newsletters,
  conferences and seminars.

- **Books**
  Many guidebooks, textbooks and manuals on
  small business are published annually. To find the
  names of books not in your local library check
  Books In Print, a directory of books currently
  available from publishers.

- **Magazine and newspaper articles**
  Business and professional magazines provide
  information that is more current than that found in
  books and textbooks. There are a number of
  indexes to help you find specific articles in
  periodicals.

In addition to books and magazines, many libraries offer
free workshops, lend skill-building tapes and have
catalogues and brochures describing continuing education
opportunities.

Excerpts from *The Catalog of Federal Domestic Assistance*

APPLYING FOR FEDERAL ASSISTANCE

- Refer to the Agency Index, Functional Index, Subject Index, and/or the Applicant Eligibility Index to locate assistance program(s) suitable to your needs as an applicant.

OR

- Have an automated program search done on the *Federal Assistance Programs Retrieval System (FAPRS)*. Access points are located throughout the country. (See narrative on *FAPRS* in this section.)

- Determine your means of approach for making an application:

  Program Objectives and Uses

  Type of Assistance Needed

  Eligibility Requirements

  Application Procedure Required

- Check for application deadline.

- Refer to *Information Contacts* section located within each program description for telephone numbers and addresses to get further information from the funding agency.

- Contact the agency to determine:

  - Applicability of your proposal or project

  - Availability of funds or assistance

  - Answers to any other questions you may have

- Apply to funding agency for assistance.

HOW TO USE THE CATALOG

The following resource aids located in the front of the Catalog will help you to locate the assistance programs in which you are interested.

WHAT'S IN THE *HOW TO USE THE CATALOG* SECTION

- Information that will familiarize potential applicants with the contents of the Catalog, and pertinent criteria to consider before applying for Federal assistance

- Definitions for the 15 types of assistance, including both financial and non-financial types of assistance

- Explanation of the organizational layout of the Catalog, the program descriptions, indexes, and appendixes

- A sample program description illustrating the kind of information found in each section of program descriptions

FOUR WAYS TO IDENTIFY A PROGRAM FOR FEDERAL ASSISTANCE

Agency Index - Page AI–1

Identify assistance programs categorized by agency (subagency, or designated commission), listed by program number and title, or listed alphabetically at the end of the Agency Index. Review program(s).

Functional Index - Page FI–1

Identify assistance programs by cross-referencing programs within 20 broad functional categories and 176 subcategories. Refer to the preceding Functional Index Summary on Page FIS–1 for a complete listing. Review program(s).

Subject Index - Page SI–1

Identify assistance programs by subject categories, popular names, or common keywords associated with the subject matter of the program objectives for the type of assistance you are seeking. Review program(s).

Applicant Eligibility Index - Page AE–1

Identify assistance programs according to the type of applicant who is eligible to apply for each program listed in the Catalog. Review program(s).

Federal Assistance Programs Retrieval System (FAPRS)

The Federal Assistance Programs Retrieval System (FAPRS) is a computerized question-answer system designed to provide rapid access to Federal domestic assistance program information. The system provides information on Federal programs which meet the developmental needs of the applicant and for which the applicant meets basic eligibility criteria. Program information provided by FAPRS is determined from input supplied by the requestor. Input includes the types of applicant (e.g., State or local governments, federally-designated Indian tribal governments, nonprofit organizations, small businesses, individuals), the type of assistance under which programs are administered (e.g., grants, loans); and the specific functional categories and subcategories of interest. Based upon the input supplied, the output consists of: (1) a list of program numbers and titles; (2) the full text of selected programs; or (3) specific sections of the program text.

The keyword search facility of FAPRS was added as the direct result of users' requests. The new features allow the applicant to (1) perform a program search of all Catalog programs by using up to five "keywords" or phrases with several operators; (2) position the keyword options in the same order, paragraph or program or within a selected range of words; and (3) determine the number of programs and occurrences selected. (This allows programs to be listed by program number and titles, with the option to view each occurrence in context.) Keyword search is designed for experienced users and provides greater search specificity. The original menu-driven FAPRS category search facility is still available to all users.

As originally developed, FAPRS was designed to aid small, rural, isolated communities unfamiliar with Federal assistance programs or unable to locate Federal aid programs that had the greatest funding potential. The present FAPRS is an enhanced version which was developed by incorporating data provided from an analysis of FAPRS users and an OMB study of the overall requirements for Federal information systems. FAPRS may now be accessed by both rural and urban communities.

FAPRS consists of the following features:

1. Functional search criteria—20 functional categories and 175 subcategories to specify areas of interest, as listed in the Functional Index of the Catalog.

2. Applicant eligibility search criteria—10 government related and 11 non-government related applicant types.

3. Type(s) of assistance search criteria—15 types of assistance categories.

4. A display of definitions for functional subcategories, applicant types, and types of assistance to assist the user in selecting the desired search criteria.

5. Program text printout selection to print entire text(s) or only specified sections of text(s) if desired.

6. Formatted display of Federal circular coordination requirements for a selected list of programs.

States have designated access points where FAPRS searches may be requested. In addition, bulletins on FAPRS are available from the system to inform users of the addition or deletion of programs, changes to program numbers from one update cycle to the next, and enhancements or changes to the system. For volume users, direct access to FAPRS is available through GSA on a cost-reimbursable basis. For further information on FAPRS, the location of the nearest State access point, or procedures for directly accessing the system, write or call:

Federal Domestic Assistance Catalog Staff (WKU)
General Services Administration
Ground Floor, Reporters Building
300 7th Street, S.W.
Washington, DC 20407
Telephone: (202) 708-5126
Toll-Free Answering Service: 1-800-669-8331

The Agency Program Index lists all programs in the Catalog in numerical order by the five-digit program identification number, the program title, the Federal agency responsible for administering the program, and whether the program offers financial assistance, nonfinancial assistance, or a combination of both.

The Functional Index Summary lists the basic functional categories and the subcategories which further identify specific areas of interest. Following the Summary is the Functional Index listing each program number and title under the appropriate basic category and subcategory.

The Subject Index provides a detailed listing of programs by various topics, popular name, general functional terms, categories of services, and selected beneficiaries, and is followed by the applicable program numbers.

The Applicant Eligibility Index is a listing in program number sequence, along with program titles, indicating the applicants eligible to apply. The index lists programs which may be applied for by:

— any of the several States of the United States, the District of Columbia, or any agency or instrumentality of a State exclusive of State institutions of higher education and hospitals;

— local governments which include a county, parish, municipality, city, town, township, village, State-designated Indian tribal government, local public authority, school district, special district, intrastate district, council of governments, sponsor group representative organizations, and other regional or interstate government entity, or any agency or instrumentality of a local government;

— U.S. Territories (and possessions) of the United States which include the Commonwealths of Puerto Rico and the Northern Mariana Islands, the Virgin Islands, Guam, Trust Territory of the Pacific Islands, and American Samoa;

— Federally-recognized Indian Tribal governments which include the governing body or a governmental agency of any Indian tribe, band, nation, or other organized group or community (including any Native village as defined in Section 3 of the Alaska Native Claims Settlement Act, 85 Stat. 688) certified by the Secretary of the Interior as eligible for the special programs and services provided by him through the Bureau of Indian Affairs;

— nonprofit organizations and institutions which include quasi-public, public and private institutions of higher education and hospitals, Native American Indian Organizations, and other quasi-public and private nonprofit organizations such as, but not limited to, community action agencies (CAAs), Head Start agencies, research institutes, educational associations, and health centers. Excluded under this definition are government-owned contractor operated facilities or research centers providing support for mission-oriented, large scale programs that are government-owned or controlled, or are designed as federally-funded research and development centers; and

— private individuals such as Native Americans, homeowners, students, farmers, artists, scientists, consumers, small business, refugees, aliens, veterans, senior citizens, low-income persons, health and education professionals, builders, contractors, developers, handicapped persons, the physically afflicted.

The Deadlines Index (for program applications) is a listing of program numbers and titles and the deadline date(s) by which funding agencies must receive applications. This information is also contained in the Deadlines Section of the program descriptions.

Users should also consult the following listings:

The Deleted Programs list identifies programs that have been deleted since the previous edition of the Catalog due to: expiration of budget authority; rescission of budget authority for the current fiscal year; program consolidation which has rendered the former program number(s) obsolete; the replacement of a categorical grant program by a block grant program; the replacement of two or more categorical programs by a block grant program; the abolishment of an agency; or the criteria for including a program [that is no longer valid] in the Catalog (e.g., a program which no longer operates under Federal funding).

The Added Programs list identifies programs that have been added since the previous edition of the Catalog due to: the appropriation of new budget authority; the consolidation of two or more programs creating a new program; the splitting of elements from a former program creating two or more new programs; the transformation of a single categorical grant program into a block program; or the consolidation of two or more categorical grant programs into a block program.

The Crosswalk of Changes to Program Numbers and Titles which lists programs that have undergone a title change, or a program number change due to restructuring of programs, or reorganization of a Federal agency.

PROGRAM DESCRIPTIONS—The center section of the Catalog contains descriptions of Federal programs listed by program number in the same numerical sequence as in the Agency Program Index. Detailed information concerning programs is contained under the description headings of each Catalog program. The following is an explanation of each program description heading followed by examples of the type of information found under each heading.

Note: The program used in the example below does not exist. It is provided for the purpose of illustration only.

PROGRAM NUMBER, TITLE, AND POPULAR NAME—each program in the Catalog is preceded by a five-digit program identification number. The first two digits identify the Federal department or agency that administers the program, and the last three numbers are assigned in numerical sequence. Thus, program number 10.500 is administered by the Department of Agriculture, 11.500 by the Department of Commerce, 12.500 by the Department of Defense, 93.500 by the Department of Health and Human Services, and so on. (In the numerical sequence of program numbers, some numbers do not appear due to program deletions or consolidations. To accommodate users' systems and records, the numbers are not reassigned to other programs but are reserved for the reinstated programs.) The program title is the descriptive name given to a program. The popular name, which is less descriptive than the program title, is the name by which programs are commonly known or most often used by applicants and agencies.

Example: 93.259 Mental Health—Children's Services

FEDERAL AGENCY—The Federal agency is the Federal department, agency, commission, council or instrumentality of the government, and the primary organizational sub-unit (the administering office) that has direct operational responsibility for managing a program.

Example: Alcohol, Drug Abuse and Mental Health Administration, Public Health Service, Department of Health and Human Services

AUTHORIZATION—This section lists the legal authority upon which a program is based (acts, amendments to acts, Public Law numbers, titles, sections, Statute Codes, citations to the U.S. Code, Executive Orders, Presidential Reorganization Plans, and Memoranda from an agency head). Information provided here is used to produce Appendix II, the Authorization Appendix.

Example: Community Mental Health Centers Act of 1975, Part A, Section 203(e), Public Law 94–63, 42 U.S.C. 2689.

OBJECTIVES—This is a brief statement of specific objectives stated in terms of what the program is intended to accomplish along with the goals toward which the program is directed.

Example: To stimulate innovative approaches to children's mental health problems emphasizing prevention and coordination of community services; to expand training activities; and, to broaden resources for children's mental health services.

TYPES OF ASSISTANCE—This section indicates the form in which the assistance is transmitted from the Federal government and is initially received for use or distribution by the applicant.

Example: Project Grants.

USES AND USE RESTRICTIONS—This section describes the potential uses for the assistance provided to meet stated objectives, and the specific restrictions placed upon the use of funds. The section cites one or more applications depending upon the nature of a particular program. Since this section translates objectives into the uses of a program, users may develop a clearer understanding of the program's objectives.

Example: Support for Continuation Grants only. Program authorizes funds on a matching basis for initial staffing of facilities offering mental health services for children. Staffing grants may be used for a portion of the costs of professional and technical personnel to operate a facility for child mental health services; a higher percentage may be paid if an area has been designated a poverty area by the Secretary, HHS. The proposed program must provide consultation and coordinating services with other community agencies serving children in service area, and must include a plan with the means by which it will be evaluated.

ELIGIBILITY REQUIREMENTS:

Applicant Eligibility—This section indicates who can apply to the Federal government for assistance and the criteria the potential applicant must satisfy. For example, individuals may be eligible for research grants, and the criteria to be satisfied may be that they have a professional or scientific degree, 3 years of research experience, and be a citizen of the United States. Universities, medical schools, hospitals, or State and local governments may also be eligible. Where State governments are eligible, the type of State agency will be indicated (State welfare agency or State agency on aging) and the criteria that they must satisfy.

Certain programs in the Catalog (e.g., the Pell Grant program which provides grants to students) involve intermediate levels of application processing, i.e., applications are transmitted through colleges or universities that are neither the direct applicant nor the ultimate beneficiary. For these programs, the criteria that the intermediaries must satisfy are also indicated, along with intermediaries who are not eligible.

Example: To be eligible for staffing grants, applicants must be part of, or affiliated with, a community mental health center, unless there is no center serving the community. Applicants may then be any public or private non-profit agency providing, or coordinating with programs which will provide a full range of mental health services for children and their families residing in the service area.

Beneficiary Eligibility—This section lists the ultimate beneficiaries of a program, the criteria they must satisfy and who specifically is not eligible. The applicant and beneficiary will generally be the same for programs that provide assistance directly from a Federal agency. However, financial assistance that passes through State or local governments will have different applicants and beneficiaries since the assistance is transmitted to private sector beneficiaries who are not obligated to request or apply for the assistance.

Example: Children and their families in the service area as well as personnel of schools and other community agencies serving children.

Credentials/Documentation—This is a brief description of the credentials or documentation required prior to, or along with, an application for assistance. The eligibility factors that must be proven, certified, or established are indicated in this section. This section also indicates whether OMB Circular No. A-87 requirements, "Cost Principles Applicable to Grants and Contracts with State and Local Governments," are applicable. In cases where specific Federal circulars or other regulatory requirements are not applicable to the program, disclaimer statements may be included referencing the requirement(s) from which the program is excluded, e.g., "This program is excluded from coverage under (applicable requirement)."

Example: Proof of nonprofit status is required of nonprofit organizations and institutions. This program is excluded from coverage under OMB Circular No. A-87.

APPLICATION AND AWARD PROCESS:

Preapplication Coordination—This section indicates whether any prior coordination or approval is required with governmental or nongovernmental units prior to the submission of a formal application to the Federal funding agency. For example, programs may require: (1) State agency approval prior to the submission of an application to a Federal agency; (2) the submission of environmental impact information as required by the National Environmental Policy Act of 1969, and Executive Order 11514 of March 4, 1970; (3) coordination with the policies of the recently revised OMB Circular No. A-102, "Uniform Administrative Requirements for Grants and Cooperative Agreements to State and Local Governments" (referenced here for construction, land acquisition, and land development projects for which Federal funding exceeds $100,000); (4) coverage for eligibility under Executive Order 12372, "Intergovernmental Review of Federal Programs"; or (5) a preapplication or preapplication conference. Applicants should also ascertain from the Federal agency the existence of other circular requirements not indicated by this section, and from the State, any State requirements which may be in effect. In cases where E.O. 12372 is not applicable to the program, a disclaimer statement is included referencing the exclusion, e.g., "This program is excluded from coverage under E.O. 12372."

Example: Preapplication consultation with the ADAMHA Branch of the HHS Regional Office is not mandatory. Application must be accompanied by evidence of approval and recommendation by the appropriate State agency or agencies. The standard application forms, as furnished by the Federal agency and required by OMB Circular No. A-102, must be used for this program. This program is excluded from coverage under E.O. 12372.

Application Procedure—This section discusses the basic procedural steps required by the Federal agency in the application process, beginning with the lowest level (e.g., State and local government units, institutions or organizations) and ending eventually with the Federal government. Each program will indicate whether applications are to be submitted to the Federal headquarters, regional or local office, or to a State or local government office. Numerous programs in the Catalog require the standard application forms in OMB Circular No. A-102 (Attachment M). Other applications may be in the form of a written request to the funding agency stating the need for assistance and requesting available services, or a formal proposal prepared in response to an announcement in the Federal Register or the Commerce Business Daily. Also indicated in this section is guidance concerning the applicability of OMB Circular No. A-110, "Grants and Agreements with Institutions of Higher Education, Hospitals, and Other Nonprofit Organizations." In cases where specific Federal circulars or other regulatory requirements are not applicable to the program, disclaimer statements may be included referencing the requirement(s) from which the program is excluded, e.g., "This program is excluded from coverage under (applicable requirement)."

Example: Continuation Application Form ADM-115 should be used for staffing. Instructions and consultation may be obtained from the mental health section of the appropriate HHS Regional Office. Applications are sent to the Regional Office with copies to Acting Director, Division of Mental Health Service Programs, NIMH, 5600 Fishers Lane, Rockville, MD 20857. This program is subject to the provisions of OMB Circular No. A-110. This program is excluded from coverage under OMB Circular No. A-102.

Award Procedure—This section lists the basic procedural steps for awarding assistance, beginning with the organizational components of the Federal agency that has final approval authority for the application and ending with the lowest level at which Federal resources are expended. Also indicated is whether assistance passes through the initial applicant for further distribution by intermediate level applicants to groups or individuals in the private sector.

Accepted applications are subject to evaluation by the headquarters, regional, local or district office to determine the feasibility of the proposed project to include consistency with Federal and individual agency policies concerning its scope and purpose. Grant payment may be made by a letter of credit, advance by Treasury check, or reimbursement by Treasury check. Awards may be made by the headquarters office directly to the applicant, an agency field office, a regional office, or by an authorized county office.

Example: The Regional Health Administrator makes awards to approved applicants.

Deadlines— When available, this section indicates the deadlines for applications to the funding agency which will be stated in terms of the date(s) or between what dates the application should be received. Reference is made to new applications, continuations, renewals, and supplementals. Application deadline information is also indicated in the Deadlines Index, in the agency's program guidelines, or announced in the Federal Register. Where not available, applicants should contact the funding agency for deadline information.

Example: Staffing: Determined by award period (contact the Regional Office).

Range of Approval or Disapproval Time— This section informs the applicant of the representative range of time required for the application to be processed (in terms of days or months) at the Federal level.

Example: From 90 to 120 days.

Appeals— In some cases, there are no provisions for appeal. Where applicable, this section discusses appeal procedures or allowable rework time for resubmission of applications to be processed by the funding agency. Appeal procedures vary with individual programs and are either listed in this section or applicants are referred to appeal procedures documented in the relevant Code of Federal Regulations (CFR).

Example: Not applicable. (An appeal was not applicable in this case. A related program (93.231) allows applicants to reapply if revised applications are submitted.)

Renewals— This section advises the applicant as to whether renewals or extensions of applications are available and indicates the appropriate procedures to follow. In some instances, renewal procedures may be the same as for the application procedure, e.g., for projects of a non-continuing nature renewals will be treated as new, competing applications; for projects of an ongoing nature, renewals may be given annually.

Example: This program is renewed annually. Grantees are required to update their plan and submit a current year budget.

ASSISTANCE CONSIDERATIONS:

Formula and Matching Requirements— This section indicates the formula and matching requirements prescribed in the allocation of funds or maintenance of effort requirements. A formula may be based on population, per capita income, and other statistical factors. Applicants are informed whether there are any matching requirements to be met when participating in the cost of a project. In general, the matching share represents that portion of the project costs not borne by the Federal government. Usually, a minimum percentage for matching share is prescribed by program legislation, and matching share requirements are included in the grant agreement. Attachment F of OMB Circular No. A-102 sets forth the criteria and procedures for the evaluation of matching share requirements which may be cash or in-kind contributions made by State and local governments or other agencies, institutions, private organizations, or individuals to satisfy matching requirements of Federal grants or loans.

Cash contributions represent the grantees' cash outlay, including the outlay of money contributed to the grantee by other public agencies, institutions, private organizations, or individuals. When authorized by Federal regulation, Federal funds received from other grants may be considered as the grantees' cash contribution.

In-kind contributions represent the value of noncash contributions provided by the grantee, other public agencies and institutions, private organizations or individuals. In-kind contributions may consist of charges for real property and equipment, and value of goods and services directly benefiting and specifically identifiable to the grant program. When authorized by Federal legislation, property purchased with Federal funds may be considered as grantees' in-kind contribution.

Maintenance of effort (MOE) is a requirement contained in certain legislation, regulations, or administrative policies stating that a grantee must maintain a specified level of financial effort in a specific area in order to receive Federal grant funds, and that the Federal grant funds may be used only to supplement, not supplant, the level of grantee funds. Programs that have maintenance of effort requirements and have total allocations over $100 million (current FY) should have the following statement in this section: This program has maintenance of effort (MOE) requirements, see funding agency for further details.

Example: Staffing: Federal funds on a decreasing percentage basis over a period of 8 years 90 percent - 1st and 2nd years; 80 percent - 3rd year; 75 percent - 4th and 5th years; 70 percent - 6th, 7th and 8th years. Nonpoverty areas are entitled to: 80 percent - 1st and 2nd years; 75 percent - 3rd year; 60 percent - 4th year; 45 percent - 5th year; 30 percent - 6th, 7th and 8th years.

Length and Time Phasing of Assistance— This section indicates the time period during which the assistance is normally available, whether there are any restrictions placed on the time permitted to use the funds awarded, and the timing of disbursement of the assistance, e.g., lump sum, annually, quarterly, or as required.

Example: Staffing grants are limited to 8 years by law. Payments are made on a Monthly Cash Request System or under a Letter of Credit.

POST ASSISTANCE REQUIREMENTS:

Reports— This section indicates whether program reports, expenditure reports, cash reports or performance monitoring is required by the Federal funding agency, and specifies at what time intervals (monthly, annually, etc.) this must be accomplished.

Example: Interim progress reports must be submitted annually as part of a non-competing application; report of expenditures are due annually. Immediate reporting of any inventions is required.

Audits— This section discusses audits required by the Federal agency. The procedures and requirements for State and local governments are set forth in OMB Circular No. A-128, which supersedes the provisions of Attachment P of OMB Circular No. A-102 that formerly governed audit requirements for State and local governments. This pertains to awards made within the respective State's fiscal year—not the Federal fiscal year, as some State and local governments may use the calendar year or other variation of time span designated as the fiscal year period, rather than that commonly know as the Federal fiscal year (from October 1st through September 30th). The procedures and requirements for nonprofit organizations and institutions are set forth in OMB Circular No. A-133, "Audits of Institutions of Higher Education and Other Nonprofit Organizations," and should also be referenced here, as appropriate.

Example: In accordance with the provisions of OMB Circular No. A-128, "Audits of State and Local Governments," State and local governments that receive financial assistance of $100,000 or more within the State's fiscal year shall have an audit made for that year. State and local governments that receive between $25,000 and $100,000 within the State's fiscal year shall have an audit made in accordance with Circular No. A-128, or in accordance with Federal laws and regulations governing the programs in which they participate. For nonprofit grant recipients, audits are to be carried out in accordance with the provisions set forth in OMB Circular No. A-133.

Records— This section indicates the record retention requirements and the type of records the Federal agency may require. Not included are the normally imposed requirements of the General Accounting Office. For programs falling under the purview of OMB Circular No. A-102, record retention is set forth in Attachment C. For other programs, record retention is governed by the funding agency's requirements.

Example: Records must be retained at least 3 years; records shall be retained beyond the 3-year period if audit findings have not been resolved.

FINANCIAL INFORMATION:

Account Identification— This 11-digit budget account identification code represents the account which funds a particular program. This code should be consistent with the code given for the program area as specified in Appendix III of the Budget of the United States Government. (See Appendix III for further information on the meaning of the 11 digits of this code.)

Example: 75-1361-0-1-550.

Obligations— The dollar amounts listed in this section represent obligations for the past fiscal year (PY), estimates for the current fiscal year (CY), and estimates for the budget fiscal year (BY) as reported by the Federal agencies. In each succeeding edition of the Catalog, the dollar amounts are revised to reflect changes which may result from supplemental appropriations or amendments. Each program indicates what the obligation figures represent in terms of the type of assistance provided. Obligations for nonfinancial assistance programs indicate the administrative expenses involved in the operation of a program as an indication of the magnitude of the services being provided, or the items involved in obligations.

Example:(Grants) PY $19,853,000; CY est $20,407,000; and BY est $14,830,000.

Range and Average of Financial Assistance— This section lists the representative range (smallest to largest) of the amount of financial assistance available. These figures are based upon funds awarded in the past fiscal year and the current fiscal year to date. Also indicated is an approximate average amount of awards which were made in the past and current fiscal years.

Example: Formula: $26,355 to $691,481; $235,305.

PROGRAM ACCOMPLISHMENTS— This section briefly describes the accomplishments of a program using quantitative data, focusing on program output, results achieved, or services rendered during the past fiscal year, the current fiscal year, and projections for the coming fiscal year.

Example: In the past fiscal year, 140 applications were received and 140 staffing awards were issued. Approximately 147 continuation grants were funded during the current fiscal year and 103 are estimated to be funded in the budget fiscal year.

REGULATIONS, GUIDELINES, AND LITERATURE— This section lists the title, number, and price of guidelines, handbooks, manuals, and other officially published information pertinent to a program. Since program regulations are published first in the Federal Register (FR) and later in the Code of Federal Regulations (CFR), citations to the CFR are listed.

Example: Interim guidelines available in application kits.

INFORMATION CONTACTS:

Regional or Local Office— This section lists the agency contact person, address and telephone number of the Federal Regional or Local Office(s) to be contacted for detailed information regarding a program such as: (1) current availability of funds and the likelihood of receiving assistance within a given period; (2) preapplication and application forms required; (3) whether a preapplication conference is recommended; (4) assistance available in preparation of applications; (5) whether funding decisions are made at the headquarters, regional or local level; (6) application renewal procedures (including continuations and supplementals) or appeal procedures for rejected applications; and (7) recently published program guidelines and material.

However, for most programs in the Catalog, this section will instruct the reader to consult Appendix IV of the Catalog (Agency Regional and Local Office Addresses) due to the volume of Regional and Local Office Contacts for most agencies. For those agencies with fewer contacts, the actual information will be provided in this section.

Example: ADAMHA Branch of the appropriate HHS Regional Office (see Appendix IV of the Catalog for listing).

(Appendix IV Listing) Region 1
(Connecticut, Maine, Massachusetts, New Hampshire, Rhode Island, Vermont)

William Farrow
John F. Kennedy Federal Building
Government Center
Boston, MA 02203
(617) 123-4567
(Use same 7-digit number for FTS)

Headquarters Office— This section lists names and addresses of the office at the headquarters level with direct operational responsibility for managing a program. A telephone number is provided in cases where a Regional or Local Office is not normally able to answer detailed inquiries concerning a program. Also listed are the name(s) and telephone number(s) of the information contact person(s) who can provide additional program information to applicants.

Example: Dr. Steven Sharfstein, Acting Director, Division of Mental Health Service Programs, National Institutes of Mental Health, 5600 Fishers Lane, Rockville, MD 20857. Telephone (301) 123-4567. (Use same 7-digit number for FTS.)

RELATED PROGRAMS— This section of the program description lists all programs in the Catalog that are closely related based on objectives and program uses. Applicants should also refer to these programs, as they may provide additional assistance in a related area of interest.

Example: 93.232, Maternal and Child Health Services; 93.233, Maternal and Child Health Training; 93.242, Mental Health Research Grants; 93.295, Community Mental Health Centers—Comprehensive Support; 93.630, Developmental Disabilities—Basic Support.

EXAMPLES OF FUNDED PROJECTS: This section indicates the different types of projects which have been funded in the past. Only projects funded under Project Grants or Direct Payments for Specified Use should be listed here. The examples give potential applicants an idea of the types of projects that may be accepted for funding. The agency should list at least five examples of the most recently funded projects.

Example: Awards are made only for staffing of facilities offering mental health services for children.

CRITERIA FOR SELECTING PROPOSALS: This section indicates the criteria used by the Federal grantor agency to evaluate proposals in order to inform potential applicants for the application review process and the criteria used to award funds for projects.

Example: The criteria for selecting proposals are based upon the extent the project will contribute to needed services and training, capability of applicant to provide services and training, more effective utilization of personnel providing mental health services, and development of new methods or information.

APPENDICES—The last section of the Catalog contains the following appendices: Programs Requiring Executive Order 12372 Review (Appendix I); Authorization Appendix (Appendix II); Budget Functional Code Appendix (Appendix III); Agency Regional and Local Office Addresses (Appendix IV); Sources of Additional Information (Appendix V); in each Basic edition, Historical Profile of Catalog Programs (Appendix VI); and Developing and Writing Grants Proposals (Appendix VII).

Appendix I— Programs Requiring Executive Order 12372 Review: This Appendix gives a brief description of Executive Order 12372. The description explains its purpose, identifies a listing of all Catalog program numbers and titles to which it applies, the general procedures to follow in applying for assistance, and the State Single Point of Contact List to which the States may refer for application coordination purposes.

Appendix II— Authorization Appendix: This appendix lists Acts, Executive Orders and Public Law numbers which mandate programs in the Catalog. Acts and Executive Order citations are listed in alphabetic sequence and Public Law citations are listed numerically by the Congress. The citations are followed by their corresponding program numbers.

Appendix III— Budget Functional Code Appendix: This appendix lists programs by the Budget functional classification. The three digits listed are the major and minor functional classifications used to identify the major purpose of the programs.

Appendix IV— Agency Regional and Local Office Addresses: This appendix lists the names, addresses and telephone numbers of the regional and local offices which should be contacted for detailed information concerning a program and for initiating the process for applying for assistance. In cases where a Federal agency does not have a regional or local office, the headquarters office listed in the program description should be contacted.

Appendix V— Sources of Additional Information: Information pertaining to Federal programs is available from Federal Information Centers and Federal Executive Boards as listed in this Appendix. Also listed are other government sources of information, including the 24 U.S. locations for the Government Printing Office Bookstores that sell the Catalog and other Federal publications.

Appendix VI— Historical Profile of Catalog Programs: This appendix lists all programs that have been published in the Catalog of Federal Domestic Assistance beginning with the 1965 edition, and the subsequent action taken related to those programs. (Published in the Basic editions only.)

Appendix VII— Developing and Writing Grants Proposals: General overview of the grants proposal process and suggested guidelines for developing and writing a well-prepared proposal to obtain Federal funding.

Appendix VII: Developing and Writing Grant Proposals
Part One: Developing a Grant Proposal

Preparation

A successful grant proposal is one that is well-prepared, thoughtfully planned, and concisely packaged. The potential applicant should become familiar with all of the pertinent program criteria related to the Catalog program from which assistance is sought. Refer to the information contact person listed in the Catalog program description before developing a proposal to obtain information such as whether funding is available, when applicable deadlines occur, and the process used by the grantor agency for accepting applications. Applicants should remember that the basic requirements, application forms, information and procedures vary with the Federal agency making the grant award.

Individuals without prior grant proposal writing experience may find it useful to attend a grantsmanship workshop. A workshop can amplify the basic information presented here. Applicants interested in additional readings on grantsmanship and proposal development should consult the references listed at the end of this section and explore other library resources.

INITIAL PROPOSAL DEVELOPMENT

Developing Ideas for the Proposal

When developing an idea for a proposal it is important to determine if the idea has been considered in the applicant's locality or State. A careful check should be made with legislators and area government agencies and related public and private agencies which may currently have grant awards or contracts to do similar work. If a similar program already exists, the applicant may need to reconsider submitting the proposed project, particularly if duplication of effort is perceived. If significant differences or improvements in the proposed project's goals can be clearly established, it may be worthwhile to pursue Federal assistance.

Community Support

Community support for most proposals is essential. Once proposal summary is developed, look for individuals or groups representing academic, political, professional, and lay organizations which may be willing to support the proposal in writing. The type and caliber of community support is critical in the initial and subsequent review phases. Numerous letters of support can be persuasive to a grantor agency. Do not overlook support from local government agencies and public officials. Letters of endorsement detailing exact areas of project sanction and commitment are often requested as part of a proposal to a Federal agency. Several months may be required to develop letters of endorsement since something of value (e.g., buildings, staff, services) is sometimes negotiated between the parties involved.

Many agencies require, in writing, affiliation agreements (a mutual agreement to share services between agencies) and building space commitments prior to either grant approval or award. A useful method of generating community support may be to hold meetings with the top decision makers in the community who would be concerned with the subject matter of the proposal. The forum for discussion may include a query into the merits of the proposal, development of a contract of support for the proposal, to generate data in support of the proposal, or development of a strategy to create proposal support from a large number of community groups.

Identification of a Funding Resource

A review of the Objectives and Uses and Use Restrictions sections of the Catalog program description can point out which programs might provide funding for an idea. Do not overlook the related programs as potential resources. Both the applicant and the grantor agency should have the same interests, intentions, and needs if a proposal is to be considered an acceptable candidate for funding.

Once a potential grantor agency is identified, call the contact telephone number identified in Information Contacts and ask for a grant application kit. Later, get to know some of the grantor agency personnel. Ask for suggestions, criticisms, and advice about the proposed project. In many cases, the more agency personnel know about the proposal, the better the chance of support and of an eventual favorable decision. Sometimes it is useful to send the proposal summary to a specific agency official in a separate cover letter, and ask for review and comment at the earliest possible convenience. Always check with the Federal agency to determine its preference if this approach is under consideration. If the review is unfavorable and differences cannot be resolved, ask the examining agency (official) to suggest another department or agency which may be interested in the proposal. A personal visit to the agency's regional office or headquarters is also important. A visit not only establishes face-to-face contact, but also may bring out some essential details about the proposal or help secure literature and references from the agency's library.

Federal agencies are required to report funding information as funds are approved, increased or decreased among projects within a given State depending on the type of required reporting. Also, consider reviewing the Federal Budget for the current and budget fiscal years to determine proposed dollar amounts for particular budget functions.

The applicant should carefully study the eligibility requirements for each Federal program under consideration (see the Applicant Eligibility section of the Catalog program description). The applicant may learn that he or she is required to provide services otherwise unintended such as a service to particular client groups, or involvement of specific institutions. It may necessitate the modification of the original concept in order for the project to be eligible for funding. Questions about eligibility should be discussed with the appropriate program officer.

Deadlines for submitting applications are often not negotiable. They are usually associated with strict timetables for agency review. Some programs have more than one application deadline during the fiscal year. Applicants should plan proposal development around the established deadlines.

Getting Organized to Write the Proposal

Throughout the proposal writing stage keep a notebook handy to write down ideas. Periodically, try to connect ideas by reviewing the notebook. Never throw away written ideas during the grant writing stage. Maintain a file labeled "Ideas" or by some other convenient title and review the ideas from time to time. The file should be easily accessible. The gathering of documents such as articles of incorporation, tax exemption certificates, and bylaws should be completed, if possible, before the writing begins.

REVIEW

Criticism

At some point, perhaps after the first or second draft is completed, seek out a neutral third party to review the proposal working draft for continuity, clarity and reasoning. Ask for constructive criticism at this point, rather than wait for the Federal grantor agency to volunteer this information during the review cycle. For example, has the writer made unsupported assumptions or used jargon or excessive language in the proposal?

Signature

Most proposals are made to institutions rather than individuals. Often signatures of chief administrative officials are required. Check to make sure they are included in the proposal where appropriate.

Neatness

Proposals should be typed, collated, copied, and packaged correctly and neatly (according to agency instructions, if any). Each package should be inspected to ensure uniformity from cover to cover. Binding may require either clamps or hard covers. Check with the Federal agency to determine its preference. A neat, organized, and attractive proposal package can leave a positive impression with the reader about the proposal contents.

Mailing

A cover letter should always accompany a proposal. Standard U.S. Postal Service requirements apply unless otherwise indicated by the Federal agency. Make sure there is enough time for the proposals to reach their destinations. Otherwise, special arrangements may be necessary. Always coordinate such arrangements with the Federal grantor agency project office (the agency which will ultimately have the responsibility for the project), the grant office (the agency which will coordinate the grant review), and the contract office (the agency responsible for disbursement and grant award notices), if necessary.

Part Two: Writing the Grant Proposal

The Basic Components of a Proposal

There are eight basic components to creating a solid proposal package: (1) the proposal summary; (2) introduction of organization; (3) the problem statement (or needs assessment); (4) project objectives; (5) project methods or design; (6) project evaluation; (7) future funding; and (8) the project budget. The following will provide an overview of these components.

The Proposal Summary: Outline of Project Goals

The proposal summary outlines the proposed project and should appear at the beginning of the proposal. It could be in the form of a cover letter or a separate page, but should definitely be brief—no longer than two or three paragraphs. The summary would be most useful if it were prepared after the proposal has been developed in order to encompass all the key summary points necessary to communicate the objectives of the project. It is this document that becomes the cornerstone of your proposal, and the initial impression it gives will be critical to the success of your venture. In many cases, the summary will be the first part of the proposal package seen by agency officials and very possibly could be the only part of the package that is carefully reviewed before the decision is made to consider the project any further.

The applicant must select a fundable project which can be supported in view of the local need. Alternatives, in the absence of Federal support, should be pointed out. The influence of the project both during and after the project period should be explained. The consequences of the project as a result of funding should be highlighted.

Introduction: Presenting a Credible Applicant or Organization

The applicant should gather data about its organization from all available sources. Most proposals require a description of an applicant's organization to describe its past and present operations. Some features to consider are:

- A brief biography of board members and key staff members;

- The organization's goals, philosophy, track record with other grantors, and any success stories.

- The data should be relevant to the goals of the Federal grantor agency and should establish the applicant's credibility.

The Problem Statement: Stating the Purpose at Hand

The problem statement (or needs assessment) is a key element of a proposal that makes a clear, concise, and well-supported statement of the problem to be addressed. The best way to collect information about the problem is to conduct and document both a formal and informal needs assessment for a program in the target or service area. The information provided should be both factual and directly related to the problem addressed by the proposal. Areas to document are:

- The purpose for developing the proposal.

- The beneficiaries—who are they and how will they benefit.

- The social and economic costs to be affected.

- The nature of the problem (provide as much hard evidence as possible).

- How the applicant organization came to realize the problem exists, and what is currently being done about the problem.

- The remaining alternatives available when funding has been exhausted. Explain what will happen to the project and the impending implications.

- Most importantly, the specific manner through which problems might be solved. Review the resources needed, considering how they will be used and to what end.

There is a considerable body of literature on the exact assessment techniques to be used. Any local, regional, or State government planning office, or local university offering course work in planning and evaluation techniques should be able to provide excellent background references. Types of data that may be collected include: historical, geographic, quantitative, factual, statistical, and philosophical information, as well as studies completed by colleges, and literature searches from public or university libraries. Local colleges or universities which have a department or section related to the proposal topic may help determine if there is interest in developing a student or faculty project to conduct a needs assessment. It may be helpful to include examples of the findings for highlighting in the proposal.

Project Objectives: Goals and Desired Outcome

Program objectives refer to specific activities in a proposal. It is necessary to identify all objectives related to the goals to be reached, and the methods to be employed to achieve the stated objectives. Consider quantities or things measurable and refer to a problem statement and the outcome of proposed activities when developing a well-stated objective. The figures used should be verifiable. Remember, if the proposal is funded, the stated objectives will probably be used to evaluate program progress, so be realistic. There is literature available to help identify and write program objectives.

Program Methods and Program Design: A Plan of Action

The program design refers to how the project is expected to work and solve the stated problem. Sketch out the following:

- The activities to occur along with the related resources and staff needed to operate the project (inputs).

- A flow chart of the organizational features of the project. Describe how the parts interrelate, where personnel will be needed, and what they are expected to do. Identify the kinds of facilities, transportation, and support services required (throughputs).

- Explain what will be achieved through 1 and 2 above (outputs); i.e., plan for measurable results. Project staff may be required to produce evidence of program performance through an examination of stated objectives during either a site visit by the Federal grantor agency and or grant reviews which may involve peer review committees.

- It may be useful to devise a diagram of the program design. For example, draw a three column block. Each column is headed by one of the parts (inputs, throughputs and outputs), and on the left (next to the first column) specific program features should be identified (i.e., implementation, staffing, procurement, and systems development). In the grid specify something about the program design, for example, assume the first column is labeled inputs and the first row is labeled staff. On the grid one might specify under inputs five nurses to operate a child care unit. The throughput might be to maintain charts, counsel the children, and set up a daily routine; outputs might be to discharge 25 healthy children per week. This type of procedure will help to conceptualize both the scope and detail of the project.

- Wherever possible, justify in the narrative the course of action taken. The most economical method should be used that does not compromise or sacrifice project quality. The financial expenses associated with performance of the project will later become points of negotiation with the Federal program staff. If everything is not carefully justified in writing in the proposal, after negotiation with the Federal grantor agencies, the approved project may resemble less of the original concept. Carefully consider the pressures of the proposed implementation, that is, the time and money needed to acquire each part of the plan. A Program Evaluation and Review Technique (PERT) chart could be useful and supportive in justifying some proposals.

- Highlight the innovative features of the proposal which could be considered distinct from other proposals under consideration.

- Whenever possible use appendices to provide details, supplementary data, references, and information requiring in-depth analysis. These types of data, although supportive of the proposal, if included in the body of the design, could detract from its readability. Appendices provide the proposal reader with immediate access to details if and when clarification of an idea, sequence or conclusion is required. Time tables, work plans, schedules, activities, methodologies, legal papers, personal vitae, letters of support, and endorsements are examples of appendices.

Evaluation: Product and Process Analysis

The evaluation component is two-fold: (1) product evaluation: and (2) process evaluation. Product evaluation addresses results that can be attributed to the project, as well as the extent to which the project has satisfied its desired objectives. Process evaluation addresses how the project was conducted, in terms of consistency with the stated plan of action and the effectiveness of the various activities within the plan.

Most Federal agencies now require some form of program evaluation among grantees. The requirements of the proposed project should be explored carefully. Evaluations may be conducted by an internal staff member, an evaluation firm or both. The applicant should state the amount of time needed to evaluate, how the feedback will be distributed among the proposed staff, and a schedule for review and comment for this type of communication. Evaluation designs may start at the beginning, middle or end of a project, but the applicant should specify a start-up time. It is practical to submit an evaluation design at the start of a project for two reasons:

- Convincing evaluations require the collection of appropriate data before and during program operations; and,

- If the evaluation design cannot be prepared at the outset then a critical review of the program design may be advisable.

Even if the evaluation design has to be revised as the project progresses, it is much easier and cheaper to modify a good design. If the problem is not well defined and carefully analyzed for cause and effect relationships then a good evaluation design may be difficult to achieve. Sometimes a pilot study is needed to begin the identification of facts and relationships. Often a thorough literature search may be sufficient.

Evaluation requires both coordination and agreement among program decision makers (if known). Above all, the Federal grantor agency's requirements should be highlighted in the evaluation design. Also, Federal grantor agencies may require specific evaluation techniques such as designated data formats (an existing information collection system) or they may offer financial inducements for voluntary participation in a national evaluation study. The applicant should ask specifically about these points. Also, consult the Criteria For Funding Proposals section of the Catalog program description to determine the exact evaluation methods to be required for the program if funded.

Future Funding: Long-Term Project Planning

Describe a plan for continuation beyond the grant period, and/or the availability of other resources necessary to implement the grant. Discuss maintenance and future program funding if program is for construction activity. Account for other needed expenditures if program includes purchase of equipment.

The Proposal Budget: Planning the Budget

Funding levels in Federal assistance programs change yearly. It is useful to review the appropriations over the past several years to try to project future funding levels (see Financial Information section of the Catalog program description).

However, it is safer to never anticipate that the income from the grant will be the sole support for the project. This consideration should be given to the overall budget requirements, and in particular, to budget line items most subject to inflationary pressures. Restraint is important in determining inflationary cost projections (avoid padding budget line items), but attempt to anticipate possible future increases.

Some vulnerable budget areas are: utilities, rental of buildings and equipment, salary increases, food, telephones, insurance, and transportation. Budget adjustments are sometimes made after the grant award, but this can be a lengthy process. Be certain that implementation, continuation and phase-down costs can be met. Consider costs associated with leases, evaluation systems, hard/soft match requirements, audits, development, implementation and maintenance of information and accounting systems, and other long-term financial commitments.

A well-prepared budget justifies all expenses and is consistent with the proposal narrative. Some areas in need of an evaluation for consistency are: (1) the salaries in the proposal in relation to those of the applicant organization should be similar; (2) if new staff persons are being hired, additional space and equipment should be considered, as necessary; (3) if the budget calls for an equipment purchase, it should be the type allowed by the grantor agency; (4) if additional space is rented, the increase in insurance should be supported; (5) if an indirect cost rate applies to the proposal, the division between direct and indirect costs should not be in conflict, and the aggregate budget totals should refer directly to the approved formula; and (6) if matching costs are required, the contributions to the matching fund should be taken out of the budget unless otherwise specified in the application instructions.

It is very important to become familiar with government-wide circular requirements. The Catalog identifies in the program description section (as information is provided from the agencies) the particular circulars applicable to a Federal program, and summarizes coordination of Executive Order 12372, "Intergovernmental Review of Programs" requirements in Appendix I. The applicant should thoroughly review the appropriate circulars since they are essential in determining items such as cost principles and conforming with government guidelines for Federal domestic assistance.

GUIDELINES AND LITERATURE

United States Government Manual
Superintendent of Documents
U.S. Government Printing Office
Washington, DC 20402

OMB Circular Nos. A-87, A-102, A-110, and A-128, and Executive Order 12372:
Publications Office
Office of Administration

Government Foundation Program: National Science Foundation

47.009 GRADUATE RESEARCH FELLOWSHIPS

FEDERAL AGENCY: NATIONAL SCIENCE FOUNDATION AUTHORIZATION: National Science Foundation Act of 1950, as amended, 42 U.S.C. 1861 et seq.

OBJECTIVES: To provide tangible Federal encouragement to highly talented graduate students for advanced study in the sciences, mathematics, and engineering.

TYPES OF ASSISTANCE: Project Grants.

USES AND USE RESTRICTIONS: Fellowships provide for stipends and allowances to be paid to the awardee through his or her institution. A fixed cost-of-education allowance is paid directly to the institution. A fellow must remain a full-time student for the duration of the award. Both Graduate and Minority Graduate Research Fellowships are available.

ELIGIBILITY REQUIREMENTS:

Applicant Eligibility: Beginning graduate students are eligible to apply for support in accordance with requirements and procedures specifically described in program announcements.

Beneficiary Eligibility: Beginning graduate students.

Credentials/Documentation: Applicants for fellowship support must show evidence of ability such as academic records, letters of recommendation, Graduate Record Examination scores, and grade point average. This program is excluded from coverage under OMB Circular No. A-87.

APPLICATION AND AWARD PROCESS:

Preapplication Coordination: None. This program is excluded from coverage under Executive Order No. 12372.

Application Procedure: Application forms for graduate fellowships are available from National Research Council Fellowship Office, 2101 Constitution Avenue, NW., Washington, DC 20418. Completed application, including plan of study, is forwarded to the National Research Council (NRC) which serves as an advisory body to the Foundation for this program. This program is subject to the provisions of OMB Circular No. A-110. This program is excluded from coverage under OMB Circular No. A-102.

Award Procedure: NRC panelists members who are conversant with the field covered by the application review and evaluate all applications. Awards are made by NSF on a competitive basis in order of merit to the extent permitted by available funds.

Deadlines: Mid-November. Contact National Research Council at address indicated under the Information Contacts section of this program for specific dates.

Range of Approval/Disapproval Time: Approximately 6 months.

Appeals: Denials, 90 days.

Renewals: Not applicable.

ASSISTANCE CONSIDERATIONS:

Formula and Matching Requirements: This program has no statutory formula. This program has no matching requirements.

Length and Time Phasing of Assistance: For fellowships, typically 9 to 12 months; up to 3 years of support. Assistance is disbursed to the institution for monthly stipend allotment to the fellow.

POST ASSISTANCE REQUIREMENTS:

Reports: Brief annual activities report required.

Audits: Under the total audit concept, audits will be made on an organization-wide basis (rather than grant-by-grant) under GAO guidelines, "Standards for Audit of Government Organizations, Programs, Activities and Functions."

Records: Not applicable to fellowships.

FINANCIAL INFORMATION:

Account Identification: 49-0106-0-1-251.

Obligations: (Grants) FY 90 $30,288,000; FY 91 est $38,900,000; and FY 92 est $50,000,000.

Range and Average of Financial Assistance: For fellowships, $14,000 stipends plus $6,000 cost of education allowance.

PROGRAM ACCOMPLISHMENTS: In fiscal year 1990, 7,190 applications were received; 1,000 new awards and approximately 1,320 continuing awards will be made. In fiscal year 1991, 8,615 applications were received and 1,100 new awards will be made. Data unavailable for fiscal year 1992.

REGULATIONS, GUIDELINES, AND LITERATURE: 45 CFR Parts 610 and 630. Program announcements (at no charge) are available from the National Research Council at the address indicated under Information Contacts section of this program.

INFORMATION CONTACTS:

Regional or Local Office: Fellowship Office, National Research Council, 2101 Constitution Avenue, Washington, DC 20814.

Headquarters Office: Ms. Susan Sherman, Graduate Fellowships, Division of Research Career Development, National Science Foundation, 1800 G Street, NW., Washington, DC 20550. Telephone: (202) 357-7856.

RELATED PROGRAMS: None.

EXAMPLES OF FUNDED PROJECTS: (1) Objectives of one graduate student is to earn a Ph.D in Molecular Systematics of algae. (2) one graduate student hopes to pursue research in acid deposition or the enhanced greenhouse effect. (3) an exact plan of study for one graduate student has not been finalized; however, the student would like to do research in some aspects of neural development. (4) during graduate study, a student plans to go in the field of space science and will concentrate on structural design. (5) a graduate student will further study the areas of communication systems.

CRITERIA FOR SELECTING PROPOSALS: Decisions are based primarily on the ability of the applicant in conformance with the objectives of the program. In the case of applications of substantially equal merit, program and geographic balance are additional decision criteria.

Government Foundation Program: National Foundation on the Arts and Humanities

45.004 PROMOTION OF THE ARTS—LITERATURE

FEDERAL AGENCY: National Endowment for the Arts, National Foundation on the Arts and the Humanities

AUTHORIZATION: National Foundation on the Arts and the Humanities Act of 1965, as amended, Public Law 89-209, Section 5, 20 U.S.C. 951 et seq.

OBJECTIVES: To aid creative writers of fiction and non-fiction, poets, and translators of literary works (into English) through fellowships, funding of residencies for writers and reading series and support for noncommercial literary magazines and small presses, literary service organizations, and literary centers.

TYPES OF ASSISTANCE: Project Grants (Fellowships).

USES AND USE RESTRICTIONS: Grants are given for publication to noncommercial literary magazines and small presses. Grants are awarded for the following: to publish, distribute, or promote volumes of poetry, fiction, and creative non-fiction by contemporary writers; to publish journals of contemporary creative literature; residencies for writers and reading series; for assistance to national literary service organizations and literary centers; and to promote and develop audiences for contemporary creative writing. There are no funds for construction or rehabilitation of facilities.

ELIGIBILITY REQUIREMENTS:

Applicant Eligibility: Grants may be made to: 1) Nonprofit organizations, including State and local governments and State arts agencies, if donations to such organizations qualify as charitable deductions under Section 170(c) of the Internal Revenue Code; and to 2) individuals (ordinarily U.S. citizens or permanent residents only) who, according to Public Law 89-209, Section 5(c) must possess exceptional talent.

Beneficiary Eligibility: Nonprofit organizations including State and local governments and State arts agencies and individual artists.

Credentials/Documentation: Applying organizations are required to submit a copy of their Internal Revenue Service tax exemption determination letter with their applications. Costs will be determined in accordance with OMB Circular No. A-87 for State and local governments. For institutions of higher education, allowable costs will be determined according to OMB Circular No. A-21; for other nonprofit organizations making application, allowable costs will be determined according to OMB Circular No. A-122.

APPLICATION AND AWARD PROCESS:

Preapplication Coordination: The standard application forms as furnished by the Federal agency and required by OMB Circular No. A-102 must be used for this program for State and local governments only. This program is excluded from coverage under E.O. 12372.

Application Procedure: Applicants should request guidelines for this program area and appropriate standard application forms (NEA-2 for individuals and NEA-3 for organizations) from headquarters office. This program is subject to the provisions of OMB Circular No. A-110.

Award Procedure: The Chairman of the Endowment makes the final decision on all awards based on recommendations from the National Council on the Arts (the NEA advisory body) and the consulting panels to the agency. The Endowment Headquarters will determine on a case-by-case basis those applicants who can further disburse grant money to sub-grantees.

Deadlines: Fellowships: The date for fellowships for creative writers: fiction, poetry, and creative non-fiction is March 5, 1991. The date for translators is January 11, 1991. The date for nominations for senior fellowships for literature is July 2, 1991. Literary Publishing: The date for assistance to literary magazines is July 2, 1991. The date for small press assistance is August 1, 1991. The date for distribution projects is September 11, 1991. Audience Development: The date for residencies for writers and reading series, literary centers, and audience development projects was December 4, 1990. The date for professional development was January 11, 1991.

Range of Approval/Disapproval Time: Dependent on meetings of the National Council on the Arts.

Appeals: Information on the appeals process may be obtained from the headquarters office listed below.

Renewals: Renewal grants are processed as new applications.

ASSISTANCE CONSIDERATIONS:

Formula and Matching Requirements: Grants to organizations, with few exceptions, must be matched, at least dollar-for-dollar with nonfederal funds.

Length and Time Phasing of Assistance: Length and time may vary with project. Generally, requests may be received at any time for payment to cover immediate project expenses.

POST ASSISTANCE REQUIREMENTS:

Reports: A financial report plus a narrative of accomplishments must by submitted within 90 days after termination of the grant period.

Audits: Provided in accordance with the provisions of OMB Circular No. A-110 for organizations other than State and local governments. In accordance with the provisions of OMB Circular No. A-128, "Audits of State and Local Governments," State and local governments that receive financial assistance of $100,000 or more within the State's fiscal year shall have an audit made for that year. State and local governments that receive between $25,000 and $100,000 within the State's fiscal year shall have an audit made in accordance with Circular No. A-128, or in accordance with Federal laws and regulations governing the programs in which they participate.

Records: Financial records to be retained by grantee for three years following submission of final reports.

FINANCIAL INFORMATION:

Account Identifications: 59-0100-0-1-503.

Obligations: (Grants) FY 90 $5,007,000; FY 91 est $4,435,000; and FY 92 est $4,635,000.

Range and Average of Financial Assistance: Individuals:

$10,000 to $20,000 (Senior Fellowships $40,000) in fiscal years 1990 and 1991. Organizations: $2,000 to $200,000 in fiscal years 1990 and 1991.

PROGRAM ACCOMPLISHMENTS: In fiscal year 1990, 2,531 applications were received and 282 grants were awarded. In fiscal year 1991, we estimate receiving 2,572 applications and awarding 241 grants. In fiscal year 1992: 2,621 applications and 250 grants.

REGULATIONS, GUIDELINES, AND LITERATURE: The following publications are available from Public Information, National Endowment for the Arts, 1100 Pennsylvania Avenue, NW., Washington, DC 20506: "National Endowment for the Arts, Guide to Programs" and "Literature Guidelines" for appropriate fiscal year.

INFORMATION CONTACTS:

Regional or Local Office: Not applicable.

Headquarters Office: Director, Literature Program, National Endowment for the Arts, 1100 Pennsylvania Avenue, NW., Washington, DC 20506. Telephone: (202) 682-5451 (use same 7-digit number for FTS).

RELATED PROGRAMS: 45.003, Promotion of the Arts—Arts in Education; 45.005, Promotion of the Arts—Music; 45.006, Promotion of the Arts—Media Arts: Film/Radio/Television; 45.008, Promotion of the Arts—Theater; 45.010, Promotion of the Arts—Expansion Arts; 45.011, Promotion of the Arts—Inter-Arts; 45.013, Promotion of the Arts—Challenge Grants.

EXAMPLES OF FUNDED PROJECTS: 1) To support essential services to literary translators; 2) to support the distribution of small press volumes and literary magazines; 3) to support the publication of an issue of a literary journal; 4) to support a series of writers' residencies which has brought nationally known writers for formal readings and informal workshops to a region of the country; 5) to support a statewide traveling book display and reading series; and 6) to support creative writers in setting aside time for writing, research, or travel in order to advance their careers.

CRITERIA FOR SELECTING PROPOSALS: Applications are generally reviewed according to the following standards: Literary merit of the proposed project; potential impact of the project; applicant's ability to carry out the project; evidence that the applicant has budgeted appropriately for the project; general fiscal and organizational responsibility of the applicant; completeness and clarity of the application package. Creative writing fellowships are reviewed on the basis of the literary quality of the manuscript submitted.

45.005 PROMOTION OF THE ARTS—MUSIC

FEDERAL AGENCY: National Endowment for the Arts, National Foundation on the Arts and the Humanities

AUTHORIZATION: National Foundation on the Arts and the Humanities Act of 1965, as amended, Public Law 89-209, 20 U.S.C. 951 et seq.

OBJECTIVES: To support excellence in music performance and creativity and to develop informed audiences for music throughout the country.

TYPES OF ASSISTANCE: Project Grants.

USES AND USE RESTRICTIONS: Grants may be used to assist exceptionally talented individuals and a wide range of organizations including professional symphony orchestras, new music ensembles, groups engaged in jazz, national service organizations, choruses, chamber music ensembles, music festivals, and others. The types of activities supported vary depending upon the guidelines under which assistance is requested. There are no funds for construction or rehabilitation of facilities, summer music camps, research, publication costs, purchase of musical instruments or uniforms.

ELIGIBILITY REQUIREMENTS:

Applicant Eligibility: Grants may be made to: 1) Nonprofit organizations, including State and local governments and State arts agencies, if donations to such organizations qualify as charitable deductions under Section 170(c) of the Internal Revenue Code; 2) to individuals (ordinarily U.S. citizens only) who, according to Public Law 89-209, Section 5(c) must possess exceptional talent.

Beneficiary Eligibility: Nonprofit organizations including State and local governments, State arts agencies and individual artists.

Credentials/Documentation: Applying organizations are required to submit a copy of their Internal Revenue Service tax exemption determination letter with their applications. Costs will be determined in accordance with OMB Circular No. A-87 for State and local governments. For institutions of higher education, allowable costs will be determined according to OMB Circular No. A-21; for other nonprofit organizations making application, costs will be determined according to OMB Circular No. A-122.

APPLICATION AND AWARD PROCESS:

Preapplication Coordination: This program is excluded from coverage under OMB Circular No. A-102. This program is excluded from coverage under E.O. 12372.

Application Procedure: The Chairman of the Endowment makes the final decision on all awards based on recommendations from the National Council on the Arts (the NEA advisory body) and the consulting panels to the agency. The Endowment Headquarters will determine on a case-by-case basis those applicants who can further disburse grant money to subgrantees. This program is subject to the provisions of OMB Circular No. A-110.

Award Procedure: The Chairman of the Endowment makes the final decision on all awards based on recommendations from the National Council on the Arts (the NEA advisory body) and the consulting panels in this field. Headquarters office will determine on a case-by-case basis those applicants which can further dispense grant money to subgrantees.

Deadlines: Dates differ for various projects. The date for fellowships is January 3, 1992. For Chamber/Solo Recitalists/New Music Presenters the date is April 5, 1991. For all other presenters and for festivals the date is April 26, 1991. Ensembles: The deadline date for jazz ensembles and choruses is July 12, 1991. The deadline date for chamber music (including early and new) ensembles, orchestras, and composer in residence is July 26, 1991. Training/Recording/Centers: For music recording, centers for new music resources, services to composers, and career development, the date is September 27, 1991. For music professional training the date is October 25, 1991. For special projects the date is February 14, 1992.

Range of Approval/Disapproval Time: Dependent on meetings of the National Council on the Arts.

Appeals: Information on the appeals process may be obtained from the headquarters office listed below.

Renewals: Renewal grants may be made and are processed as new applications.

ASSISTANCE CONSIDERATIONS:

Formula and Matching Requirements: Grants to organizations, with few exceptions, must be matched, at least dollar-for-dollar (some grants require a three to one match), with nonfederal funds.

Length and Time Phasing of Assistance: Length and time may vary with project. Generally, requests may be received at any time for payment.

POST ASSISTANCE REQUIREMENTS:

Reports: Organizations: Financial report within 90 days after termination of grant period or as requested, plus narrative of accomplishment. Individuals: Narrative report within 90 days after termination of grant period plus financial report.

Audits: Provided in accordance with the provisions of OMB Circular No. A-110 for organizations other than State and local governments. In accordance with the provisions of OMB Circular No. A-128, "Audits of State and Local Governments," State and local governments that receive financial assistance of $100,000 or more within the State's fiscal year shall have an audit made for that year. State and local governments that receive between $25,000 and $100,000 within the State's fiscal year shall have an audit made in accordance with Circular No. A-128, or in accordance with Federal laws and regulations governing the programs in which they participate.

Records: Financial records to be retained by grantee for three years following termination of grant.

FINANCIAL INFORMATION:

Account Identification: 59-0100-0-1-503.

Obligations: (Grants) FY 90 $15,792,000; FY 91 est $14,167,000; and FY 92 est $14,247,000.

Range and Average of Financial Assistance: Individuals : $2,000 to $35,000 in fiscal years 1991 and 1992. Organizations: $3,000 to $290,000 in fiscal years 1991 and 1992.

PROGRAM ACCOMPLISHMENTS: In fiscal year 1990, 1,846 applications were received and 792 grants were awarded. In fiscal year 1991, it is anticipated that 1,803 applications will be received and 731 grants will be awarded. In fiscal year 1992, it is anticipated that 1,843 applications will be received and 680 grants will be awarded.

REGULATIONS, GUIDELINES, AND LITERATURE: The following are available from Public Information, National Endowment for the Arts, 1100 Pennsylvania Avenue, NW., Washington DC 20506: "National Endowment for the Arts, Guide to Programs," "Fellowship Guidelines," (Composers, Jazz, Solo Recitalists); "Presenters and Festivals Guidelines," (Chamber Music, New Music, Solo Recitalists, Jazz, Multi-Music, Music Festivals); "Ensembles Guidelines," (Chamber Music (including early and new), Jazz, Chorus, Orchestra, and Composer-in-Residence); "Training/Recording/Centers Guidelines," (Music Professional Training, Career Development, Music Recording, Centers for New Music Resources, Services to Composers, and Special Projects).

INFORMATION CONTACTS:
Regional or Local Office: Not applicable.
Headquarters Office: Director, Music Program, National Endowment for the Arts, 1100 Pennsylvania Avenue, NW., Washington, DC 20506. Telephone (202) 682-5445 (use same 7-digit number for FTS).

RELATED PROGRAMS: 45.002, Promotion of the Arts—Dance; 45.006, Promotion of the Arts—Media Arts: Film/Radio/Television; 45.008, Promotion of the Arts—Theater; 45.009, Promotion of the Arts—Visual Arts; 45.011, Promotion of the Arts—Inter-Arts; 45.013, Promotion of the Arts—Challenge Grants; 45.014, Promotion of the Arts—Opera-Musical Theater; 45.015, Promotion of the Arts-Folk Arts.

EXAMPLES OF FUNDED PROJECTS: (1) A summer music festival featuring orchestral, choral, jazz, and opera performances; (2) assisting an orchestra's season to include the performance of contemporary American works, young people's concerts, touring, and an audience development campaign; (3) a series of tour concerts and mini-residencies by chamber ensembles; (4) a fellowship to compose a concerto for clarinet and chamber ensemble; and (5) a regional touring jazz festival of residencies and concerts, workshops, clinics, and outreach performance activities.

CRITERIA FOR SELECTING PROPOSALS: All applications are reviewed according to the following standards: artistic quality, the merit of the project, and the applicant's capacity to accomplish it.

45.002 PROMOTION OF THE ARTS—DANCE

FEDERAL AGENCY: National Endowment for the Arts, National Foundation on the Arts and the Humanities

AUTHORIZATION: National Foundation on the Arts and the Humanities Act of 1965, as amended, Public Law 89-209, 20 U.S.C. 951 et seq.

OBJECTIVES: The Dance Program provides support for professional choreographers, dance companies, organizations and individuals that present or serve dance.

TYPES OF ASSISTANCE: Project Grants; Direct Payments for Specified Use.

USES AND USE RESTRICTIONS: Grants may be used for the creation of new dance works, rehearsal support, experimentation with a new technique, dance touring, and presenting dance workshops, management improvement, study with another choreographer, rehearsal space subsidy, national services to the field, and dance films and video. Generally, there are no funds for construction or rehabilitation of facilities, general operating support, foreign study and travel, scholarships, publications other than newsletters, research, or student performing groups. Support is also provided for dance presentation through cooperative programs with 45.007, Promotion of Arts—State Programs and 45.011, Promotion of the Arts—Inter-Arts.

ELIGIBILITY REQUIREMENTS:

Applicant Eligibility: Grants may be made to: 1) Nonprofit organizations, including State and local governments and State arts agencies, if donations to such organizations qualify as charitable deductions under Section 170(c) of the Internal Revenue Code; and 2) individuals (U.S. citizens and permanent residents) who, according to Public Law 89-209, Section 5(c) must possess exceptional talent.

Beneficiary Eligibility: Individuals and nonprofit organizations including State and local governments and State arts agencies.

Credentials/Documentation: Applying organizations are required to submit a copy of their Internal Revenue Service tax exemption determination letter with their applications. Costs will be determined in accordance with OMB Circular No. A-87 for State and local governments. For institutions of higher education, allowable costs will be determined according to OMB Circular No. A-21; and other nonprofit organizations making application, allowable costs will be determined according to OMB Circular No. A-122.

APPLICATION AND AWARD PROCESS:

Preapplication Coordination: The standard application forms as furnished by the Federal agency and required by OMB Circular No. A-102 must be used for this program. This program is excluded from coverage under E.O. 12372.

Application Procedure: Applicants should request guidelines for this program area and appropriate standard application forms from: Dance Program, National Endowment for the Arts, 1100 Pennsylvania Avenue, NW., Washington, DC 20506. This program is subject to the provisions of OMB Circular No. A-110.

Award Procedure: The Chairperson of the Endowment makes the final decision on all awards based on recommendations from the National Council on the Arts (the NEA advisory body) and the consulting panels to the agency. The Endowment Headquarters will determine on a case-by-case basis those applicants who can further disburse grant money to sub-grantees.

Deadlines: Call program office for deadlines.

Range of Approval/Disapproval Time: Dependent on meetings of the National Council on the Arts.

Appeals: Information on the appeals process may be obtained from the headquarters office listed below.

Renewals: Renewal grants may be made and are processed as new applications.

ASSISTANCE CONSIDERATIONS:

Formula and Matching Requirements: Grants to organizations must be matched at least dollar-for-dollar with nonfederal funds.

Length and Time Phasing of Assistance: Length and time may vary with project. Generally, requests may be received at any time for payment to cover immediate project expenses.

POST ASSISTANCE REQUIREMENTS:

Reports: Financial report within 90 days after termination of grant period or as requested, plus narrative of accomplishment.

Audits: In accordance with the provisions of OMB Circular No. A-128, "Audits of State and Local Governments," State and local governments that receive financial assistance of $100,000 or more within the State's fiscal year shall have an audit made for that year. State and local governments that receive between $25,000 and $100,000 within the State's fiscal year shall have an audit made in accordance with Circular No. A-128, or in accordance with Federal laws and regulations governing the programs in which they participate.

Records: Financial records to be retained by grantee for three years following termination of grant.

FINANCIAL INFORMATION:

Account Identification: 59-0100-0-1-503.

Obligations: (Grants) FY 90 $9,565,000; FY 91 est $8,545,000; and FY 92 est $8,630,000.

Range and Average of Financial Assistance: Individuals: $45,000; Organizations: $2,000 to $400,000.

PROGRAM ACCOMPLISHMENTS: In fiscal year 1990, 1,078 applications were received and 355 grants were awarded. In fiscal year 1991, it is anticipated that 1,029 applications will be received and 290 grants will be awarded. In fiscal year 1992, it is anticipated that 1,033 applications will be received and 267 grants will be awarded.

REGULATIONS, GUIDELINES, AND LITERATURE: The following publications are available from Public Information, National Endowment for the Arts, 1100 Pennsylvania Ave., NW., Washington, DC 20506: "National Endowment for the Arts, Guide to Programs" and "Dance Program Guidelines."

INFORMATION CONTACTS:

Regional or Local Office: Not applicable.

Headquarters Office: Dance Program, National Endowment for the Arts, 1100 Pennsylvania Avenue, NW., Washington, DC 20506. Telephone: (202) 682-5435 (use same 7-digit number for FTS).

RELATED PROGRAMS: 45.001, Promotion of the Arts—Design Arts; 45.003, Promotion of the Arts—Arts in Education; 45.005, Promotion of the Arts—Music; 45.006, Promotion of the Arts—Media Arts: Film/Radio/Television; 45.008, Promotion of the Arts—Theater; 45.009, Promotion of the Arts—Visual Arts; 45.010, Promotion of the Arts—Expansion Arts; 45.011, Promotion of the Arts—Inter-Arts; 45.013, Promotion of the Arts—Challenge Grants; 45.014, Promotion of the Arts—Opera-Musical Theater; 45.015, Promotion of the Arts—Folk Arts; 45.022, Promotion of the Arts—Advancement Grants; 45.023, Promotion of the Arts—Locals Program.

EXAMPLES OF FUNDED PROJECTS: (1) Support for the costs associated with rehearsal time and facility rental necessary to develop and sustain new work for a dance company; (2) a choreography fellowship to allow an independent choreographer to work with several professional dancers and a composer to create a new piece; (3) presentation of several professional dance companies throughout the year; (4) assist in support of administrative costs to enable an organization to provide space and promotional services at low cost to small companies and individual artists; and (5) support of the creation of a dance videotape through the collaboration of a choreographer and a videographer.

CRITERIA FOR SELECTING PROPOSALS: Review criteria vary according to the type of application, but all applications are reviewed first according to artistic quality.

Surviving in the Workplace of the 1990s

The first six chapters of *How to Hold It All Together When You've Lost Your Job* have provided you with the tools for financially surviving your period of unemployment so that you can devote your energy to forge a successful job search campaign. With Chapter 1 you laid the foundation for your job search. Chapters 7 and 8 form the logical conclusion of your book.

- Your financial house is in order

- You are networking and interviewing

- You are following up on your résumés and cover letters

- You are beginning to receive positive feedback from your efforts

You need to learn how to position yourself to your best advantage in case you are ever laid off again. From personal experience, I can tell you that being laid off the second time is just as painful as the first. Within six months after taking a new position I was downsized. Now, however, my networking skills were keen. Our family continued to live within our survival budget. My experience taught me two important principles:

- Understand every benefit that your company offers you—*read your employee benefits handbook*

- Understand every phase of the exit interview so you can use your power points to obtain your best severance and benefits package

In this chapter you will learn to develop a "sixth sense" about your company's activities. In Chapter 8 we will analyze the exit interview. Both of these chapters are essential reading for those who are employed as well as for those who are unemployed. Be alert and plan for every contingency.

Your Employee Benefits Manual

Just about every employer, even if they aren't large enough to have a human resources department, has a written statement that describes employee benefits and lays out the company's policies regarding vacation time, sick leave, insurance coverage, and any pension, profit sharing, and/or 401K plans. Even the smallest companies discuss these matters with employees at time of hire.

The excitement associated with starting a new job and meeting co-workers can make many new employees simply glance quickly at their policy and benefits manual. They promise themselves that they will read it when they need it, and then tuck the manual away in a desk drawer. In doing this they deprive themselves of an opportunity to learn what their new company will do for them. Benefits are an important part of your compensation. If your company withdrew its benefits it could be paying higher wages. I recommend that you:

- Find your benefits manual

- Read it carefully

- Make sure you understand all its provisions

- Keep your manual current

Your employer provides benefits in order to attract productive employees like you. These benefits are part of your compensation. Understand them so you can use them. Familiarize yourself with the details so that you can negotiate the greatest number of employer-provided benefits into your severance package if you are laid off. It is your responsibility to understand:

- Your group health, life, and disability coverage policy provisions

- Your employer pension and profit-sharing plans, flexible spending accounts, and your own 401K Plan

- Your employer's retirement policies

- Other employee benefits such as holiday and vacation pay, sick leave, pregnancy leave, day care, and tuition reimbursement

- Any early retirement plans and severance policies

Be sure to keep your department head or supervisor informed about any unusual personal and family circumstances for which you are responsible. Are there unusual health problems? Are you caring for dependents who have disabilities? Are you responsible for your elderly parents? Are you a single parent who is solely responsible for child care? Write this information in a memo and give one copy to your superior and another to your human resources department to include on your personnel file. Keep a copy for yourself.

By making your employer formally aware of your special circumstances, you differentiate yourself from your peers. You will also be able to use your personal situation to help negotiate and extract a better severance package for yourself. This holds true whether you are laid off individually or as part of a mass downsizing.

Keeping Your Ear to the Ground

Even just knowing that companies in your industry are downsizing can make you feel uneasy. It doesn't matter if you are employed in banking, defense, or consumer goods. If you work for a company that is currently downsizing, chances are that you have become tense, untrusting, saddened by your co-workers' sudden departures, and wary of your boss's silence about what might come next. Become a savvy worker. Keep an open ear to what your co-workers say about the company in informal conversation. Read your company newsletter. Be aware of words like "spin-off," "buyout," and "restructuring," and of any articles that dwell on the gloomy condition of your industry. This could be your company's way of bracing you for something unpleasant in the future.

Do your homework. Learn which departments or divisions in your company are growing and profitable. You might read about them in the company newsletter or in magazine and newspaper articles. Companies enjoy broadcasting their success. Try to negotiate a transfer into one of these growth areas even if it means taking a temporary cut in pay. Offer to obtain the training you need to acquire new skills, either through the company or on your own. If you are successful, you will maintain your income, benefits, and perquisites, such as vacations. You will continue to participate in your company's pension and profit-sharing plans, and have the opportunity to continue on your successful career path. Do this and you will have negotiated a smart career move. In your company's eyes, you will be a "known quantity." Your work record will speak for itself. Your company would much rather transfer an internal candidate into a position than hire from the outside.

Keep informed about economic conditions and industry trends. Read periodicals such as *Newsweek*, *Time*, *Fortune*, *Business Week* and *Forbes*. If your company is large, you might find an article that reveals how your president views the future of your firm. Always read the business section of your local newspaper. Look for and read articles about the growing companies in your area. Network with people you know who work for these companies.

Some dos and don'ts

- Don't panic. The savvy worker avoids the high-anxiety and self-destructive behavior that tends to flourish in tense environments.

- Never goad your supervisor with questions as "How many more of us will be axed this month?" or "Please level with me—am I next?"

- Never take revenge by destroying company property or by slacking off on your job because you believe "I'm going to be let go anyway, so what's the use?" Your supervisor could be your best source for a future job reference.

- Don't deny that your job is at risk. Don't allow yourself the luxury of fatalistically believing that "the situation is totally out of my control." This is exactly the time when you should begin networking to find a new position.

- Try to put yourself into your boss's shoes. Downsizing and consolidation might mean that he or she will be responsible for the same amount or additional production from fewer workers and, possibly, with reduced resources. His or her future could be uncertain. Your superior is under intense pressure and is as frustrated as you are.

- Do take care of "number one." Prepare a contingency job search plan, network, and pare down your living expenses.

If you were recently laid off and you don't understand your benefits available to you under COBRA, don't hesitate to contact your previous employer's human resources department. Your previous employer is legally responsible to give you this information or be liable for violating the Employers' Fair Practices Act.

Negotiating Your Best Separation Package

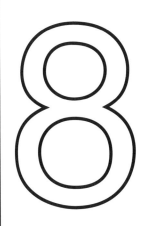

Employers can be very creative when it comes to describing the act of terminating workers. Autoworkers are "temporarily laid off." Teachers and military personnel are part of a reduction in force or "RIF-ed." Government workers are "furloughed." The euphemisms preferred by most corporations are "downsizing" or "rightsizing" for a layoff due to a major reorganization.

The exit interview, theoretically, is a confidential separation procedure during which departing workers can talk candidly about the company and vent their frustrations. For employers it represents an opportunity to gather valuable feedback about employment issues, such as working conditions, wages, and personnel practices.

In reality, the exit interview can be an unpleasant and traumatic experience for both employer and employee. What makes this situation worse is that, unlike hiring, there is no well-developed method for firing.

Inept handling of layoffs is as bad for the company as it is for the terminated employee. Callous treatment of former employees can destroy the loyalty and morale of the remaining workforce. It can tarnish a company's image and damage sales. Mass layoffs are the ones most likely to be mishandled by corporate management. Many companies have little or no experience with this procedure.

Fortunately, there are many times when corporations handle the process in a fair and equitable manner. In these cases, management keeps workers well-informed and current about the company's financial condition, any potential changes in ownership, planned manpower reductions, and other issues. Such candor reduces worker stress and helps workers anticipate the future. It gives employees lead time to plan for a transition period, and enables them to look for a new job while they are still employed and receiving benefits.

The Exit Interview

A well-handled exit interview rarely lasts more than fifteen minutes. You must realize, however, that once the interview is over, the positive relationship between company and employee may disappear and the company may assume a posture of self-defense. Security matters now take precedence over hurt feelings. Most companies deny terminated workers access to any files, records, or tools, and usually escort them immediately off the premises. Your ex-manager or supervisor may even collect your personal belongings and mail them to you. These procedures can seem quite degrading to a loyal employee who was not terminated for misconduct on the job. From the company's point of view, however, it is essential to return to normal as soon as possible and to minimize any chance for revenge or theft.

The exit interview is a painful experience for both sides. Since most managers or supervisors are themselves in a guilt-ridden state during the interview, they are vulnerable. When employees realize this fact, they can turn this guilt to their advantage to negotiate their best severance package.

The path to success in most adversarial situations is to stay cool and use the facts of the situation to your best advantage. The graphic illustration of the phases of the exit interview that follows will help you see how and when you can turn this process to your advantage.

The Exit Interview

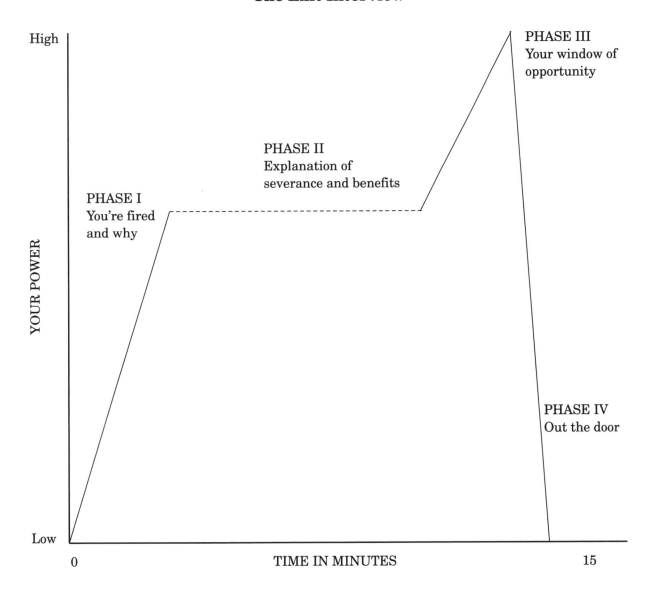

Phase I: You're fired

Most companies require someone at a higher level than your immediate manager or supervisor to approve layoffs. The decision to lay off whole groups of workers occurs only after careful deliberation at the highest management levels. Upper echelons want to be certain they have just cause for termination and are not leaving themselves and their company open to legal action. This is especially true in the areas of age, minority and sex discrimination. If you feel that you have just cause to believe you were terminated for any of these reasons, contact your Equal

Employment Opportunity Commission (listed in the Yellow Pages under U.S. Government) and your attorney immediately.

Phase II: Explanation of any severance and COBRA

Because the exit interview is traumatic and only takes a short time, your employer might forget to mention the important benefits to which you are entitled. As you learned in Chapter 7, you must be familiar with the benefits your company offers you. It is key for you to thoroughly discuss your benefits. Your goal is to extend these benefits for yourself. Remember, after the interview is over, it is next to impossible to reopen these issues.

Here is a definition of employee benefits and a list of benefits many companies offer their employees. Employee benefits include any form of compensation for time worked other than direct wages, such as:

- Group health, life and disability insurance

- Retirement income arrangements (pension, 401K Plans, etc.)

- Payments for time not worked (vacation, holiday, and sick leave)

- Social insurance programs (Social Security, unemployment, and workers' compensation)

- Flexible spending accounts for medical and dependent care expenses

- Miscellaneous benefits (daycare, education, legal services, wellness programs, and fitness centers)

- Payment for non-productive time at work (breaks, lunch periods, wash-up times)

Let's examine each of these benefits so that you know what you should request and what you should receive.

Group health, life and disability insurance. You should receive a summary of information about:

- The continuation of your group medical insurance, conversion of your group life insurance, and termination and conversion privileges of any disability insurance coverage

- Forms for COBRA continuation of group health and for conversion of your group life to individual coverage

- Names of the company's life and disability agents to contact for conversion

These benefits form part of the safety net that protects you from catastrophic events that could cause financial ruin to you and your family. They are critical to your financial and physical wellbeing and were discussed in great detail in Chapter 3.

Retirement income arrangements. These include your qualified pension and profit-sharing, 401K or 401B, stock bonus, or annuity plans. The company's plan administrator will evaluate their market value as of the day of your termination and at the end of the quarter-year after you left the company. Ask for and make sure you receive the market value of your vested benefits and contributions. Request rollover forms so that you can open a rollover IRA with the proceeds. In order to avoid penalties, the law requires you to rollover your pension and thrift plan lump-sum distributions within 60 days after receipt. Special treatment of lump-sum distributions is only available to those who have reached the age of 59 and a half. In the addenda you will find sample IRS Form W-4P (Withholding Certificate for Pension and Annuity Payments) and Form 5329 (Return for Additional Taxes Attributable to Qualified Retirement Plans [including IRAs], Annuities, and Modified Endowment Contracts), as well as instructions for each form. These are complex areas. It is best to contact a tax specialist if you have a complex retirement package or do not understand the mechanics of rolling over your retirement distribution.

Payments for time not worked. Make sure that the company pays you for the vacation days and paid holidays you have accrued up to the date of your separation. This payment should be in addition to any severance compensation you receive.

Social insurance programs. Both your and your employer's taxes fund these programs. One goal of this book has been to introduce you to these programs and explain how you can use them to help you survive during your job search—and possibly to retrain for a new career.

Flexible spending accounts. These plans allow employees to pay for their health and dependent care costs with pre-tax dollars. Your may put up to $5,000 each year into child-care accounts. Employers usually set limits of a percentage of salary or a dollar amount for medical reimbursement accounts. The catch is that, at the end of the year, you forfeit the money you haven't spent in your account.

If you are enrolled in a flexible spending plan, ask your benefits manager for the dollar amount of health and/or dependent care expenses you have contributed to your account up to the date of your separation. Be sure you submit all expenses incurred up to the date of your separation. See that your portion of group health premiums are credited to your FlexPlan account. You have until the end of the calendar year to do this. If you forget to do this, you lose the money you have already contributed to your account.

Miscellaneous benefits. Try to negotiate as many as you can into your severance package. Read the case studies in this chapter to learn how others took advantage of them.

Phase III: Your window of opportunity— negotiating your best severance package

Even if your company has an established severance policy—for example, one week's severance pay for each year of company service or, in the case of mass layoffs due to financial problems, similar packages for everyone regardless of seniority—you need not passively accept whatever you are offered. Deliberately, confidently, and with complete control over your emotions, state your case as to why you, a productive worker who has given your best to your company, deserve and expect humane financial treatment. In Chapter 7 I emphasized that you should inform your manager or supervisor about any special situation that affects you and your family—recurring illness, a large number of dependents, caring for an aged parent, etc. Now is the time to talk about your additional responsibilities and to ask for special consideration on your behalf.

Be tough. This interview is difficult and unpleasant for your employer as well as for you. If your company offers you two weeks of severance pay, plead for 45 days. If you're offered three months, try for 120 days. Your company has already approved your separation package; chances are slim they will renege. This is the time to negotiate for miscellaneous benefits: daycare for your children since your job search could necessitate that both you and your spouse search for work; tuition reimbursement to pay for the continuing education courses you take during your severance pay period; and fitness programs that will help you reduce stress during your job search. It is your last chance to ask for a transfer to another department, even if it means taking a temporary cut in pay for you. As was discussed in Chapter 7, a transfer means you preserve your income, benefits, and perks, and could redirect you on your successful career path. It also buys you time to look for other employment. If, in a worst case scenario, you are not offered any severance in the form of salary continuation, try to negotiate at least one month's extension in company-paid insurance benefits.

If your employer offers you the option of accepting your severance in a lump-sum payment, *don't accept it* unless your company is on the verge of bankruptcy or already bankrupt. All company-sponsored benefits cease the moment you receive your final severance check. Your group health insurance premiums will probably double and your group life, which is term insurance, converts to whole life (at your option), thus increasing your premiums significantly.

Accept any outplacement counseling you are offered. If you are not offered counseling, ask for it during your exit interview. It is a widely accepted practice for companies to offer outplacement counseling services as part of the severance package. It creates a positive image of a company as a good public servant that cares about what happens to its employees. It also helps maintain the morale of the remaining employees. These services are usually structured to:

- Fit everyones' needs—not just your specific needs

- Last just a few days

- Teach you only the basic job search skills

Above all, during your exit interview, curb your anger. "You can't fire me, I quit," are the six most expensive words you can utter during your career. Quitting is voluntary. Quitting relieves your employer of all responsibility to provide you severance. Very rarely can you undo this mistake. Even the most benevolent human resources department would be hard-pressed to offer you the same or any separation package that it would have originally offered you had you not "blown your stack" and come back begging for pardon.

If you are asked to submit a letter of resignation or are politely—or bluntly—told to resign, *don't do it* until you have negotiated the termination of your employment and have received a summary of those terms in writing. Unscrupulous employers have been know to accept resignations and then renege on benefits. They understand that few lawyers will accept a case on a contingency basis that might involve just a few thousand dollars, although as you well know, those dollars mean so much to your wellbeing.

Additionally, damages aside from discrimination are hard to prove. Get your separation agreement in writing!

Before considering the financial issues involved in rollovers, let's consider how two people handled themselves during their exit interviews.

> Richard had been dissatisfied with his job for months and blamed top management for freezing all employee wages for one year. His job was eliminated as part of a major downsizing. During his exit interview, Richard "blew up" and told his supervisor "I quit." His voluntary action caused him to lose any chance for severance pay and possible unused holiday and vacation pay, plus prevented him from qualifying for unemployment compensation benefits. Richard left empty-handed. *This is the worst way to leave an exit interview.*

> Linda was aware of rumors that her entire department might be eliminated. She had kept her supervisor and her human resources department informed about her accomplishments. They also knew that she had sole economic responsibility for her two young children. During her exit interview she used these facts about her situation to negotiate an extra two months of severance pay and the use of the company daycare center for her children while she searched for work. *Take note: this is the best way to handle an exit interview.*

Phase IV: Your interview has ended

You've done the best you could. Put the matter behind you. Find out what you need to do about the financial issues that are associated with your separation. Prepare for this transition time called unemployment. Craft an effective job search plan.

What You Need to Know About Pension, Profit-Sharing, and Savings Plans

- You have 60 days from when you receive your qualified plan lump-sum payment to roll it over into another plan. A rollover is a tax-free transfer of cash or other assets from one retirement account into another, or into a rollover IRA. You want to keep your rollover IRA separate from any personal IRAs. Your company has contributed to your pension and profit-sharing plans, and probably to your 401K plan as well. Pension plans are counted as exempt assets in qualifying for government entitlements.

- Whether you directly rollover, decide to take a distribution to provide yourself with living expenses, or opt to receive monthly payments from your pension as income, you must complete an IRS Form W-4P, Withholding Certificate for Pension or Annuity Payments. Your human resources department will provide you with this form, which is used for one of the following purposes:

  1. To calculate the amount of federal income tax to withhold from pension and annuity payments

  2. To claim exemption from withholding for non-periodic (lump-sum) payments

  Review the IRS forms in the addenda to this chapter. You will find a completed Form W-4P with instructions, a completed IRS Form 5329 demonstrating how to compute your tax on early distributions, and an IRS Form 1040 showing where you write the early distribution amount and where you write the 10 percent additional tax penalty for early withdrawal. If you are over the age of 59 and a half, separated from military service in or after the year of reaching age 55, or qualify for any of the other exceptions listed in Part II of IRS Form 5329, you may not have to pay additional taxes on an early distribution.

Two IRS documents that will help you are Publication 575, *Pension and Annuity Income (including simplified general rule)* and Publication 505, *Tax Withholding and Estimated Tax*. Publication 575 explains how to report pension and annuity income on your federal income tax return. Publication 505 explains the special tax treatment used for lump-sum and for periodic distributions from pension, profit-sharing and 401K Plans. You can find these publications at your local public library or request them from the IRS.

It is critical that you meet the time requirements for rolling over your qualified retirement plan and for completing Form W-4P if you plan to receive periodic payments from your qualified plan. Let's consider two examples.

Your qualified plan rollover

Mark was terminated in a downsizing and believed he could find another job within two months. He decided he would roll over his pension into his new employer's plan. He told himself he would not worry about "paperwork and taxes" until next April 15. Unfortunately, Mark did not find employment in two months and forgot about his 60-day rollover time limit. Mark's eligible pension rollover value was $100,000. Here is what happened to Mark:

- His former employer withheld 20 percent ($20,000). He received $80,000 to rollover.

- In order for Mark to roll over the entire amount ($100,000) into a rollover IRA or qualified pension plan, he will have to roll over $80,000 *plus $20,000 from his own funds*. He will recover the withheld $20,000 when he files his next tax return.

   Mark now has these choices:

- He can use his own funds. However, he loses what he could have earned by investing his $20,000.

- He can borrow the money, but he has to pay interest on his loan.

- He can roll over his $80,000 and pay income taxes on the $20,000 plus an additional 10 percent ($2,000) tax for his early withdrawal (distribution) from a qualified retirement plan. Mark is under age 59 and a half and meets none of the exceptions listed in the memorandum to IRS Form 5329 (found in the addenda to this chapter).

Your Form W-4P withholding certificate

Louise, age 56, accepted her company's early retirement package. She elected to receive monthly payments from her pension as income. These payments are treated by the IRS as wages for the purpose of withholding. By completing the Personal Allowances and the Deductions and Adjustments worksheets of Form W-4P, Louise tailored the amount of tax withheld to her own situation.

If Louise did not complete Form W-4P, the IRS would automatically compute her personal allowances as if she were married with three children. This could cause her to over-withhold or to under-withhold. If she under-withheld, Louise could be subject to a tax penalty for insufficient taxes withheld. Since Louise is under age 59 and a half, and meets no other exceptions, she must pay an additional tax equal to ten percent of the taxable portion of her monthly distributions.

Keep in contact with your former company's plan administrator. If you miss deadlines or fail to complete tax forms, the consequences can be quite expensive. If you are unemployed when your rollover period is about to end and have not established a rollover IRA, talk to your banker or broker and establish one. If you plan to receive periodic distributions, insist that your plan administrator explain the tax consequences of these distributions to you. This is a complex area and tax regulations can change. Seek professional advice *before* you elect to receive early or lump-sum distributions from your qualified plan.

Addenda to
Chapter 8

19__ Form W-4P

Department of the Treasury
Internal Revenue Service

What Is Form W-4P? This form is for recipients of income from annuity, pension, and certain other deferred compensation plans to tell payers whether income tax is to be withheld and on what basis. Your options depend on whether the payment is periodic or nonperiodic (including an eligible rollover distribution) as explained on page 3.

You can use this form to choose to have no income tax withheld from the payment (except for eligible rollover distributions or payments to U.S. citizens delivered outside the United States or its possessions) or to have an additional amount of tax withheld.

What Do I Need To Do? If you want no tax to be withheld, you can skip the worksheet below and go directly to the form at the bottom of this page. Otherwise, complete lines A through F of the worksheet. Many recipients can stop at line F.

Other Income? If you have a large amount of income from other sources not subject to withholding (such as interest, dividends, or taxable social security), you should consider making estimated tax payments using **Form 1040-ES,** Estimated Tax for Individuals. Call 1-800-829-3676 for copies of Form 1040-ES, and **Pub. 505,** Tax Withholding and Estimated Tax.

When Should I File? File as soon as possible to avoid underwithholding problems.

Multiple Pensions? More Than One Income? To figure the number of allowances you may claim, combine allowances and income subject to withholding from all sources on one worksheet. You can file a Form W-4P with each pension payer, but do not claim the same allowances more than once. Your withholding will usually be more accurate if you claim all allowances on the Form W-4P for the largest source of income subject to withholding.

Personal Allowances Worksheet

A Enter "1" for **yourself** if no one else can claim you as a dependent . . . . **A** __1__

B Enter "1" if:
- You are single and have only one pension; or
- You are married, have only one pension, and your spouse has no income subject to withholding; or
- Your income from a second pension or a job, or your spouse's pension or wages (or the total of all) is $1,000 or less.

. . . . **B** __1__

C Enter "1" for your **spouse.** You may choose to enter -0- if you are married and have either a spouse who has income subject to withholding or you have more than one source of income subject to withholding. (This may help you avoid having too little tax withheld.) . . . . **C** __1__

D Enter number of **dependents** (other than your spouse or yourself) you will claim on your return . . . . **D** __1__

E Enter "1" if you will file as a **head of household** on your tax return . . . . ▶ **E** ____

F Add lines A through E and enter total here . . . . ▶ **F** __4__

For accuracy, do all worksheets that apply.

- If you plan to itemize or claim other deductions and want to reduce your withholding, use the **Deductions and Adjustments Worksheet** on page 2.
- If you have more than one source of income subject to withholding or a spouse with income subject to withholding AND your combined earnings from all sources exceed $30,000, ($50,000 if married filing jointly), use the **Multiple Pensions/More Than One Income Worksheet** on page 2 if you want to avoid having too little tax withheld.
- If **neither** situation applies, **stop here** and enter the number from line F above on line 2 of Form W-4P below.

------------- Cut here and give the certificate to the payer of your pension or annuity. Keep the top portion for your records. -------------

Form **W-4P**

Department of the Treasury
Internal Revenue Service

Withholding Certificate for Pension or Annuity Payments

OMB No. 1545-0415

19__

Type or print your full name	Your social security number
DONALD P. JONES	123 : 45 : 6789

Home address (number and street or rural route)	Claim or identification number (if any) of your pension or annuity contract
1265 Highland Ave.	
City or town, state, and ZIP code	F-12748
Garden Grove, CA 92143	

Complete the following applicable lines:

1 I elect not to have income tax withheld from my pension or annuity. (Do not complete lines 2 or 3.) . . . . . ▶ ☐

2 I want my withholding from each **periodic** pension or annuity payment to be figured using the number of allowances and marital status shown. (You may also designate a dollar amount on line 3.) . . . . ▶ __13__

(Enter number of allowances.)

Marital status: ☐ Single   ☐ Married   ☐ Married, but withhold at higher Single rate

3 I want the following additional amount withheld from each pension or annuity payment. **Note:** *For periodic payments, you cannot enter an amount here without entering the number (including zero) of allowances on line 2* . . . ▶ $ ____

Your signature ▶ *Donald P. Jones*   Date ▶

Cat. No. 10225T

Deductions and Adjustments Worksheet

NOTE: *Complete only if you plan to itemize deductions or claim adjustments to income on your 1995 tax return.*

1. Enter an estimate of your 1995 itemized deductions. These include qualifying home mortgage interest, charitable contributions, state and local taxes (but not sales taxes), medical expenses in excess of 7.5% of your income, and miscellaneous deductions in excess of 2% of your income. (For 1995, you may have to reduce your itemized deductions if your income is over $114,700 ($57,350 if married filing separately). Get Pub. 919 for details.). . . **1** $ 30,000

2. Enter:
   $6,550 if married filing jointly or qualifying widow(er)
   $5,750 if head of household
   $3,900 if single
   $3,275 if married filing separately
   . . . . **2** $ 6,550

3. **Subtract** line 2 from line 1. If line 2 is greater than line 1, enter -0- . . . . **3** $ 23,450
4. Enter estimate of your 1995 adjustments to income. These include alimony paid and deductible IRA contributions . **4** $ -0-
5. **Add** lines 3 and 4 and enter the total . . . . **5** $ 23,450
6. Enter an estimate of your 1995 income not subject to withholding (such as dividends or interest income) **6** $ -0-
7. **Subtract** line 6 from line 5. Enter the result, but not less than zero. **7** 23,450
8. **Divide** the amount on line 7 by $2,500 and enter the result here. Drop any fraction **8** 9
9. Enter the number from **Personal Allowances Worksheet,** line F, on page 1 . . . . **9** 4
10. **Add** lines 8 and 9 and enter the total here. If you plan to use the **Multiple Pensions/More Than One Income Worksheet,** also enter this total on line 1 below. Otherwise **stop here** and enter this total on Form W-4P, line 2, on page 1 . . . . **10** 13

Multiple Pensions/More Than One Income Worksheet

NOTE: *Complete only if the instructions under line F on page 1 direct you here. This applies if you (and your spouse if married filing a joint return) have more than one source of income subject to withholding (such as more than one pension, or a pension and a job, or you have a pension and your spouse works).*

1. Enter the number from line F on page 1 (or from line 10 above if you used the **Deductions and Adjustments Worksheet**) . . . . **1** _____
2. Find the number in **Table 1** below that applies to the **LOWEST** paying pension or job and enter it here **2** _____
3. If line 1 is **GREATER THAN OR EQUAL TO** line 2, subtract line 2 from line 1. Enter the result here (if zero, enter -0-) and on Form W-4P, line 2, page 1. **Do not** use the rest of this worksheet . . . . . **3** _____
4. If line 1 is **LESS THAN** line 2, enter -0- on Form W-4P, line 2, page 1, and enter the number from line 2 of this worksheet here . . . . **4** _____
5. Enter the number from line 1 of this worksheet . . . . **5** _____
6. **Subtract** line 5 from line 4 and enter the result here . . . . **6** _____
7. Find the amount in **Table 2** below that applies to the **HIGHEST** paying pension or job and enter it here **7** $ _____
8. **Multiply** line 7 by line 6 and enter the result here . . . . **8** $ _____
9. **Divide** line 8 by the number of pay periods in each year. (For example, divide by 12 if you are paid every month.) Enter the result here and on Form W-4P, line 3, page 1. This is the additional amount to be withheld from each payment . . . . **9** $ _____

Table 1: Multiple Pensions/More Than One Income Worksheet

Married Filing Jointly				All Others	
If amounts from **LOWEST** paying pension or job is—	Enter on line 2 above	If amounts from **LOWEST** paying pension or job is—	Enter on line 2 above	If amounts from **LOWEST** paying pension or job is—	Enter on line 2 above
0 - $3,000	0	39,001 - 50,000	9	0 - $4,000	0
3,001 - 6,000	1	50,001 - 55,000	10	4,001 - 10,000	1
6,001 - 11,000	2	55,001 - 60,000	11	10,001 - 14,000	2
11,001 - 16,000	3	60,001 - 70,000	12	14,001 - 19,000	3
16,001 - 21,000	4	70,001 - 80,000	13	19,001 - 23,000	4
21,001 - 27,000	5	80,001 - 90,000	14	23,001 - 45,000	5
27,001 - 31,000	6	90,001 and over	15	45,001 - 60,000	6
31,001 - 34,000	7			60,001 - 70,000	7
34,001 - 39,000	8			70,001 and over	8

Table 2: Multiple Pensions/More Than One Income Worksheet

Married Filing Jointly		All Others	
If amounts from **HIGHEST** paying pension or job is—	Enter on line 7 above	If amounts from **HIGHEST** paying pension or job is—	Enter on line 7 above
0 - $50,000	$380	0 - $30,000	$380
50,001 - 100,000	700	30,001 - 60,000	700
100,001 - 130,000	780	60,001 - 110,000	780
130,001 - 230,000	900	110,001 - 230,000	900
230,001 and over	990	230,001 and over	990

Form **5329** Department of the Treasury Internal Revenue Service	**Additional Taxes Attributable to Qualified Retirement Plans (Including IRAs), Annuities, and Modified Endowment Contracts** (Under Sections 72, 4973, 4974, and 4980A of the Internal Revenue Code) ▶ **Attach to Form 1040. See separate instructions.**	OMB No. 1545-0203 19__ Attachment Sequence No. **29**

Name of individual subject to additional tax. (If married filing jointly, see instructions.) DONALD P. JONES	Your social security number 123 45 6789

Fill in Your Address Only If You Are Filing This Form by Itself and Not With Your Tax Return ▷	Home address (number and street), or P.O. box if mail is not delivered to your home 1265 Highland Ave.	Apt. no.
	City, town or post office, state, and ZIP code Garden Grove, CA 92143	If this is an amended return, check here ▶ ☐

If you are subject to the 10% tax on early distributions **only,** see **Who Must File** in the instructions before continuing. You may be able to report this tax directly on Form 1040 without filing Form 5329.

Part I   Tax on Early Distributions

Complete this part if a taxable distribution was made from your qualified retirement plan (including an IRA), annuity contract, or modified endowment contract before you reached age 59½ (or was incorrectly indicated as such on your Form 1099-R—see instructions). **Note:** *You must include the amount of the distribution on line 15b or 16b of Form 1040 or on the appropriate line of Form 4972.*

1	Early distributions included in gross income (see instructions)	**1**	12,000 00
2	Distributions excepted from additional tax (see instructions). Enter appropriate exception number from instructions ▶ _____	**2**	-0-
3	Amount subject to additional tax. Subtract line 2 from line 1	**3**	12,000 00
4	**Tax due.** Multiply line 3 by 10% (.10). Enter here and on Form 1040, line 51	**4**	1,200 00

Part II   Tax on Excess Contributions to Individual Retirement Arrangements

Complete this part if, either in this year or in earlier years, you contributed more to your IRA than is or was allowable and you have an excess contribution subject to tax.

5	Excess contributions for 1994 (see instructions). Do not include this amount on Form 1040, line 23a or 23b	**5**	
6	Earlier year excess contributions not previously eliminated (see instructions)	**6**	
7	Contribution credit. If your actual contribution for 1994 is less than your maximum allowable contribution, see instructions; otherwise, enter -0-	**7**	
8	1994 distributions from your IRA account that are includible in taxable income	**8**	
9	1993 tax year excess contributions (if any) withdrawn after the due date (including extensions) of your 1993 income tax return, and 1992 and earlier tax year excess contributions withdrawn in 1994 . . .	**9**	
10	Add lines 7, 8, and 9	**10**	
11	Adjusted earlier year excess contributions. Subtract line 10 from line 6. Enter the result, but not less than zero	**11**	
12	Total excess contributions. Add lines 5 and 11	**12**	
13	**Tax due.** Enter the **smaller** of 6% (.06) of line 12 or 6% (.06) of the value of your IRA on the last day of 1994. Also enter this amount on Form 1040, line 51	**13**	

For Paperwork Reduction Act Notice, see page 1 of separate instructions.   Cat. No. 13329Q   Form **5329** (1994)

Form 5329 (1994)   Page **2**

Part III	Tax on Excess Accumulation in Qualified Retirement Plans (Including IRAs)			

14	Minimum required distribution (see instructions)	14		
15	Amount actually distributed to you	15		
16	Subtract line 15 from line 14. If line 15 is more than line 14, enter -0-	16		
17	**Tax due.** Multiply line 16 by 50% (.50). Enter here and on Form 1040, line 51	17		

Part IV	Tax on Excess Distributions From Qualified Retirement Plans (Including IRAs)			

Complete Column A for regular distributions. Complete Column B for lump-sum distributions.

			Column A Regular Distributions	Column B Lump-Sum Distributions
18	Total amount of regular retirement or lump-sum distributions	18		
19	Amount excluded from additional tax. Enter appropriate exception number from instructions ▶ _____	19		
20	Subtract line 19 from line 18.	20		
21	Enter the **greater** of the threshold amount or the 1994 recovery of the grandfather amount (from Worksheet 1 or 2). See instructions	21		
22	Excess distributions. Subtract line 21 from line 20. If less than zero, enter -0-	22		
23	Tentative tax. Multiply line 22 by 15% (.15)	23		
24	Early distributions tax offset (see instructions)	24		
25	Subtract line 24 from line 23.	25		
26	**Tax due.** Combine columns (a) and (b) of line 25. Enter here and on Form 1040, line 51. . .	26		

Acceleration Elections (see the instructions for Part IV)

1   If you elected the discretionary method in 1987 or 1988 and wish to make an acceleration election beginning in 1994 under Temporary Regulations section 54.4981A-1T, Q&A b-12, check here ▶ ☐ .

2   If you previously made an acceleration election and wish to revoke that election, check here ▶ ☐ .

Signature. *Complete **ONLY** if you are filing this form by itself and not with your tax return.*

Please Sign Here   Under penalties of perjury, I declare that I have examined this form, including accompanying schedules and statements, and to the best of my knowledge and belief, it is true, correct, and complete. Declaration of preparer (other than taxpayer) is based on all information of which preparer has any knowledge.

▶ *Donald P. Jones*
Your signature   ▶ Date

Paid Preparer's Use Only	Preparer's signature ▶	Date	Check if self-employed ▶ ☐	Preparer's social security no.
	Firm's name (or yours, if self-employed) and address ▶		E.I. No. ▶	
			ZIP code ▶	

♲ *Printed on recycled paper*

19

Department of the Treasury
Internal Revenue Service

Instructions for Form 5329

Additional Taxes Attributable to Qualified Retirement Plans (Including IRAs), Annuities, and Modified Endowment Contracts

Section references are to the Internal Revenue Code unless otherwise noted.

Paperwork Reduction Act Notice

We ask for the information on this form to carry out the Internal Revenue laws of the United States. You are required to give us the information. We need it to ensure that you are complying with these laws and to allow us to figure and collect the right amount of tax.

The time needed to complete and file this form will vary depending on individual circumstances. The estimated average time is:

Recordkeeping	2 hr., 24 min.
Learning about the law or the form	31 min.
Preparing the form	1 hr., 17 min.
Copying, assembling, and sending the form to the IRS	34 min.

If you have comments concerning the accuracy of these time estimates or suggestions for making this form simpler, we would be happy to hear from you. You can write to both the IRS and the Office of Management and Budget at the addresses listed in the Instructions for Form 1040. DO NOT send this form to either of these offices. Instead, see **When and Where To File** on this page.

General Instructions

Purpose of Form

Use Form 5329 to report any additional income tax or excise tax you may owe in connection with your qualified retirement plan (including your individual retirement arrangement (IRA)), annuity, or modified endowment contract.

Do not use Form 5329 to report your deduction for contributions to your IRA. Report this deduction on your **Form 1040** or **1040A.** If you make nondeductible contributions to your IRA, use **Form 8606,** Nondeductible IRAs (Contributions, Distributions, and Basis), to report the nondeductible contribution. Also, if you previously made nondeductible IRA contributions, use Form 8606 to figure the taxable part of your IRA distributions.

Who Must File

You **MUST** file Form 5329 if any of the following apply.

● You owe a tax on early distributions from your qualified retirement plan (including an IRA), annuity, or modified endowment contract but distribution code 1 is not shown in box 7 of **Form 1099-R,** Distributions From Pensions, Annuities, Retirement or Profit-Sharing Plans, IRAs, Insurance Contracts, etc. (complete Part I).

● You meet an exception to the tax on early distributions, but distribution code 2, 3, or 4 is not shown in box 7 of Form 1099-R, or the distribution code shown is incorrect.

● You owe a tax because of excess contributions to your IRA (complete Part II).

● You owe a tax because you did not receive a minimum required distribution from your qualified retirement plan (complete Part III).

● You received distributions from a qualified retirement plan that exceed the applicable threshold amount, whether or not you owe a tax (complete Part IV).

You **DO NOT** have to file Form 5329 if:

● You owe **only** the 10% tax on early distributions (distribution code 1 must be shown in box 7 of Form 1099-R). If you are filing **Form 1040,** U.S. Individual Income Tax Return, do not complete Form 5329. Enter 10% of the taxable part of your distribution on Form 1040, line 51. Write "No" on the dotted line next to line 51 to indicate that you do not have to file Form 5329.

● You received an early distribution from your plan, but meet an exception to the tax (distribution code 2, 3, or 4 must be correctly shown on Form 1099-R).

● You rolled over the taxable part of all distributions you received during the year.

When and Where To File

Attach your 1994 Form 5329 to your 1994 Form 1040 and file both by the due date for your Form 1040 (including extensions).

If you do not have to file Form 1040 but owe a tax on Form 5329 or otherwise have to file Form 5329 (see above), you **must** still complete and file it with the IRS at the time and place you would be required to file Form 1040. If you are filing your 1994 Form 5329 by itself, be sure to include your address on page 1 and your signature and date on page 2. Enclose, but do not attach, a check or money order payable to the "Internal Revenue Service" for the total of any taxes due. Include your social security number and "1994 Form 5329" on the check or money order.

Filing for Previous Tax Years

If you are filing a Form 5329 to pay a tax for a previous year, you must use that year's version of the form. For example, if you are paying tax for 1992, you must use the 1992 version of the form to report the tax.

If you owe a tax for that previous year because of an early distribution, complete the appropriate part of Form 5329 for that year and attach it to **Form 1040X,** Amended U.S. Income Tax Return. Be sure to include the distribution as additional income on Form 1040X if not previously reported.

If you owe only a tax other than the tax on early distributions for a previous year, file Form 5329 by itself for that year. Be sure to include your signature and date on page 2. Enclose, but do not attach, a check or money order payable to the "Internal Revenue Service" for the amount of tax due. Include your social security number, "Form 5329," and the year for which the form is being filed on the check or money order.

Definitions

Qualified Retirement Plan

A qualified retirement plan includes:

● A qualified pension, profit-sharing, and stock bonus plan (including a qualified cash or deferred arrangement (CODA) under section 401(k)),

● A qualified annuity plan,

● A tax-sheltered annuity contract,

● An individual retirement account, and

● An individual retirement annuity.

Cat. No. 13330R

Early Distribution

Generally, any distribution from your qualified retirement plan, annuity, or modified endowment contract that you receive before you reach age 59½ is an early distribution. See **Part I—Tax on Early Distributions** below for details on early distributions that are subject to an additional tax.

Rollover

A rollover is a tax-free distribution (withdrawal) of assets from one qualified retirement plan that is reinvested in another plan. Generally, you must complete the rollover within 60 days following the distribution to qualify it for tax-free treatment. Get **Pub. 590**, Individual Retirement Arrangements (IRAs), for more details and additional requirements regarding rollovers.

Note: *If you instruct the trustee of your plan to transfer funds directly to another plan, the transfer is **not** considered a rollover. Do not include the amount transferred in income or deduct the amount transferred as a contribution. A transfer from a qualified employee plan to an IRA, however, is considered a rollover.*

Compensation

Compensation includes wages, salaries, professional fees, and other pay you receive for services you perform. It also includes sales commissions, commissions on insurance premiums, pay based on a percentage of profit, tips, and bonuses. It includes net earnings from self-employment, but only for a trade or business in which your personal services are a material income-producing factor.

For IRAs, treat all taxable alimony received from a former or current spouse under a decree of divorce or separate maintenance as compensation.

Compensation does not include any amounts received as a pension or annuity and does not include any amount received as deferred compensation.

Additional Information

For more details, see Pub. 590. Also get **Pub. 575,** Pension and Annuity Income.

Specific Instructions

Joint Returns

Each spouse must complete a **separate** Form 5329 for taxes attributable to his or her own qualified retirement plan, annuity, or modified endowment contract. If both spouses owe penalty taxes and are filing a joint return, enter the combined total tax from Forms 5329 on Form 1040, line 51.

Amended Return

If you are filing an amended 1994 Form 5329, check the box at the top of page 1 of the form. **Do not** use this version of Form 5329 to amend your return for any year other than 1994. See **Filing for Previous Tax Years** on page 1.

Part I—Tax on Early Distributions

In general, if you receive an early distribution from a qualified retirement plan, an annuity, or a modified endowment contract (including an involuntary cashout under section 411(a)(11) or 417(e)), the part of the distribution that is includible in gross income is subject to an additional 10% tax.

The tax on early distributions from qualified retirement plans does **not** apply to:

• 1994 IRA contributions withdrawn during the year or 1993 excess contributions withdrawn in 1994 before the filing date (including extensions) of your 1993 income tax return;

• Excess IRA contributions for years before 1993 that were withdrawn in 1994, and 1993 excess contributions withdrawn after the due date (including extensions) of your 1993 income tax return, if no deduction was allowed for the excess contributions, and the total IRA contributions for the tax year for which the excess contributions were made were not more than $2,250 (or if the total contributions for the year included employer contributions to a SEP, $2,250 increased by the smaller of the amount of the employer contributions to the SEP or $30,000);

• The part of your IRA distributions that represents a return of nondeductible IRA contributions figured on Form 8606;

• Distributions rolled over to another retirement arrangement or plan;

• Distributions of excess contributions from a qualified cash or deferred arrangement;

• Distributions of excess aggregate contributions to meet nondiscrimination requirements for employer matching and employee contributions;

• Distributions of excess deferrals; and

• Amounts distributed from unfunded deferred compensation plans of tax-exempt or state and local government employers.

See the instructions for **Line 2** below for other distributions that are not subject to the tax.

Line 1

Enter the taxable amount of early distributions made to you from a qualified pension plan, including your

IRA (and income earned on excess contributions to your IRA), an annuity contract, or a modified endowment contract (as defined in section 7702(A), entered into after June 20, 1988). The taxable amount of a distribution is the amount you include in gross income.

Prohibited transactions.—If you engaged in a prohibited transaction, such as **borrowing** from your individual retirement **account** or **annuity,** or pledging your individual retirement **annuity** as security for a loan, your account or annuity no longer qualified as an IRA on the first day of the tax year in which you did the borrowing or pledging. You are considered to have received a distribution of the entire value of your account or annuity at that time. Using your IRA as a basis for obtaining a benefit is also a prohibited transaction. If you were under age 59½ on the first day of the year, report the entire value of the account or annuity on line 1.

Pledging individual retirement account.—If you pledged any part of your individual retirement **account** as security for a loan, that **part** is considered distributed to you at the time pledged. If you were under age 59½ at the time of the pledge, enter the amount pledged on line 1.

Collectibles.—If your IRA trustee invested your funds in collectibles, you are considered to have received a distribution equal to the cost of any "collectible." Collectibles include works of art, rugs, antiques, metals, gems, stamps, coins, alcoholic beverages, and certain other tangible personal property.

If you were under age 59½ when the funds were invested, include the cost of the collectible on line 1. Also, include the total cost of the collectible as income on your 1994 Form 1040, line 15b.

Exception. Your IRA trustee may invest your IRA funds in U.S. one, one-half, one-quarter, and one-tenth ounce gold coins, and one ounce silver coins, minted after September 30, 1986.

Note: *You must include the taxable amount of all distributions (including income earned on investments) from line 1, on either line 15b or 16b, Form 1040, or the appropriate line of **Form 4972,** Tax on Lump-Sum Distributions, whichever applies.*

Line 2

The 10% additional tax does not apply to certain distributions specifically excepted by the Code. Enter on line 2 the amount that can be excluded. In the space provided, enter the applicable exception number (01-07) from the chart on the next page.

No. **Exception**

01 Distribution due to death (does not apply to modified endowment contracts)

02 Distribution due to total and permanent disability

03 Distribution made as part of a series of substantially equal periodic payments (made at least annually) for your life (or life expectancy) or the joint lives (or joint life expectancies) of you and your designated beneficiary (if from a qualified employee plan, payments must begin after separation from service)

04 Distribution due to separation from service in or after the year of reaching age 55 (applies only to qualified employee plans)

05 Distribution to the extent you have medical expenses deductible under section 213 (applies only to qualified employee plans)

06 Distributions made to an alternate payee under a qualified domestic relations order (applies only to qualified employee plans)

07 Other (see instructions below)

Other exceptions.—In addition to the exceptions listed above, the tax does not apply to the following:

● Any distributions from a plan maintained by an employer if:

1. You separated from service by March 1, 1986;

2. As of March 1, 1986, your entire interest was in pay status under a written election that provides a specific schedule for distribution of your entire interest; and

3. The distribution is actually being made under the written election.

● Distributions that are dividends paid with respect to stock described in section 404(k).

● Distributions from annuity contracts to the extent that the distributions are allocable to investment in the contract before August 14, 1982.

For additional exceptions applicable to annuities, see Pub. 575.

If any of these exceptions applies, include the amount that can be excluded on line 2. Enter Exception No. 07 in the space provided.

Also, if you received a Form 1099-R for a distribution that incorrectly indicated an early distribution (code 1 was entered in box 7 of the Form 1099-R), include on line 2 the amount of the distribution that you received when you were age 59½ or older. Enter Exception No. 07 in the space provided.

Worksheet for line 7 (Keep for your records)

1 Enter amount from line 2, column (a) or (b), IRA Worksheet 1, or line 7, column (a) or (b), IRA Worksheet 2, in the Form 1040 Instructions, but not more than $2,000 ($2,250 if you contributed to your nonworking spouse's account) . **1.** _____

2 Enter amount actually contributed either to your account or to your and your nonworking spouse's accounts . . . . **2.** _____

3 **Contribution credit.—**Subtract line 2 from line 1 (but do not enter more than $2,000). Enter this amount on line 7 of Form 5329. You should also add to the amount calculated on line 3 or 8 (whichever is applicable) of IRA Worksheet 1, or line 9 or 19 (whichever is applicable) of IRA Worksheet 2, the **smaller** of either: (a) this amount; or (b) your earlier years' excess contributions not previously eliminated . . . . **3.** _____

Part II—Tax on Excess Contributions to Individual Retirement Arrangements

If you contributed, either this year or in earlier years, more to your IRA than is allowable, you may have to pay a tax on excess contributions. Your allowable contribution is the smaller of your taxable compensation or $2,000 ($2,250 if you contributed to an IRA for a nonworking spouse).

However, you can withdraw some or all of your excess contributions for 1994 and they will not be taxed as a distribution if:

● You make the withdrawal by the due date (including extensions) of your 1994 income tax return,

● You do not claim a deduction for the amount of the contribution withdrawn, and

● You also withdraw from your IRA any income earned on the withdrawn contributions.

Do not include the withdrawn contributions as excess contributions on line 5.

You **must** include the income earned on the contributions withdrawn before the due date of your income tax return on Form 1040 for the year in which you made the contribution. Also, if you had not reached age 59½ at the time you received the distribution, report the income (but not the withdrawn contributions) as an early withdrawal in Part I, line 1.

Line 5

Enter the excess contributions you made in 1994. To figure this amount, subtract your contributions limit from your actual contributions. To figure your contributions limit, use IRA Worksheet 1 in the Form 1040 instructions. For this purpose, use the amount from line 3, column (a) or (b), or line 8 (as applicable) of Worksheet 1 regardless of your adjusted gross income (AGI) and even though you use Worksheet 2 to figure your IRA deduction limit.

Do not include any rollover contributions in figuring your excess contributions.

Line 6

Enter the total amount of 1993 excess contributions not withdrawn from your IRA by the due date of your 1993 income tax return, plus the 1992 and earlier excess contributions not withdrawn or otherwise eliminated before January 1, 1994.

This entry should be the same as the amount from line 12 of your 1993 Form 5329.

Line 7

If you contributed less to your IRA for 1994 than your contributions limit, and your excess contributions from earlier years have not been eliminated, complete the worksheet above to see if you have a contribution credit. **Do not** enter an amount on line 7 if you have an amount on line 5.

Line 8

If you withdrew any money from your IRA in 1994 that must be included in your income for 1994, enter that amount on line 8. Do not include any contributions withdrawn that will be reported on line 9.

Line 9

Enter any excess contributions to your IRA for 1976 through 1992 that you withdrew in 1994, and any 1993 excess contributions that you withdrew after the due date (including any extensions) for your 1993 income tax return, if:

● You did not claim a deduction for the excess, and

● The total contributions to your IRA for the tax year for which the excess contributions were made were not more than $2,250 (or if the total contributions for the year included employer contributions to a SEP, $2,250 increased by the smaller of the amount of the employer contributions to the SEP or $30,000).

Part III—Tax on Excess Accumulation in Qualified Retirement Plans (Including IRAs)

If you do not receive the minimum required distribution from your qualified retirement plan, you have an excess

Page 3

accumulation subject to an additional tax.

For purposes of the tax on excess accumulations, a qualified retirement plan also includes an eligible deferred compensation plan under section 457.

The additional tax is equal to 50% of the difference between the amount that was required to be distributed and the amount that was actually distributed.

Required Distributions

IRA.—You must start receiving distributions from your IRA by April 1 of the year following the year in which you reach age 70½. At that time, you may receive your entire interest in the IRA, or begin receiving periodic distributions over your life expectancy or over the joint life expectancy of you and your designated beneficiary (or over a shorter period).

If you choose to receive periodic distributions, you must receive a minimum required distribution each year. For each year after the year in which you reach age 70½, you must receive the minimum required distribution by December 31 of that year.

Figure the minimum required distribution by dividing the account balance of the IRA on December 31 of the year preceding the distribution by the applicable life expectancy.

For applicable life expectancies, you must use the expected return multiples from the tables in Pub. 590 or **Pub. 939,** Pension General Rule (Nonsimplified Method).

Under an alternative method, if you have more than one IRA, you may take the minimum distribution from any one or more of the individual IRAs.

For more details on the minimum distribution rules, with examples, and the life expectancy tables, see Pub. 590.

Qualified pension, profit-sharing, stock bonus, or section 457 deferred compensation plan.—In general, you must begin receiving distributions from your plan no later than April 1 of the year following the year in which you reach age 70½.

Your plan administrator figures the amount that must be distributed each year.

Exceptions. If you reached age 70½ before 1988 and were not a 5% owner, or are covered by a governmental or church plan, you must start receiving distributions from your qualified retirement plan no later than April 1 following the **later** of (1) the year in which you reached age 70½, or (2) the year in which you retired.

If you reached age 70½ in 1988 but had not retired by January 1, 1989, you were required to start receiving distributions no later than April 1, 1990. If you reached age 70½ in 1988 and

retired in 1988, you were required to start receiving distributions no later than April 1, 1989.

However, if you were a 5% owner of the employer maintaining the plan, you must begin receiving distributions no later than April 1 of the year following the year in which you reached age 70½, regardless of when you retire.

Note: *The IRS may waive this tax on excess accumulations if you can show that any shortfall in the amount of withdrawals from your qualified retirement plan was due to reasonable error, and that you are taking appropriate steps to remedy the shortfall. If you believe you qualify for this relief, file Form 5329, pay this excise tax, and attach your letter of explanation. If the IRS grants your request, we will send you a refund.*

Part IV—Tax On Excess Distributions From Qualified Retirement Plans (Including IRAs)

Generally, if you received distributions in 1994 from qualified retirement plans (including IRAs) in excess of $150,000 (or $148,500 if you made a special grandfather election), you may have to pay an additional 15% tax on the excess.

Line 18

There are two types of retirement distributions: regular and lump-sum. See Form 4972 for details on distributions that can be treated as lump-sum distributions. You must make certain elections under section 402 or 403, such as the 5-year tax option, for those distributions.

If you rolled over part of a distribution, you must treat the entire distribution as a regular, not a lump-sum, distribution.

Line 19

The 15% additional tax does not apply to certain distributions specifically excepted by the Code. Enter on line 19 the amount that is to be excluded. In the space provided, enter the applicable exception number (01–06) from the chart below.

No.	Exception
01	Distribution made as a result of death
02	Distribution paid to an alternate payee under a qualified domestic relations order
03	Distribution attributable to investment in contract
04	Distribution rolled over
05	Distribution of an annuity contract
06	Distribution of excess deferrals or excess contributions

Line 21

The threshold amount depends on whether you made a grandfather election in 1987 or 1988 under Temp. Regs. section 54.4981A-1T. For regular distributions, if you did not elect the special grandfather rule, use the $150,000 threshold amount. If you made a special grandfather election, use $148,500 for 1994. For lump-sum distributions, use $750,000 if you did not elect the special grandfather rule. If you made a grandfather election, the threshold amount for 1994 is $742,500.

If you made the special grandfather election, use either Worksheet 1—Discretionary Method or Worksheet 2—Attained Age Method on page 5 to figure your 1994 recovery amount and your unrecovered grandfather amount for 1995. See the worksheets on page 5.

Attach a copy of the applicable worksheet to your return if you are required to file Form 5329. Also, keep the completed worksheet as part of your permanent records to help you figure your 1995 recovery amount. In the case of your death, the executor or administrator of your estate will need to know the unrecovered amount to figure any increase in estate tax that may be due under section 4980A(d) on Schedule S of Form 706.

See Temp. Regs. section 54.4981A-1T for more details on the two grandfather recovery methods and recordkeeping requirements.

Line 24

The 15% excise tax on excess distributions is offset by the 10% tax on early distributions, to the extent that the 10% tax applies to excess distributions. If you entered an amount on line 4, figure the offset amount, if any, as follows.

1. Add the amounts included on line 1 that were attributable to distributions from a qualified retirement plan (including an IRA), prohibited transactions, pledging of accounts as security for loans, or acquisition of collectibles,

2. Subtract any amount on line 2 that is attributable to the distributions included in **1** above, and

3. Subtract line 21 from the result obtained in **2** above.

If the result is zero or less, you are not eligible for an offset. If the result is greater than zero, multiply the result by 10% (the rate for tax on early distributions), and enter that result on line 24.

Page 4

Acceleration Elections

If you elected the special grandfather rule using the discretionary method, you may make (or revoke) an acceleration election for a prior year (and all later years) on a timely filed Form 1040X for any prior years to which the discretionary method of recovery applied. Indicate on Form 1040X that you are amending your return to make (or revoke) an acceleration election under Internal Revenue Code section 4980A. Attach the version of Form 5329 that was used for the year you are amending. Be sure to check the "amended return" box on page 1 and item 1 or 2 under **Acceleration Elections** on each applicable Form 5329. You may need to amend more than one return because an amendment of an earlier year return to elect (or revoke) 100% acceleration will also require consistent treatment on later year returns.

An acceleration election becomes irrevocable once the period for amending your return for the year of the election has expired. Acceleration applies to all distributions received during a calendar year and all later calendar years. If you have a fiscal tax year, you make the acceleration election on your return for your tax year that begins within the first calendar year for which the election applies.

Note: *You cannot revoke a basic grandfather election you made in 1987 or 1988.*

Worksheet 1—Discretionary Method

*Use this worksheet to figure your unrecovered grandfather amount under the discretionary method. Under this method, 10% of the distributions you receive during the calendar year is generally treated as a recovery of the grandfather amount. You may elect to accelerate the rate of recovery (on line 3) to 100%. If you make the election, the rate of recovery is accelerated to 100% for the calendar year for which the election is made and for all later years. See **Acceleration Elections** above for details on making or revoking an election for a prior year. Attach a completed copy of this worksheet to your 1994 return if you entered a recovery of the grandfather amount on line 21. Otherwise, keep for your records.*

1 Remaining unrecovered grandfather amount as of 1/1/94 (from line 4 of your 1993 worksheet) . **1.** _____

2 Distributions received during 1994 . . . . **2.** _____

3 1994 recovery of grandfather amount. Enter the **smaller** of line 1 **or** 10% (.10) or, if elected, 100% (1.00) of line 2. Enter here and in Column **A** or **B** on line 21 of Form 5329 (ratably if both) . . **3.** _____

4 Remaining unrecovered grandfather amount for 1995. Subtract line 3 from line 1 . . . . . . **4.** _____

Worksheet 2—Attained Age Method

Use this worksheet to figure your unrecovered grandfather amount under the attained age method. Under this method, you figure the part of the distributions you received during the year that is treated as a recovery of the grandfather amount by multiplying the distributions you received by a fraction. The numerator of the fraction is the difference between your attained age in completed months on August 1, 1986, and age 35 (420 months). The denominator of the fraction is the difference between your attained age in completed months on December 31, 1994, and age 35 (420 months). Attach a completed copy of this worksheet to your 1994 return if you entered a recovery of the grandfather amount on line 21. Otherwise, keep for your records.

Note: *If you were born after August 1, 1951, you cannot use this method.*

1 Remaining unrecovered grandfather amount as of 1/1/94 (from line 7 of your 1993 worksheet) . **1.** _____

2 Distributions received during 1994 . . . . **2.** _____

3a Attained age in completed months on 8/1/86 . . . . **3a.** _____

  b Number of completed months at age 35 . . . . **b.** ___420___

  c Subtract line 3b from line 3a . . . . **c.** _____

4a Attained age in completed months on 12/31/94 . . . . **4a.** _____

  b Number of completed months at age 35 . . . . **b.** ___420___

  c Subtract line 4b from line 4a . . . . **c.** _____

5 Divide line 3c by line 4c. Enter the result as a percentage . . . . **5.** _____ %

6 1994 recovery of grandfather amount. Enter the **smaller** of (a) line 1 **or** (b) line 2 multiplied by the percentage on line 5. Enter here and in Column **A** or **B** on line 21 of Form 5329 (ratably if both) **6.** _____

7 Remaining unrecovered grandfather amount for 1995. Subtract line 6 from line 1 . . . . . . **7.** _____

♻ *Printed on recycled paper*

Form 1040

Department of the Treasury—Internal Revenue Service

U.S. Individual Income Tax Return (L) 19__

For the year Jan. 1–Dec. 31, 1994, or other tax year beginning _____ 19___, ending _____, 19___   OMB No. 1545-0074

IRS Use Only—Do not write or staple in this space.

Label

(See instructions on page 12.)

Use the IRS label. Otherwise, please print or type.

Your first name and initial DONALD P.	Last name JONES
If a joint return, spouse's first name and initial SHEILA F.	Last name JONES

Home address (number and street). If you have a P.O. box, see page 12.   1265 Highland Ave.   Apt. no.

City, town or post office, state, and ZIP code. If you have a foreign address, see page 12.   Garden Grove, CA 92143

Your social security number   123 : 45 : 6789

Spouse's social security number   987 : 65 : 4321

For Privacy Act and Paperwork Reduction Act Notice, see page 4.

Presidential Election Campaign (See page 12.)

Do you want $3 to go to this fund? . . . .

If a joint return, does your spouse want $3 to go to this fund? . . . .

Yes | No

Note: *Checking "Yes" will not change your tax or reduce your refund.*

Filing Status

(See page 12.)

Check only one box.

1 ☐ Single

2 ☐ Married filing joint return (even if only one had income)

3 ☐ Married filing separate return. Enter spouse's social security no. above and full name here. ▶ _____

4 ☐ Head of household (with qualifying person). (See page 13.) If the qualifying person is a child but not your dependent, enter this child's name here. ▶ _____

5 ☐ Qualifying widow(er) with dependent child (year spouse died ▶ 19___). (See page 13.)

Exemptions

(See page 13.)

6a ☐ **Yourself.** If your parent (or someone else) can claim you as a dependent on his or her tax return, **do not** check box 6a. But be sure to check the box on line 33b on page 2

b ☐ **Spouse** . . . .

c **Dependents:**

(1) Name (first, initial, and last name)	(2) Check if under age 1	(3) If age 1 or older, dependent's social security number	(4) Dependent's relationship to you	(5) No. of months lived in your home in 1994
Glenda P. Jones		415 20 6789	Daughter	12

If more than six dependents, see page 14.

No. of boxes checked on 6a and 6b

No. of your children on 6c who:
- lived with you
- didn't live with you due to divorce or separation (see page 14)

Dependents on 6c not entered above

d If your child didn't live with you but is claimed as your dependent under a pre-1985 agreement, check here ▶ ☐

e Total number of exemptions claimed . . . .

Add numbers entered on lines above ▶

Income

Attach Copy B of your Forms W-2, W-2G, and 1099-R here.

If you did not get a W-2, see page 15.

Enclose, but do not attach, any payment with your return.

7	Wages, salaries, tips, etc. Attach Form(s) W-2	7	
8a	**Taxable** interest income (see page 15). Attach Schedule B if over $400	8a	
b	**Tax-exempt** interest (see page 16). DON'T include on line 8a	8b		
9	Dividend income. Attach Schedule B if over $400	9	
10	Taxable refunds, credits, or offsets of state and local income taxes (see page 16) . .	10	
11	Alimony received	11	
12	Business income or (loss). Attach Schedule C or C-EZ	12	
13	Capital gain or (loss). If required, attach Schedule D (see page 16)	13	
14	Other gains or (losses). Attach Form 4797	14	
15a	Total IRA distributions .	15a		b Taxable amount (see page 17)	15b	
16a	Total pensions and annuities	16a	12000 00	b Taxable amount (see page 17)	16b	
17	Rental real estate, royalties, partnerships, S corporations, trusts, etc. Attach Schedule E	17	12000 00
18	Farm income or (loss). Attach Schedule F	18	
19	Unemployment compensation (see page 18)	19	
20a	Social security benefits	20a		b Taxable amount (see page 18)	20b	
21	Other income. List type and amount—see page 18	21	
22	Add the amounts in the far right column for lines 7 through 21. This is your **total income** ▶	22	

Adjustments to Income

Caution: See instructions . . ▶

23a	Your IRA deduction (see page 19)	23a		
b	Spouse's IRA deduction (see page 19)	23b		
24	Moving expenses. Attach Form 3903 or 3903-F . .	24		
25	One-half of self-employment tax	25		
26	Self-employed health insurance deduction (see page 21)	26		
27	Keogh retirement plan and self-employed SEP deduction	27		
28	Penalty on early withdrawal of savings	28		
29	Alimony paid. Recipient's SSN ▶	29		
30	Add lines 23a through 29. These are your **total adjustments** . . . . ▶	30	

Adjusted Gross Income

31 Subtract line 30 from line 22. This is your **adjusted gross income.** If less than $25,296 and a child lived with you (less than $9,000 if a child didn't live with you), see "Earned Income Credit" on page 27 ▶ | 31 | |

Cat. No. 12600W

Form **1040** (1994)

Form 1040 (1994)   Page **2**

Tax Compu-tation (See page 23.)	**32**	Amount from line 31 (adjusted gross income)	**32**	
	33a	Check if: ☐ **You** were 65 or older, ☐ Blind; ☐ **Spouse** was 65 or older, ☐ Blind. Add the number of boxes checked above and enter the total here . . . . ▶ **33a**		
	b	If your parent (or someone else) can claim you as a dependent, check here . ▶ **33b** ☐		
	c	If you are married filing separately and your spouse itemizes deductions or you are a dual-status alien, see page 23 and check here . . . . ▶ **33c** ☐		
	34	Enter the **larger** of your: { **Itemized deductions** from Schedule A, line 29, **OR** **Standard deduction** shown below for your filing status. **But if you checked any box on line 33a or b,** go to page 23 to find your standard deduction. If you checked **box 33c,** your standard deduction is zero. ● Single—$3,800 ● Head of household—$5,600 ● Married filing jointly or Qualifying widow(er)—$6,350 ● Married filing separately—$3,175 }	**34**	
	35	Subtract line 34 from line 32	**35**	
	36	If line 32 is $83,850 or less, multiply $2,450 by the total number of exemptions claimed on line 6e. If line 32 is over $83,850, see the worksheet on page 24 for the amount to enter .	**36**	
If you want the IRS to figure your tax, see page 24.	**37**	**Taxable income.** Subtract line 36 from line 35. If line 36 is more than line 35, enter -0- .	**37**	
	38	Tax. Check if from **a** ☐ Tax Table, **b** ☐ Tax Rate Schedules, **c** ☐ Capital Gain Tax Worksheet, or **d** ☐ Form 8615 (see page 24). Amount from Form(s) 8814 ▶ **e** _____	**38**	
	39	Additional taxes. Check if from **a** ☐ Form 4970 **b** ☐ Form 4972	**39**	
	40	Add lines 38 and 39 . . . . ▶	**40**	
Credits (See page 24.)	**41**	Credit for child and dependent care expenses. Attach Form 2441	**41**		
	42	Credit for the elderly or the disabled. Attach Schedule R .	**42**		
	43	Foreign tax credit. Attach Form 1116	**43**		
	44	Other credits (see page 25). Check if from **a** ☐ Form 3800 **b** ☐ Form 8396 **c** ☐ Form 8801 **d** ☐ Form (specify) _____	**44**		
	45	Add lines 41 through 44	**45**	
	46	Subtract line 45 from line 40. If line 45 is more than line 40, enter -0- . . . . . ▶	**46**	
Other Taxes (See page 25.)	**47**	Self-employment tax. Attach Schedule SE	**47**	
	48	Alternative minimum tax. Attach Form 6251	**48**	
	49	Recapture taxes. Check if from **a** ☐ Form 4255 **b** ☐ Form 8611 **c** ☐ Form 8828 .	**49**	
	50	Social security and Medicare tax on tip income not reported to employer. Attach Form 4137	**50**	
	51	Tax on qualified retirement plans, including IRAs. If required, attach Form 5329 . . .	**51**	1200 00
	52	Advance earned income credit payments from Form W-2	**52**	
	53	Add lines 46 through 52. This is your **total tax** . . . . ▶	**53**	
Payments Attach Forms W-2, W-2G, and 1099-R on the front.	**54**	Federal income tax withheld. If any is from Form(s) 1099, check ▶ ☐	**54**		
	55	1994 estimated tax payments and amount applied from 1993 return .	**55**		
	56	**Earned income credit.** If required, attach Schedule EIC (see page 27). Nontaxable earned income: amount ▶ _____ and type ▶ _____	**56**		
	57	Amount paid with Form 4868 (extension request)	**57**		
	58	Excess social security and RRTA tax withheld (see page 32)	**58**		
	59	Other payments. Check if from **a** ☐ Form 2439 **b** ☐ Form 4136	**59**		
	60	Add lines 54 through 59. These are your **total payments** . . . . ▶	**60**	
Refund or Amount You Owe	**61**	If line 60 is more than line 53, subtract line 53 from line 60. This is the amount you **OVERPAID**. ▶	**61**	
	62	Amount of line 61 you want **REFUNDED TO YOU** . . . . ▶	**62**	
	63	Amount of line 61 you want **APPLIED TO YOUR 1995 ESTIMATED TAX** ▶	**63**		
	64	If line 53 is more than line 60, subtract line 60 from line 53. This is the **AMOUNT YOU OWE.** For details on how to pay, including what to write on your payment, see page 32 . . .	**64**	
	65	Estimated tax penalty (see page 33). Also include on line 64	**65**		

Sign Here

Keep a copy of this return for your records.

Under penalties of perjury, I declare that I have examined this return and accompanying schedules and statements, and to the best of my knowledge and belief, they are true, correct, and complete. Declaration of preparer (other than taxpayer) is based on all information of which preparer has any knowledge.

▶ Your signature *Donald P. Jones*	Date	Your occupation Job search
▶ Spouse's signature. If a joint return, BOTH must sign. *Sheila F. Jones*	Date	Spouse's occupation

Paid Preparer's Use Only

Preparer's signature ▶	Date	Check if self-employed ☐	Preparer's social security no.
Firm's name (or yours if self-employed) and address ▶		E.I. No. ZIP code	

♻ *Printed on recycled paper*

U.S.GPO:1994-375-060

Memorandum re: Tax Consequences of Distributions From Qualified Plans

This is the Internal Revenue Service's announcement on changes of the Federal tax consequences of distributions from a qualified corporate profit-sharing or retirement plan and some matters that should be considered in making elections as to the mode of distribution. The subject matter is complex, there are continuous changes in the tax law and interpretations thereof, and individual circumstances vary significantly, so professional advice should be obtained.

Summary

A payment from the plan that is eligible for "rollover" can be taken in two ways. You can have all or any portion of your payment either: *paid in a direct rollover*, or *paid to you*. A rollover is a payment of your Plan benefits to your individual retirement arrangement (IRA) or to another employer plan. This choice will affect the tax you have.

If you choose a direct rollover:

- Your payment will not be taxed in the current year and no income tax will be withheld;

- Your payment will be made directly to your IRA or, if you choose, to another employer plan that accepts your rollover;

- Your payment will be taxed later when you take it out of the IRA or the employer plan.

If you choose to have your Plan benefits paid to you:

- You will receive only 80% of the payment because the Plan Administrator is required to withhold 20% of the payment and send it to the IRS as income tax withholding to be credited against your taxes;

- Your payment will be taxed in the current year unless you roll it over. You may be able to use special tax rules that could reduce the tax you owe. However, if you receive the payment before age 59½, you also may have to pay an additional 10% tax;

- You can roll over the payment by paying it to your IRA or to another employer plan that accepts your rollover within 60 days of receiving the payment. The amount rolled over will not be taxed until you take it out of the IRA or the employer plan;

- If you want to roll over 100% of the payment to an IRA or an employer plan, *you must find other money to replace the 20% that was withheld*. If you roll over only the 80% that you received, you will be taxed on the 20% that was withheld and that is not rolled over.

Payments that can and cannot be rolled over

Payments from a Plan may be "eligible rollover distributions." This means that they can be rolled over to an IRA or to another employer plan that accepts rollovers. Your Plan Administrator should be able to tell you what portion of your payment is an eligible rollover distribution.

- Non-taxable payments: In general, only the taxable portion of your payment is an eligible rollover distribution. If you have made after tax employee contributions to the Plan, these contributions will be non-taxable when they are paid to you. They cannot be rolled over;

- Payments spread over long periods: You cannot roll over a payment if it is part of a series of equal or almost equal payments that are made at least once a year and that will last for your lifetime or life expectancy, your lifetime and your beneficiary's lifetime or life expectancy, or a period of 10 years or more.

Required Minimum Payments: Beginning in the year you reach age 70½, a certain portion of your payment cannot be rolled over because it is a required minimum payment that must be paid to you.

Direct Rollover: You can choose a direct rollover of all or any portion of your payment that is an eligible rollover distribution. In a direct rollover the eligible rollover distribution is paid directly from your Plan to an IRA or another employer plan that accepts rollovers. If you choose a direct rollover, you are not taxed on a payment until you later take it out of the IRA or the employer plan. Consult IRS Publication 590 (Individual Retirement Arrangements) for more information on IRAs including limits on how often you can roll over between IRAs.

If you are employed by a new employer that has a plan and you want a direct rollover to that plan, ask the Plan Administrator whether it will accept your rollover. An employer plan is not legally required to accept a rollover.

Direct Rollover of a Series of Payments: If you receive eligible rollover distributions that are paid in a series for less than ten years, your choice to make or not make a direct rollover for a payment will apply to all later payments in the series until you change your election. You are free to change your election for any later payment in the series.

Payment Paid To You: If you have the payment made to you, it is subject to income tax withholding. The payment is taxed in the year you receive it unless within 60 days you roll it over into an IRA or another plan that accepts rollovers. If you do not roll it over, special tax rules may apply:

Income tax withholding

- Mandatory withholding: If any portion of the payment to you is an eligible rollover distribution, the Plan is required by law to withhold 20% of that amount. When you prepare your income tax return for the year you will report the amount of the payment from the Plan. You will report the 20% of the amount as tax withheld and it will be credited against any income tax you owe for the year.

- Voluntary withholding: If any portion of your payment is not an eligible rollover distribution but is taxable, you may elect not to have withholding apply to that portion.

- Sixty-day rollover option: If you have an eligible rollover distribution paid to you, you can decide to roll over all or parts of it to an IRA or another employer plan that accepts rollovers. If you decide to rollover, *you must make the rollover within sixty days after you receive the payment*. The portion of your payment that is rolled over will not be taxed until you take it out of the IRA or the employer plan.

Additional 10% tax if you are under age 59½: If you receive a payment before you reach age 59½ and you do not roll it over, then, in addition to the regular income tax, you may have to pay an extra tax equal to 10% of the taxable portion of the payment. The additional tax does not apply to your payment if it is:

- Paid to you because you separate from service with your employer during or after the year you reach age 55;

- Paid because you retire due to disability;

- Paid to you as equal or almost equal payments over your life or life expectancy (or your beneficiaries' lives or life expectancies);

- Used to pay certain medical expenses.

Please consult IRS Form 5329 for more information on the additional 10% tax.

Special tax treatment: If your eligible rollover distribution is not rolled over it will be taxed in the year you receive it. However, if it qualifies as a "lump sum distribution", it may be eligible for special tax treatment. A lump sum distribution is a payment, within one year, of your entire balance under the Plan that is payable to you because you have reached 59½ or have separated from service with your employer. For a payment to qualify as a lump sum distribution, you must have been a participant in the Plan for at least five years.

- Five-year averaging: If you receive a lump sum distribution after you are age 59½, you may be able to make a one-time election to figure the tax on the payment by using "five-year averaging". Five-year averaging often reduces the tax you owe because it treats the payment much as if it were paid over five years. Distribution due to separation from service in or after the year of reaching age 55 applies only to qualified employee plans.

- Ten-year averaging if you were born before 1936: If you receive a lump sum distribution you can make a one-time election to figure the tax on the payment by using "ten-year averaging" using 1986 tax rates. Ten-year averaging often reduces the tax you owe.

- Capital gain treatment if you were born before 1936: If you receive a lump sum distribution, you may elect to have part of your payment that is attributable to your pre-1974 participation in the Plan taxed as a long-term capital gain at a rate of 20%.

Special tax treatment for lump sum distributions has other limits. You can generally elect this special tax treatment only once in your lifetime, and this election applies to all lump sum distributions that you receive in that same year. If you have previously rolled over a payment from the Plan you cannot use this special tax treatment for later payments from the Plan. If you roll over your payment to an IRA, you will not be able to use this special tax treatment for later payments from the IRA. If you roll over only a portion of your payment to an IRA, this special tax treatment is not available for the rest of the payment. Additional restrictions are described in IRS Form 4972.

VGM CAREER BOOKS

CAREER DIRECTORIES
Careers Encyclopedia
Dictionary of Occupational Titles
Occupational Outlook Handbook

CAREERS FOR
Animal Lovers
Bookworms
Caring People
Computer Buffs
Crafty People
Culture Lovers
Environmental Types
Film Buffs
Foreign Language Aficionados
Good Samaritans
Gourmets
History Buffs
Kids at Heart
Nature Lovers
Night Owls
Number Crunchers
Plant Lovers
Shutterbugs
Sports Nuts
Travel Buffs
Writers

CAREERS IN
Accounting; Advertising;
Business; Child Care;
Communications; Computers;
Education; Engineering;
the Environment; Finance;
Government; Health Care; High
Tech; International Business;
Journalism; Law; Marketing;
Medicine; Science; Social &
Rehabilitation Services

CAREER PLANNING
Admissions Guide to Selective
  Business Schools
Beating Job Burnout
Beginning Entrepreneur
Career Planning & Development
  for College Students & Recent
  Graduates
Career Change
Careers Checklists
Complete Guide to Career
  Etiquette
Cover Letters They Don't Forget
Dr. Job's Complete Career Guide

Executive Job Search Strategies
Guide to Basic Cover Letter
  Writing
Guide to Basic Résumé Writing
Guide to Temporary
  Employment
Job Interviewing for College
  Students
Joyce Lain Kennedy's Career
  Book
Out of Uniform
Slam Dunk Résumés

CAREER PORTRAITS
Animals; Cars; Computers;
Electronics; Fashion;
Firefighting; Music; Nursing;
Sports; Teaching; Travel; Writing

GREAT JOBS FOR
Communications Majors
Engineering Majors
English Majors
Foreign Language Majors
History Majors
Psychology Majors

HOW TO
Approach an Advertising Agency
  and Walk Away with the Job
  You Want
Bounce Back Quickly After
  Losing Your Job
Choose the Right Career
Cómo escribir un currículum
  vitae en inglés que tenga éxito
Find Your New Career Upon
  Retirement
Get & Keep Your First Job
Get Hired Today
Get into the Right Business
  School
Get into the Right Law School
Get People to Do Things Your
  Way
Have a Winning Job Interview
Hit the Ground Running in Your
  New Job
Hold It All Together When
  You've Lost Your Job
Improve Your Study Skills
Jump Start a Stalled Career
Land a Better Job

Launch Your Career in TV News
Make the Right Career Moves
Market Your College Degree
Move from College into a
  Secure Job
Negotiate the Raise You Deserve
Prepare a Curriculum Vitae
Prepare for College
Run Your Own Home Business
Succeed in College
Succeed in High School
Take Charge of Your Child's
  Early Education
Write a Winning Résumé
Write Successful Cover Letters
Write Term Papers & Reports
Write Your College Application
  Essay

MADE EASY
Cover Letters
Job Hunting
Job Interviews
Résumés

OPPORTUNITIES IN
This extensive series provides
detailed information on nearly
150 individual career fields.

RÉSUMÉS FOR
Advertising Careers
Banking and Financial Careers
Business Management Careers
College Students &
  Recent Graduates
Communications Careers
Education Careers
Engineering Careers
Environmental Careers
Ex-Military Personnel
50+ Job Hunters
Health and Medical Careers
High School Graduates
High Tech Careers
Law Careers
Midcareer Job Changes
Re-Entering the Job Market
Sales and Marketing Careers
Scientific and Technical Careers
Social Service Careers
The First-Time Job Hunter

 VGM Career Horizons
a division of *NTC Publishing Group*
4255 West Touhy Avenue
Lincolnwood, Illinois 60646–1975